# BULLY!

## THE LIFE AND TIMES OF
## THEODORE ROOSEVELT

*Illustrated with*
## MORE THAN 250 VINTAGE POLITICAL CARTOONS

## RICK MARSCHALL

REGNERY
HISTORY

Library of Congress Cataloging-in-Publication Data

Marschall, Richard.
Bully! : the life and times of Theodore Roosevelt / by Rick Marschall.
p. cm.
Includes bibliographical references.
ISBN 978-1-59698-154-6
1. Roosevelt, Theodore, 1858-1919. 2. Roosevelt, Theodore, 1858-1919--Caricatures and cartoons. 3. Presidents--United States--Biography. I. Title.
E757.M377 2011
973.91'1092--dc23
[B]
2011033513

ISBN 978-1-59698-154-6

Published in the United States by
Regnery Publishing, Inc.
One Massachusetts Avenue, NW, Washington, DC 20001
www.regnery.com

Manufactured in the United States of America
10 9 8 7 6 5 4 3 2 1

Books are available in quantity for promotional or premium use. For information on discounts and terms write to Director of Special Sales, Regnery Publishing, Inc., One Massachusetts Avenue, NW, Washington, DC, 20001, or call 202-216-0600.

Distributed to the trade by:
Perseus Distribution, 387 Park Avenue South, New York, NY 10016

Cartoon Restoration: Jon Barli, Rosebud Archives
Editorial Assistant: John Olsen

For my son

Ted Marschall

*Qui plantavit curabit*

# CONTENTS

**FOREWORD**

"AGGRESSIVE FIGHTING FOR
THE RIGHT IS THE NOBLEST SPORT
THE WORLD AFFORDS."

~THEODORE ROOSEVELT

# FOREWORD

The life of Theodore Roosevelt (1858–1919) coincided with the most colorful period of American journalism. Between the Gilded Age of illustrated magazines and the advent of the hard-boiled city rooms of *The Front Page* was the era of colored political-cartoon magazines, yellow journalism, and the muckrakers. The cartoons in *BULLY!* are collected from those vibrant but now scarce and nearly forgotten pages. Cartoonists and reporters had no better subject during those years than Theodore Roosevelt—not even frontier expansion, wars, and innovations such as railroads, telephones, motion pictures, automobiles, and flying machines would compete.

America came of age during this era, with a growing leisure class that was able to indulge an appetite for politics, current affairs, and the arts in periodicals. Technology freed cartoonists from old-fashioned chalk-plates and wood-engravings, allowing them to reproduce pen drawings with all the glorious detail they could invest. Cartoonists captured the issues of the day—war and peace, economic crises, the growing divide between rich and poor—bringing them more poignantly to the attention of readers to whom the editorial cartoon was truly worth a thousand words.

Theodore Roosevelt was the perfect subject for the cartoonists' art. One is tempted to say that if TR, in all his distinctive glory, had not come along, American culture would have had to invent him. Presidents were boring before Theodore Roosevelt, and boring after him; life, as many said after he died, seemed emptier without him.

Cartoonists did not create Theodore Roosevelt, however—not by any means. His life was a series of memorable phases: writing dozens of books and hundreds of magazine articles; living the life of a cowboy; fighting heroically on the battlefield; devoting himself to innumerable interests and physical pastimes; enjoying a vaunted circle of friends. All of this would make up TR's biography, even without the cartoonists.

Still, cartoonists of his day best conveyed his traits, keeping them alive for posterity. Press photography was still coming into its own during the period in which cartoonists drew the likenesses we know today. Movies and newsreels were new, but cartoonists told us how Roosevelt walked and ran and rode and gestured and laughed.

Theodore Roosevelt was perhaps the most caricatured president—if not the most caricatured American—in history. Here is the raw material cartoonists had to work with: TR was of average height, between 5'8" and 5'10". People noticed that he had rather small ears. He had sandy hair and was often "brown as a nut" from outdoor activities. An obsessive exerciser, Roosevelt was barrel-chested with a thick, muscular neck. He was comfortable, as a patrician, in silk vests, top hats, and *pince-nez* spectacles with a cord. But he fit just as well into riding clothes, boots, and wire-rimmed glasses. It is probable that he frequently displayed an assortment of cuts, blisters, and bruises; such was the occupational hazard of an inveterate hunter, hiker, sportsman, boxer, not to mention someone who romped crazily with his children for an hour every afternoon.

He spoke with great animation, chopping off his words as if each were a separate bite of meat. He clicked his teeth between words or sentences and elongated his "s" sounds.

He spoke in a rich baritone flavored with an East Coast aristocrat's affected "Harvard accent." But when emphasizing a point, or aiming for humor, he lapsed into a comical falsetto. TR laughed frequently, and likely had the best sense of humor of any president other than Lincoln. His military aide, Major Archie Butt, once confided in a letter to a relative that at a pompous funeral, he could scarcely keep a straight face through Roosevelt's whispered stream of sarcasms and humorous commentary. TR also relished humor at his own expense, one of many refutations against those who say he possessed a large ego.

He did not dislike many people, but he surely disliked things some people did, or things they stood for. When he was someone's opponent, they knew it. He could be withering in print to such folks, and no less to their faces.

He was a proponent of many "new" things in a new age; but in terms of morality, manners, and traditions, he was a Victorian—almost a prude, and blue-nosed. He favored women's suffrage before most politicians (and before his wife did), but maintained, as a traditionalist, that "equality of rights should not be confused with equality of function" in society. He hated to be called "Teddy," and said that anyone who used the nickname did not know him and did not respect his wishes. We respect his wishes in this biography.

For other descriptions of the physical Roosevelt—more of what the cartoonists had to work with—I present some passages from William Bayard Hale's series of articles for *The New York Times* in 1908. For "A Week in the White House," the writer was allowed an unfettered presence in all meetings and activities, and his observations provide a thorough description of the man.

*Imagine [him] at the desk sometimes, on the divan sometimes, sometimes in a chair in the farthest corner of the Cabinet room, more often on his feet—it may be anywhere within the four walls—the muscular, massive figure of Mr. Roosevelt. You know his features—the close-clipped brachycephalous head, close-clipped mustache, pince-nez, square and terribly rigid jaw.*

*Hair and moustache indeterminate in color; eyes a clear blue; cheeks and neck ruddy. He is in a frock-coat, a low collar with a four-in-hand, a light waistcoat, and grey striped trousers—not that you would ever notice all that unless you pulled yourself away from his face and looked with deliberate purpose. Remember that he is almost constantly in action, speaking earnestly and with great animation; that he gestures freely, and that his whole face is always in play. For he talks with his whole being—mouth, eyes, forehead, cheeks, and neck all taking their mobile parts.*

*The President is in the pink of condition today.... Look at him as he stands and you will see that he is rigid as a soldier on parade. His chin is in, his chest out. The line from the back of his head falls straight as a plumb-line to his heels. Never for a moment, while he is on his feet, does that line so much as waver, that neck unbend. It is a pillar of steel. Remember that steel pillar. Remember it when he laughs, as he will do a hundred times a day—heartily, freely, like an irresponsible school-boy on a lark, his face flushing ruddier, his eyes nearly closed, his utterance choked with mirth, and speech abandoned or become a weird falsetto. For the President is a joker, and (what many jokers are not) a humorist. He is always looking for fun—and always finding it. He likes it rather more than he does a fight—but that's fun too. You have to remember, then, two things to see the picture: a room filled with constant good humor, breaking literally every five minutes into a roar of laughter—and a neck of steel.*

*Not that the President always stands at attention. He doubles up when he laughs, sometimes. Sometimes—though only when a visitor whom he knows well is alone with him—he puts his foot on a chair. When he sits, however, he is very much at ease—half the time with one leg curled up on the divan or maybe on the Cabinet table top. And, curiously, when the President sits on one foot, his visitor is likely to do the same, even if, like Mr. Justice Harlan or Mr. J. J. Hill, he has to take hold of the foot and pull it up....*

*Remember that Mr. Roosevelt never speaks a word in the ordinary conversational tone.... His face energized from the base of the neck to the roots of the hair, his arms usually gesticulating, his words bursting forth like projectiles, his whole being radiating force. He does not speak fast, always pausing before an emphatic word, and letting it out with the spring of accumulated energy behind it. The President doesn't allow his witticisms to pass without enjoying them. He always stops—indeed, he has to stop till the convulsion of merriment is over and he can regain his voice.*

*The President enters into a subject which arouses him. He bursts out against his detractors. His arms begin to pump. His finger rises in the air. He beats one palm with the other fist. "They have no conception of what I'm driving at, absolutely None. It Passes Belief—the capacity of the human mind to resist intelligence. Some people Won't learn, Won't think, Won't know. The amount of—stupid Perversity that lingers in the heads of some men is a miracle."*

*The President's good-humor and candor have not been sufficiently appreciated. It is good to have a President with a laugh like Mr. Roosevelt's. That laugh is working a good deal too; hardly does half an hour, seldom do five minutes go by without a joyful cachinnation from the Presidential throat.... The fun engulfs his whole face; his eyes close, and speech expires in a silent gasp of joy.*

*He is, first of all, a physical marvel. He radiates energy as the sun radiates light and heat.... It is not merely remarkable, it is a simple miracle, that this man can keep up day after day—it is a sufficient miracle that he can exhibit for one day—the power which emanates from him like energy from a dynamo.... He radiates from morning until night, and he is nevertheless always radiant.*

*Never does the President appear to meet a personality than which he is not the stronger; an idea to which he is a stranger; a situation which disconcerts him. He is always master. He takes what he pleases, gives what he likes, and does his will upon all alike. Mr. Roosevelt never tires; the flow of his power does not fluctuate. There is never weariness on his brow nor, apparently, languor in his heart.... The President ends the day as fresh as he began it. He is a man of really phenomenal physical power, a fountain of perennial energy, a dynamic marvel.*

*The President is able to concentrate his entire attention on the subject in hand, whether it be for an hour or for thirty seconds, and then instantly to transfer it, still entirely concentrated, to another subject.... He flies from an affair of state to a hunting reminiscence; from that to an abstract ethical question; then to a literary or a historical subject; he settles a point in an army reorganization plan; the next second he is talking earnestly to a visitor on the Lake Superior whitefish, the taste of its flesh and the articulation of its skeleton as compared with the shad; in another second or two he is urging the necessity of arming for the preservation of peace, and quoting Erasmus; then he takes up the case of a suspected violation of the Sherman law, and is at the heart of it in a minute; then he listens to the tale of a Southern politician and gives him rapid instruction; turns to the intricacies of the Venezuela imbroglio, with the mass of details of a long story which everybody else has forgotten at his finger tips; stops a moment to tell a naval aide the depth and capacity of the harbor of Auckland; is instantly intent on the matter of his great and good friend of the Caribbean; takes up a few candidacies for appointments, one by one; recalls with great gusto the story of an adventure on horseback; greets a delegation; discusses with a Cabinet secretary a recommendation he is thinking of sending to Congress. All this within half an hour. Each subject gets full attention when it is up; there is never any hurrying away from it, but there is no loitering over it.*

These assessments came, by the way, from someone who was not a hero-worshiper. Hale was a Democrat, writing for a Democrat newspaper; he confessed to be out of sympathy with Roosevelt's policies, and within four years he would be writing Woodrow Wilson's campaign biography.

You will see in this book that countless cartoonists tried to capture the coruscating nature of this man Roosevelt. As cartoonists with multiple panels to fill, they perhaps had an easier job than Hale. In any event, it was more fun. "Slow news days" were solved in the city rooms of American newspapers: cartoonists could draw what TR did, or would do, or might do. He was the cartoonists' best friend.

Cartoons and comic strips—not just editorial and political cartoons—tell us about more than public affairs of the day. They describe manners and morals, fads and fancies. Cartoons tell us how people dressed, what they liked or avoided, what angered them, and what made them laugh. They truly are snapshots in a beloved American family album.

You will meet here the great cartoonists: from Nast and the Kepplers (father and son) and the Gillam brothers, in the magazines; to Opper and Davenport and McCutcheon, in the newspapers; from forgotten geniuses like Charles Green Bush and Joseph Donahey, to Winsor McCay of *Little Nemo* fame, and Pulitzer Prize-winners like Ding Darling. The cartoons herein were culled from famous magazines *Puck, Judge*, and *Life*, and from major newspapers of the turn of the last century, including New York's *Journal, World*, and *Herald*. Printed in the millions, they are almost impossible to find today. You will discover forgotten cartoonists from obscure publications…and, I hope, you will revel as I have in the discovery of prescient commentary cleverly drawn and presented in great numbers and variety. With such a rich lode to mine (for I have been fortunate to assemble what is arguably the nation's largest archive of such source-material), I endeavor in *BULLY!* to bring out the work of more obscure artists over the familiar. Thus, if textbooks have given us a Keppler or a Davenport on a certain topic, and if a "forgotten" cartoonist has made an equally trenchant observation on the same event, I introduce that cartoonist to posterity.

Through the cartoons reproduced in this book, you will experience what America was like 100 years ago. Mostly, though, I want you to meet Theodore Roosevelt in a new way. These illustrations are not just cartoons—they unveil for us the caricatured Roosevelt, revealing an aspect of the man's character that has been little explored. There has not yet been a biography of TR's entire life relying on colorful cartoons as guides. In so crafting *BULLY!,* I have aimed for a comprehensive but not exhaustive biography. The greatest value to all readers, whether you are a devotee of American history in general, or a member of the large, loyal, and increasing corps of TR fans specifically, will be the wealth of pictorial commentary and satire herein. Cartoonists had their own "bully pulpits," right at their ink-stained drawing tables, and we are all the richer from their legacy.

# CHAPTER 1

# 1858~1877

# TR: AN AMERICAN PATRICIAN...
## OF SORTS

merica has distinguished itself from other cultures throughout its history. Most notably, the first generations of Americans possessed an inherent democratic spirit, a fierce individualism. From the beginning, America had no aristocracy. Early settlers and pioneers did not arrive with pedigrees or escutcheons. In fact, America in its earliest days was largely populated by lower classes, some indentured to work, some slaves, and countless others simply desperate for land and opportunity. Many people of middle class also arrived on the continent without pretension or provision—tradesmen and farmers, entrepreneurs as we would call them today. They arrived in the New World humble but hopeful. While European courts deeded tracts of land and created a gentry class, the average early American was not defined in terms of his geographical or even mercantile empire. The average American, then as now, was just that: average.

The Roosevelt family arrived on American shores around 1640, as ordinary as many of their fellow immigrants. They were from the Netherlands and planted themselves in

New Amsterdam, right where they disembarked. "Roosevelt" means "field of roses," and was spelled in various ways before "Roosevelt" became standard in the family's third American generation. The Roosevelts were like thousands of other immigrants to the American continent: fairly comfortable, very industrious, and extremely determined. Unlike many others, they had not fled religious oppression or racial discrimination in the Netherlands. They simply wanted to experience opportunity in this beautiful, abundant, welcoming land. Klaes Maartenszen van Rosevelt, the head of the family, possessed a pioneer spirit—a spirit that would be inherited by his descendent Theodore Roosevelt, who would be born in Manhattan two centuries after the family arrived in America.

The Roosevelts involved themselves in many businesses, first farming (Klaes bought a 50-acre farm in what is now Midtown Manhattan, right where the Empire State Building stands today), and then the importation of glass. Later they expanded their activities to include banking and real-estate investment. They were a prosperous family, "patrician" in the sense of the admirable elite, those worthy by distinction, responsible leaders who rise by merit. The Roosevelts became a very wealthy family, though they never reached the heights of the famous Astor and Vanderbilt fortunes. They were also immensely generous.

The Roosevelts concerned themselves with charity work and social betterment. Klaes's son Nicholas was the first of the clan to enter politics, around 1700, elected as a city alderman. Beyond public service, the Roosevelts also recognized first of all a personal responsibility toward others, to better the conditions of people and their situations.

Many of the institutions in and around New York today bearing the Roosevelt name are assumed to have been named in honor of President Theodore Roosevelt. On the contrary, many of them were established by, or named for, other members of this patrician family, before TR made his own mark. Roosevelt Hospital was founded and funded by a distant relative, James Roosevelt. The Roosevelt Building, the distinctive New York landmark designed by Mead and White, was named for Cornelius Roosevelt, Theodore's philanthropic grandfather. Although the American Museum of Natural History boasts the Roosevelt Rotunda—named for Theodore, and located behind an equestrian statue of him—his father was actually a founder of the institution.

In fact, when TR—as we will call the subject of this biography—was born on October 27, 1858, it would have seemed impossible that he could ever surpass the fame and universal respect of his father, Theodore (whom we shall call "the elder," or his nickname Thee; he was not actually a Senior, as his son was not formally Theodore Roosevelt Junior). By that point in the family's history and fortunes, TR's father concerned himself mainly with philanthropy. He supported big projects like the Metropolitan Museum of Art, which is said to have had its genesis in the Roosevelts' living room. Thee also had smaller—sometimes virtually anonymous—pursuits. For instance, he not only endowed the Newsboys Lodging-House for orphaned street children, but he paid weekly visits there, principally to encourage the youngsters and teach Bible classes. Thee did not enlist in the Union Army during the Civil War, because his wife, Martha Bulloch, was a southern belle from Roswell, Georgia. (Her brothers were prominent in the Confederate Navy.) Roosevelt compensated for this lack of active military service during the war by perfervid charity work among Union soldiers, encouraging them and, after consulting with President Lincoln, establishing the Allotment Bureau. He ceaselessly traveled to military camps, explaining and facilitating subscriptions to the Allotment System, whereby soldiers could send part of their pay to families back home.

He came to be known so widely as an advocate and worker for private causes and public charities that friends would joke that anyone who saw him coming down the street would greet him with the words, "How much this time, Theodore?" Although he petitioned local and national governments to instate compassionate policies, it was the hallmark of the Roosevelt family to practice and encourage personal responsibility among citizens for uplift and reform.

Roosevelt was remembered by his son TR as "the best man I ever knew." His marriage to "Mittie" Bulloch was the talk of Manhattan, as well as antebellum Georgia, where they married. Her family home, Bulloch Hall, which still stands in Roswell, is widely assumed to be the model for Tara in *Gone with the Wind*, and Mittie herself was said by friends of author Margaret Mitchell to be the inspiration for Scarlett O'Hara. After moving to New York City, Mrs. Theodore Roosevelt was generally regarded as an incredible white-skinned beauty, fragile yet determined, the essence of charm, an eccentric but gracious hostess and member of Society.

The Roosevelt children worshiped their father and adored their mother. Theirs was a notably happy childhood (except for health challenges), nurtured by servants and nannies, and punctuated by two lengthy trips to Europe, one extending to a cruise on the Nile. There were four Roosevelt children: Anna, the eldest, nicknamed Bamie (a corruption of "Bambina," little girl) or Bye; Theodore; Elliott (father of Eleanor Roosevelt, who would later marry her distant cousin Franklin from another branch of the family); and Corinne.

Roosevelt family crest. Roughly translated from the Latin: "He Who Plants, Cultivates."

The two eldest children had severe health problems. Bamie suffered from the painful spinal affliction known as Pott's Disease and spent a decade of her childhood in cumbersome braces. Her father cared for her in countless tender ways, and became interested in the affliction to the extent that he helped found and endow what became the New York Orthopedic Hospital. Its primary purposes included research and care, but also to be a dispensary of assistance and equipment to poor children. Thee's son Theodore, nicknamed "Teedie" in his youth, suffered from a variety of ailments, principally asthma and cholera morbus. Naturally slight and weak, the boy's frequent asthmatic episodes frightened him and his parents alike; he would find it nearly impossible to breathe and all strength would leave him. TR's earliest memories were of his father walking him around the house hour after hour at night, soothing him to induce calmer respiration. Teedie's frailty extended to his eyesight, which evidently approached legal blindness.

TR later wrote about realizing his poor eyesight during his thirteenth year:

> *It was this summer that I got my first gun, and it puzzled me to find that my companions seemed to see things to shoot at which I could not see at all. One day they read aloud an advertisement in huge letters on a distant billboard, and I then realized that something was the matter, for not only was I unable to read the sign but I could not even see the letters. I spoke of this to my father, and soon afterwards got my first pair of spectacles, which literally opened an entirely new world to me. I had no idea how beautiful the world was until I got those spectacles. I had been a clumsy and awkward little boy, and while much of my clumsiness and awkwardness was doubtless due to general character-istics, a good deal of it was due to the fact that I could not see and yet was wholly igno-rant that I was not seeing.*

Teedie once endured a crisis of self-esteem, when he was helpless against two bullies who cornered him. He had suffered a bout of asthma and was sent to a rural location for recuperation. "On the stagecoach ride thither I encountered a couple of other boys who were about my own age, but very much more competent and also much more mischie-vous. I have no doubt they were good-hearted boys, but they were boys! They found that I was a foreordained and predestined victim, and industriously proceeded to make life miserable for me. The worst feature was that when I finally tried to fight them I discovered that either one singly could not only handle me with easy contempt, but handle me so as not to hurt me much and yet to prevent my doing any damage whatever in return."

All these factors, plus the advice of physicians, convinced the elder Roosevelt to *work* his son's physical challenges out of him. TR was twelve. He remembered the speech:

"You have the mind but not the body.... You must *make* your body." The upstairs back piazza of the family town house at 28 East 20th Street in Manhattan was converted to a gymnasium. Teedie began to exercise, working on gymnastic equipment, lifting weights, boxing, and doing calisthenics. In the country, especially at the family's estate in Oyster Bay, Long Island, Teedie rode horses and rowed boats; he hiked and ran and played sports. Although it was years before he shed all symptoms of asthma, he never stopped exercising, all the way until the time of his death. He became known as a physical fitness addict. TR would title one of his books *The Strenuous Life*—his prescription for physical, moral, and civic standards. He boxed in college; he became an avid hunter, relishing the harshest conditions and most trying challenges; he rode to hounds for a period, frequently shocking society friends with his bloody face and broken bones, a reckless enthusiast. Later, during his time in the White House, in place of other presidents' "kitchen cabinets" of friends and advisors, TR was to establish a Tennis Cabinet that played almost every day weather permitted.

Teedie's active, aggressive lifestyle was closely tied to his later famous philosophy of the strenuous life. But his regimen was not solely physical; it merely reflected other aspects of the boy's emergent personality. Family and friends noted in young Teedie a voracious interest in everything around him. He could recall virtually every detail of books read to him. Later, when he could read to himself, he often consumed a book a day, sometimes more.

His love of reading continued into his adult years, even the busiest days of his presidency. Once a friend gave him a dense volume, with several pages marked, for Roosevelt to read when he could make the time. TR immediately opened the book, seeming to glance at page after page, lingering only slightly at each one. Finally, he closed the book and began discussing its points. His friend was incredulous that Roosevelt could have read, much less retained, any information in that manner. "Ask me anything about that material," TR challenged his friend. He did. Roosevelt passed the quiz.

As a boy, Teedie started a journal and made remarkable observations, particularly during travels—some comments very funny, and some quite sagacious about history (one of the subjects he particularly enjoyed). Likewise, Teedie took an interest in natural history, and before long he was measuring fish in street markets, drawing detailed studies of rodents, and stuffing specimens in every place at every opportunity. He established a boyhood "Roosevelt Natural History Museum" that prefigured his scientific essays and explorations in Africa and Brazil. Whatever spare places were left in the family's home after the construction of the gymnasium were littered with examination-tables, specimens in jars, bloody pelts, and the malodorous omnipresence of taxidermists' chemicals.

Some described the boy as precocious. Certainly people knew that there was more to Teedie than mere hyperactivity. He held his own with adults in discussions, but he maintained a tight-knit circle among his peers, including his siblings, always close, and neighborhood children like Bamie's friend Edith Carow from the other side of Union Square. He could be headstrong, but he was sensitive too, to the point of tenderness. He seemed to take an interest in everything, and he mastered whatever interested him. Many marked him for greatness.

Because of his frailty and poor eyesight, TR never attended school. He had tutors—one wonders whether they could keep up with their pupil at times—and entered Harvard after passing examinations. He intended to secure a degree in natural history. His later natural history work in the field and in print, and his discoveries and theories, would have made TR a prominent American in that discipline alone. Yet his "landscape" was wider than that covered in typical college courses. When he began his studies, he was dismayed that the prospects of a professional naturalist might shackle him to laboratories, rather than allowing him to roam the outdoors. TR dropped this major and pursued general studies. Nonetheless, he would still make great contributions to the field. Few laymen have done more to preserve and protect the natural environment than TR would do during the rest his life. Some critics today criticize TR's love of hunting. But it should be recalled that he set aside 230,000,000 acres of American land as national forests and parks, game preserves, and bird reservations during his presidency, making countless animals, as well as future generations of the American public, beneficiaries of his passion for natural history and God's creation.

Theodore grew up in a very devout Christian family. Thee's Dutch Reformed tradition merged well with Mittie's Presbyterian faith, both in the Calvinist tradition, and the family worshiped faithfully and read the Bible at home. When TR went to Harvard, he carried his spiritual habits with him, studying the Bible daily, attending chapel, and teaching weekly Sunday school classes in Cambridge. He might have been considered a prig. Indeed, his attire, sideburns, and affected Harvard accent were all in the style of a dandy; he even had a dog cart. Yet he maintained many friendships and enjoyed a convivial lifestyle. As a student, Roosevelt's intensity asserted itself. A classmate recalled an exasperated professor in one class saying, "Now look here, Roosevelt. Let me talk! I'm running this course!" TR was invited to join the Dickey and Hasty Pudding clubs, and the most exclusive Porcellian. He was staff member of the *Advocate*. When he graduated in 1880, he was both magna cum laude and Phi Beta Kappa.

Withal, the greatest impact on TR during his four college years was not Harvard-related. In the course of the social whirl of dances and dinners, he met the cousin of a classmate and fell in love. The pretty and fragile Alice Hathaway Lee, related to several Boston Brahmin families, was seventeen when Roosevelt fell under her spell. Roosevelt, boisterous and headstrong (sometimes redolent of taxidermy fluids), the New Yorker of Dutch lineage, was initially a strong cup of tea for dainty Alice. But TR was, predictably, determined. "Do you see that girl over there?" Roosevelt once asked a friend about Alice; "She won't have me, but I'm going to have *her*!" A long and tempestuous courtship followed, marked by florid Victorian emotionalism, one of Roosevelt's hallmarks at the time. TR was rapturous when Alice finally accepted his proposal of marriage.

While at school, he continued to build his body. TR was an active boxer on campus, although ultimately unsuccessful at the sport. Still, legends grew up on campus about his sportsmanship; more than once he suffered late hits, but defended his opponents to the spectators, insisting they had not heard the bell.

Also during this time, TR went on his first extended hunting trip, an expedition to the Maine woods. He reveled not only in the chase, the kills, the new flora and fauna, but also in the brutal cold, the long treks, and the daunting challenges. He befriended the guides William Sewall and Wilmot Dow. Skeptical at first of this willowy "dude," Sewall and Dow were soon convinced of his prowess in the field. TR proceeded to wear them out, rising earlier, staying awake longer, sacrificing comfort, dismissing freezing rain, snow, and ice, and constantly talking. He loved every minute of the experience. (A few years later, TR hired Sewall and Dow to move to the Dakota Territory to manage one of his cattle ranches.) TR became an habitué of the Maine woods, the first of many happy hunting grounds in his life.

North Dutch Church inscription, 1769. Two "Roosevelts" are listed: Senior Elder Jacobus and Deacon Isaac. The spelling of the name varied during the family's first generations in Manhattan.

The establishment patrician found himself quite at home in rough sleeping bags and crude hunting lodges. He was still "Mr. Roosevelt" to his guides; he still woke up early and left camp to read the Bible at dawn every morning; but his blue-blood inheritance was mixing well with the red-bloodedness of the outdoor life.

Another important game-changer occurred in TR's life during his college years, when his father entered politics. Politics—the dirty, sordid politics of the Gilded Age—traditionally was a pursuit that "proper" men disdained. Yet that admirable icon of New York society, Theodore Roosevelt the elder, surprised family and friends alike by accepting a federal appointment from President Rutherford B. Hayes. The position was an important one, but it was also one infamous for graft and corruption: Collector of the Port of New York. Its very reputation is what persuaded the elder Roosevelt to accept the appointment: he resolved to champion Reform.

TR's father was doomed to failure and even disgrace, none of his own doing or culpability. The forces that would attack him would steel his son to redeem the Reformist vision.

## The Society for the Prevention of Cruelty to Children.

| President. | Treasurer. | Executive Committee. |
|---|---|---|
| JOHN D. WRIGHT. | WM. L. JENKINS. | BENJAMIN H. FIELD, |
| | | HENRY BERGH, |
| | Counsel. | JOHN HOWARD WRIGHT, |
| Vice-Presidents. | ELBRIDGE T. GERRY. | THOMAS C. ACTON, |
| | | FERDINAND DE LUCA, |
| JAMES BROWN, | Secretary. | SINCLAIR TOUSEY, |
| PETER COOPER, | E. FELLOWS JENKINS. | WILLIAM M. VERMILYE, |
| WILLIAM E. DODGE, | | CHARLES HAIGHT, |
| JONATHAN THORNE, | | ADRIAN ISELIN, JR. |
| ROBERT L. STUART, | | B. B. SHERMAN, |
| AUGUST BELMONT, | OFFICES, | RICHARD R. HAINES, |
| THEODORE ROOSEVELT, | 1300 BROADWAY, | JAMES STOKES, |
| HENRY BERGH, | Corner 84th Street. | WILLIAM H. WEBB, |
| ELBRIDGE T. GERRY, | | FREDERIC DE PEYSTER, |
| CORNELIUS VANDERBILT. | | HARMON HENDRICKS. |

*New York, _____ 1875.*

Letterhead of the original Society for the Prevention of Cruelty to Children, 1875. TR's father was listed as a vice president—the SPCC was one of the many charities and missions he supported. He was in the company of "old money," established families represented by Elbridge Gerry and Peter Cooper. "New money" was represented by August Belmont and Cornelius Vanderbilt. Henry Bergh established the original Society for the Prevention of Cruelty to Animals, a novel cause, much ridiculed at first.

CHAPTER 2

# 1877~1878

# "THE BEST MAN I EVER KNEW"

TR was a world away from New York City at Harvard, and he was busy. His courses seemed comparatively easy to him, and, having decided against training to be a naturalist, he chose courses already within the orbit of his interests. Still, campus activities, his clubs, a budding romance, weekend balls and dinners, and hunting trips in Maine all commanded his attention.

Amidst his activities, TR maintained close contact with his family. His father's involvement in national politics would begin suddenly and end quickly, so Theodore, safe at Harvard, scarcely experienced it. Nonetheless, the difficulties his father suffered in his political career were momentous and traumatic, and they left their mark on his son. The episode surely inspired the crusading spirit in TR that lasted a lifetime: a zeal for political reform.

The Reconstruction era, at least in the North, brought prosperity, expansion, and innovation, but it had a dark substratum. Political corruption, while not new in the United

States, suddenly spread like an aggressive, noxious weed. Its handmaidens were decadence, exploitation, and a rapid, troubling division between social classes. Periodic press exposures and efforts by reformers ultimately were ineffective in the face of the corruption and collusion of the power elites. Mark Twain criticized the era in his aptly titled *The Gilded Age*. Henry Adams (writing as the long-secret "Anonymous") wrote *Democracy*, a popular satire that certainly created a buzz, though it ignited no reforms.

In New York City, the Democrat "Tweed Ring" of Tammany Hall, engineers of spectacular civic thievery, had been thrown out of power in the municipal elections of 1871, largely due to the powerful cartoons of Thomas Nast in *Harper's Weekly*. But within a few years, Tammany was back in control of the New York City government.

On the national field, Democrat Samuel J. Tilden outpolled Republican Rutherford B. Hayes for the presidency in popular votes in 1876. He seemed to have won the electoral vote, too, but questions arose about the counts in two southern states (where the Republican national administration had maintained a virtual military occupation since the Civil War's end). After weeks of uncertainty, disputed vote-counts in various jurisdictions, and action by the House of Representatives, Hayes was finally certified. Democrats rightfully felt their victory had been stolen, but Tilden discouraged protests (perhaps due to charges that he had attempted subterfuge himself, through cipher telegrams). As part of a silent "deal" between political bosses of the two national parties, federal troops were soon withdrawn from the South, which remained solidly Democrat, while the GOP retained the White House. Unbelievably, the protracted, sordid spectacle of the bazaar-haggling presidential election did not spark major flames of reform throughout the land, either. Politicos just kept rolling along.

The recently inaugurated President Hayes (widely referred to as "His Fraudulency" and "Rutherfraud" B. Hayes) was chastened by the manner of his election, which had been totally managed by GOP bosses. As his wife Lucy reformed the White House social regime (banning wine and liquor from state functions), the new president advocated for civil-service reforms. This obliged him to lock horns with some of his own party's dirtiest scoundrels. Not particularly clever or forceful, Hayes's attempts at reform were doomed to failure. Some of his allies, like Senator James G. Blaine, the focus of many corruption allegations, were hardly spotless themselves. Hayes planned to challenge the boss of the U.S. Senate, New York Republican Roscoe Conkling, and proceed from there to reform the Republican party and the country in general. But Conkling was a formidable foe. The American political landscape was littered with the corpses of many who had tried to take him down.

Senatorial courtesy—respecting the prerogatives of matters, even federal offices, in a senator's home state—was sacrosanct within the upper chamber, so Hayes's frontal assault on Conkling was a dubious enterprise from the start. The president requested the resignation of a Conkling henchman, Chester Alan Arthur, from his post as Collector of the New York Customs House. The Collector was paid $50,000 a year, a salary equal to the president's, the equivalent of $1 million in today's dollars. The Collector was also in a position to receive many kickbacks from arriving imports as well as from a bloated staff—kickbacks for himself, and for the party in power.

In late 1877, Hayes nominated a man of spotless reputation and national respect to replace Arthur as Collector: the philanthropist Theodore Roosevelt. No one could say anything ill of the man, except that he was not subservient to Conkling or his party faction, known as "Stalwarts." Roosevelt himself, surprised and flattered by the nomination, was willing to assume the Custom House duties and its challenges, not for the salary but for the opportunity to make a major contribution to his nation, to purify his party, and to help lead the reform movement.

Roosevelt had no idea what he would be up against. Arthur refused to resign; the president would not back down, and the stand-off attracted national attention. Democrats and anti-administration Republicans were happy to defend Arthur and to vilify Roosevelt. Rumors were invented, innuendos spread, and all sorts of criticism was aimed at the noble nominee. Roosevelt frankly was bewildered and hurt by the whole affair. It was all begun and ended in the space of a few short weeks. Chester Alan Arthur remained in office.

Theodore Roosevelt, the spotless paragon of civic virtue and reform, remained on the playing field, a tattered political leftover.

TR, beginning his sophomore year at Harvard, was aware of the firestorm, but he did not immediately suffer the full force of the blow to his family. He congratulated his father upon the nomination, proud that the man was willing to sacrifice so much to become a crusader for civil-service reform. When he became aware of the campaign of vilification against his father, TR wrote letters of encouragement and sympathy to him—but often only one line. It was certainly not that he didn't care; but apparently he assumed the imbroglio was not as horrible as it, in fact, was. The family in New York was wounded because their honorable paterfamilias had been dishonored. Even at best, the elder Roosevelt found himself talked about as a man who had allowed himself to be a naïve pawn in tawdry political wars.

Shortly after this traumatic episode, the family was blindsided by a calamity worse than the first. Thee's health began to unravel; he suffered acutely, was unable to eat or sleep, and lost weight. Naturally the family attributed the malaise to the strain of the political humiliation. Soon, however, as the pain became excruciating, doctors discovered that he had virulent and inoperable stomach cancer. The cancer advanced rapidly. Theodore's faculties slowly disappeared. He became fevered and delirious, and evinced such pain that doctors could scarcely medicate with effect.

The family decided, at first, not to alarm TR at Harvard beyond general reports of his father's indisposition. But the sickroom situation deteriorated so rapidly that when the son was at last advised to rush home to see his father one last time, he arrived hours after his father's death on February 9, 1878. Theodore Roosevelt Senior was just forty-six years old.

The "best friend I ever had," as TR considered his father, was gone, and TR was stunned beyond consolation, filling his diaries with descriptions of his sorrow, and a gloomy conviction that he could not ever rise to the level of his father as a member of society, as a reformer, or as a man. TR acknowledged the comfort of knowing that his father was in the arms of God, but the comfort belonged more to the elder Roosevelt (released from the ravages of his disease) than to TR himself, bereft of his father and friend. He would feel the loss of his father's advice and guidance bitterly, and he repeatedly swore to live up to his father's ideals, to do what his father would have him do. "But I shall always live my life as he would want…that anything I do would make him proud of me," TR declared to family and friends.

TR literally owed his life to his father, who had carried the asthmatic boy in his arms at night, and walked and sleighed through the New York snows, hoping that cold, clear air would open the boy's lungs. He had built his son a state-of-the-art gymnasium and helped him exercise, hired boxing coaches, and taken him on hiking and hunting trips to the Adirondacks. Through it all, he imparted advice and counsel, extolling heroes from the Bible and world history, and providing a real-life example of compassion towards his fellow men. For the rest of his life, TR would meet people who had been helped by his father, in secret episodes never publicized. For instance, when TR was governor, he met John Green Brady, governor of the Alaska Territory, who told him how the elder Roosevelt had given him money when he was a homeless child in New York City, and sent him West to be reared. This was just one of many such stories about his father's generosity shared with TR throughout his adult life.

But in that 1878 winter, the heartbroken young man confided to his diary: "I feel that if it were not for the certainty that he is not dead but gone before, I should almost perish." He went on, "How little use I am or ever shall be."

But life went on; it had to go on—and pressing ahead with the Great Adventure, of which life and death are both parts, is what TR's father himself would have counseled.

# AMERICAN CARTOON JOURNALS

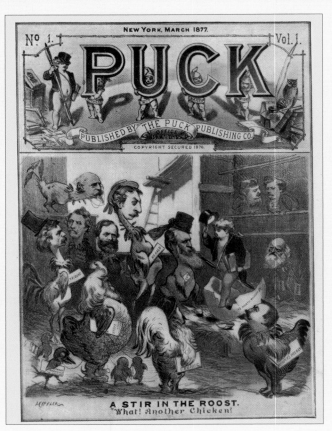

Joseph Keppler was born in Vienna and had a passion for the stage and cartooning. He drew for humor magazines in Vienna and, after emigrating to the United States, in St. Louis. When he started *Puck* as a German-language cartoon, humor, and political magazine in New York in 1876, he was already a celebrity in the artistic world. He was *Leslie's* chief cartoonist for a short time, which meant that he was Thomas Nast's major rival.

When *Puck* scored a success (partly on Keppler's innovation—front-page, back-page, and center-spread cartoons in colors), it produced an English-language edition starting in March 1877, and Keppler was thereafter the preeminent American cartoonist. In Keppler's cover of the first issue, the figure of Puck modestly appears among rival magazine and newspaper editors, with the caricature of Thomas Nast in the lower right.

The legendary illustrator and cartoonist Arthur Burdett Frost drew this encomium of his paper, *The Graphic*, in 1875. In the middle is a "typical" *Graphic* reader, urbane and comfortable. Rival newspapers and their readers are depicted via visual puns—*The Sun*, *The World*, etc. Reproduced from the original artwork. Frost's sketches and doodles can be seen in the margins, the formative working of a great artist: among Frost's many later credits were illustrations for Lewis Carroll books and *Uncle Remus* stories, as well as Theodore Roosevelt's hunting articles.

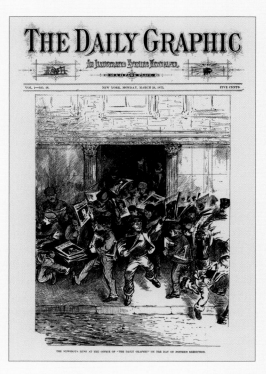

*RIGHT:* New York's *Daily Graphic* was the first American daily newspaper to run illustrations, and lots of them. It was a splashy sensation in the world of journalism, and was aided by the development of mechanical photo-engraving, although, ironically, many of its artists endeavored to make their drawings look like woodcuts. Great cartoonists like A. B. Frost and E. W. Kemble did some of their first work as cartoonists on the staff. This early issue, from its first month (March of 1873) shows newsboys rushing to hit the streets with the latest edition of the *Graphic*.

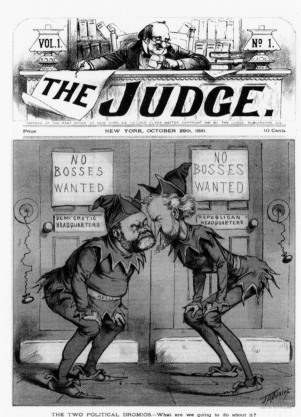

*The Judge* (later *Judge*) was an obvious imitation of *Puck*. Its chief cartoonist was James Albert Wales, a renegade *Puck* staffer. Other cartoonists were Grant Hamilton (who remained for years and became art editor), Frank Beard, and Thomas Worth, veteran of countless Currier and Ives comic lithographs. After the 1884 campaign, when the political establishment saw how effective *Puck* was, Republican investors bought *Judge*, made it a partisan voice, and lured Bernard Gillam and Eugene Zimmerman away from the former publication. *Judge* was a prominent cartoon magazine into the 1930s, and then limped along under various managements until the early 1950s.

*Life* was founded by John Ames Mitchell and Edward Sanford Martin, two Harvard grads who had worked on the first issues of the *Lampoon* there. It launched in 1883 as a black-and-white alternative to *Puck*—a society journal reminiscent of the English *Punch*. When cartoonist Charles Dana Gibson introduced the Gibson Girl to its pages, *Life*'s success was assured. The magazine was generally Democratic (founding the Fresh Air Fund for urban children and crusading against vivisection) and rather anti-Semitic. In 1936 the title was bought by Henry Luce of *Time* in order to launch the photo/news weekly.

*Truth* magazine was always a runner-up to *Puck* and *Judge*. It was usually designed for what was called the "barber shop readership," featuring mildly racy cartoons of chorus girls and the like. However, through the years it fluctuated, going heavy or light on politics, featuring high-gloss chromolithographs, and careening between slum cartoons, chorus-girl titillation, and patriotic splashes. Mostly, it is remembered as a breeding-ground for cartoonists who went on to fame in larger venues.

*The Verdict* was a short-lived color cartoon weekly of the late 1890s (like *Vim* and *The Bee*). Its chief cartoonists were MIRS and Horace Taylor. It was edited by Alfred Henry Lewis, a novelist and muckraker in the making; and its publisher was Oliver H. P. Belmont, who would long be active in Democrat politics.

# THE TRAUMATIC POLITICAL EXPERIENCE OF THEODORE ROOSEVELT'S FATHER

THE ERL KING. (NEW VERSION.)

The father groaneth, he rideth wild,        Arrived at the "White House", with fear and dread,
He holds in his arms the sobbing child.        Close in his arms, the child lay dead.—*See page 2.*

Rutherford Birchard Hayes won the presidency with a minority of the popular vote and an Electoral College victory generally assumed to be rigged. None of this was his doing, however, and he tried to atone for these circumstances by removing most federal troops from the Democratic South, and pursuing an agenda of Civil Service reform. His presidency stands, however, as an example of how good intentions can be subverted by a weak will and incompetent political instincts. In this allegorical *Puck* cartoon by Joseph Keppler, based on the Goethe poem, Hayes and his baby Civil Service Reform are haunted and pursued through the dismal swamp by shades of numerous enemies. Keppler was a clever artist, and often incorporated caricatures into tree branches and rock formations.

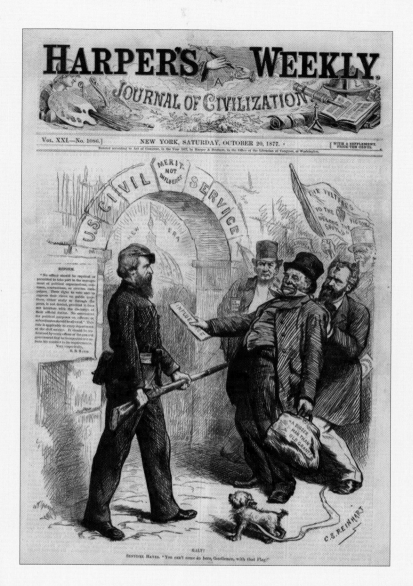

HARPER'S WEEKLY.

JOURNAL OF CIVILIZATION

Vol. XXI—No. 1086.]   NEW YORK, SATURDAY, OCTOBER 20, 1877.   [WITH A SUPPLEMENT. PRICE TEN CENTS.

HALT!

Bestidon Hayes. "You can't come in here, Gentlemen, with that Flag!"

This C. S. Reinhart cartoon depicts the nub of the GOP intra-party battle that settled in the controversy surrounding TR's father. *Harper's Weekly* portays Hayes as guardian of the gate to the new era of Civil Service reform. Conkling, right, puts forward his candidate ("a bigger man than old Grant"—a current term of hyperbolic praise) who represents Chester Arthur, Collector of the Port of New York and boss of the Customs House, and other machine appointees. The month previous to this cartoon, Hayes had announced his intention to replace Arthur; within weeks he nominated Theodore Roosevelt the elder. *Harper's Weekly* editorialized: "The selection of Mr. Theodore Roosevelt for Collector is most admirable. For all the high character and ability which the duties of the place demand, Mr. Roosevelt is known to be in full sympathy with the principles of reform, and to have the force and courage to observe the.... [I]t is impossible that a man of the energy and firmness of Mr. Roosevelt should not make himself felt as a purifying force throughout the whole institution."

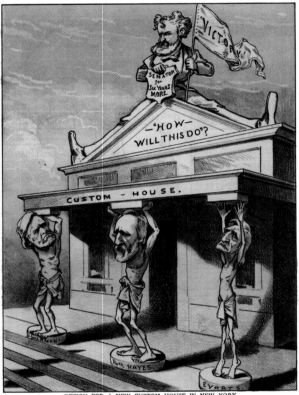

DESIGN FOR A NEW CUSTOM HOUSE IN NEW YORK.

Roscoe Conkling was vain and arrogant, but he was a spellbinding orator. In the Senate, many colleagues considered his eloquence a prelude to grandiloquence. "The Titan" was pictured by the *Graphic* shortly before the episode of his sabotage of Theodore Roosevelt the elder.

After Roscoe Conkling prevailed upon fellow senators to reject President Hayes' nomination of Theodore Roosevelt on the basis of senatorial privilege, *Puck* suggested this new design for the Port of New York headquarters.

# CHAPTER 3

# 1878~1884

# RISING LIKE A ROCKET

Indeed, life went on, and sunshine returned to TR's life in the person of Alice Hathaway Lee. His previous "understandings" (such as with childhood friend Edith Carow, who almost all their friends assumed would become his wife) were set aside. His diaries were crowded now with Alice. His letters home and chats with friends were generally on two topics: Alice and Alice. When planning hunting trips to the northern plains and the Rockies with Elliott, he told everyone how he would miss Alice. He arranged all sorts of "sprees" with common friends and with Chestnut Hill relatives of his classmates, just to see Alice. In the emotional hyperventilation common to the Victorian Era, TR was dramatic about his love, jealous of Alice's attention, and suspicious of possible rivals. Alice had rejected multiple marriage proposals from "Teddy" (her nickname for him, and one which, except for Alice, he strongly discouraged anyone from using), frustrating him often. Finally she relented, accepted his proposal, and never again confessed to anything other than head-over-heels love and devotion for him. The reasons for Alice's reluctance could have been anything from her beau's headstrong nature to her own youth (she was only seventeen when they met). Possibly she was repelled by the scent of arsenic and other singular fragrances attendant to the practice of taxidermy—for TR still collected and studied animal specimens with avidity, and his living space reeked of the hobby. But Alice evidently discovered that even a dainty debutante's nose can grow accustomed to almost anything, when the heart leads the way.

After TR's graduation from Harvard, near the top of his class, the couple married in Brookline, Massachusetts, on October 27, 1880—his twenty-second birthday. Their honeymoon was delayed due to Roosevelt's acceptance to Columbia Law School in New York. (He did not take many courses, eventually leaving law school and a possible career behind, convinced that too much of the law "was devoted to getting people off the hook.") The young couple moved in with the widowed Mittie in the Roosevelt mansion on 57th Street, discussed plans for a country home in Oyster Bay, on Long Island's North Shore, and finally honeymooned in Europe.

Before the honeymoon, the young husband was examined by a doctor who grimly diagnosed a heart malfunction, a weakness that mandated TR never again exert himself. Roosevelt responded by scaling the Matterhorn in Switzerland on his honeymoon. (It had been scarcely more than fifteen years since climbers conquered the mountain, and four members of the original eight-man party died in the attempt.) There is no record that Alice disapproved—we can wonder whether it would have dissuaded her Teddy—but neither is there any record that she showed an interest in joining his vertical spree.

Back in New York City, young Theodore was not settled about a profession, although he was certain that he needed to support his wife and (he hoped and assumed) a large family. He had a visceral aversion to the practice of law, despite applying to Columbia and briefly clerking in the office of his uncle, Robert Barnhill Roosevelt. To any of the traditional Roosevelt businesses, such as banking or glass importation, TR likewise felt no attraction. The disinclination possibly had something to do with the fact that numbers and figures flummoxed him, then and throughout his life. He had an interest in the literary life, and he invested in the publishing house of G. P. Putnam's Sons, although he never performed any managerial or editorial duties. Along with numbers, TR had a lifelong problem with spelling. Although he became a prolific author of books and magazine articles, his spelling was abysmal. To his last days, for instance, he wrote "do'n't" instead of "don't."

While Roosevelt sorted out his options for occupation, he certainly was not idle. He worked with astonishing intensity on a book he had begun at Harvard, *The Naval War of 1812*. Two uncles on his mother's side had been prominent in the Confederate Navy and had exiled themselves to England after the war. Theodore and Alice called on them during their honeymoon tour, and TR peppered them with questions for his book. He finished *The Naval War* in New York, in the midst of involvement in civic affairs, emulating his father's charitable visits around the city, and brief stints fox-hunting in the country. The lengthy book was released in 1882, and was widely praised for its thoroughgoing accuracy and impartiality. It was accepted into libraries of Royal war colleges, as well as those of American historians and military personnel. *The Naval War of 1812* continues to be one of the standard works on the subject. Theodore Roosevelt was twenty-three at the time.

The American political scene had recently experienced changes. In the presidential year of 1880, President Hayes declined to stand for reelection. Former president U. S. Grant allowed himself to be pushed for a third term by the Roosevelts' nemesis Roscoe Conkling. Various anti-Grant politicians, including Senators John Sherman and James G. Blaine (commonly called Half-Breeds) jockeyed for the nomination, eventually creating a convention stalemate. Dark horse Representative James A. Garfield of Ohio was the compromise candidate. The convention attempted to placate the defeated boss Conkling by nominating Chester Alan Arthur for the vice presidency.

Thus the Roosevelt name echoed once again in national political discussions, referring to the recent imbroglio involving TR's father; one can imagine how personal—and personally offensive—the reminders must have seemed to the younger Roosevelt.

The Garfield-Arthur ticket was successful, defeating the Democrat nominee, Civil War hero of Gettysburg General Winfield S. Hancock. The Roosevelt family's association with Arthur took an even more bizarre turn when, during TR's honeymoon, President Garfield was assassinated, shot in the back at a train station by disappointed office-seeker Charles Guiteau. In a symbolic and dramatic manifestation of the entire cesspool of grasping ambition and political corruption of the time, Guiteau shouted, "Garfield is dead, and now Chet Arthur is president!"

Would reform of the civil service and party politics *finally* attract adherents of substance? Gentlemen were disgusted by the state of politics at the time, and "decent people" eschewed politics. For this reason friends had been startled when the elder Roosevelt accepted the president's nomination to manage the notoriously graft-ridden Customs House. The same friends would be doubly surprised at young TR, who decided to explore becoming what he called "part of the governing class" rather than to disdain it, and to enter at the ground floor, although he shared the general disgust with politics. The 21st District Republican Association was technically on the second floor, over a saloon, and TR must have looked out of place at the meetings. Young, nattily attired, with side-whiskers, he socialized with men who were, precisely as his proper friends had warned him, saloon-keepers and horse-car conductors. But TR had determined to be a member of "the governing class," and not leave it to the proprietorship of anyone not a "gentleman." The district was "silk stocking," a mixture of wealthy and working-class families; the smoke-filled meetings themselves were dominated by rough types whose experience in politics was closer to stealing ballot boxes and "influencing" voters than quoting the Federalist Papers.

The local Republican boss was a former Tammany Democrat, Jake Hess, and the organizational rival was Irish immigrant Joe Murray. TR became the beneficiary of a minor power struggle when Hess's choice for the state Assembly seat was checkmated by Murray's successful nomination of young Roosevelt. Hess took his own defeat good-naturedly and joined the canvass for TR. It was a campaign that would require attention, the political leaders soon realized.

While doing the rounds of the district's influential supporters, Roosevelt was introduced to a saloon-keeper, who hinted that he expected favors to the liquor interests to continue, and that he thought operating licenses for saloons were priced too high. Roosevelt replied that he intended to treat all constituents evenly, with no favors; he added that, personally, he considered the saloons should pay higher, not lower, license fees. For the balance of the campaign his appearances were arranged with his "father's friends," the bluebloods and upper-class residents of the district; guys like Jake and Joe visited the rest. Endorsements of TR by prominent citizens included the signatures of Joseph Choate (noted attorney and later a distinguished diplomat), and Elihu Root (later Secretary of War under presidents McKinley and Roosevelt, Secretary of State under TR, and eventually a U.S. senator). Roosevelt easily won election, supported by disparate constituencies of a hybrid electorate, and as the son of his prominent father, the noted reformer.

TR was a quick study in parliamentary procedures; he was also headstrong. It was not the custom for freshmen to introduce much legislation in their first year, but within a month of being sworn in, TR introduced four reform bills; one passed. Because his reform efforts drew attention, he quickly drew prominent committee assignments and became a member the GOP leadership in the Assembly.

Newspapers, rivals, and even members of his own party did not exactly know what to make of the intense 23-year-old. In those days, Roosevelt was seen as a "dandy"—and indeed, he cultivated the impression. He wore tight pants and colorful vests; he often wore sashes and carried a gold-headed cane; he sported tan kidskin gloves and wore spats. He affected a Harvard

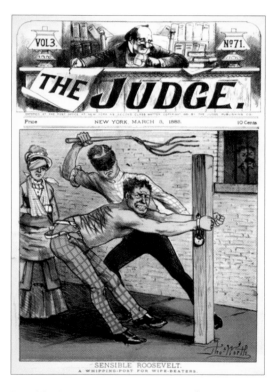

SENSIBLE ROOSEVELT.
A WHIPPING-POST FOR WIFE-BEATERS.

Possibly the first cartoon mentioning (and perhaps picturing, through the window) Theodore Roosevelt, Thomas Worth's cover cartoon in *Judge*, March 3, 1883, praises "Sensible Roosevelt" for sponsoring a bill that sanctioned the whipping post for men convicted of beating their wives. It failed to become law.

accent (which he chose to employ his whole life) and was derisively pictured in a newspaper report as applauding with the tips of his fingers and uttering phrases like, "I am rawther re-lieved." But many stories survive of surprises delivered to those who thought him a sissy or a pushover. When TR heard that one Assemblyman wanted to recruit cronies to toss TR in a blanket outside the Capitol, he immediately confronted the bully, telling him: "If you try anything like that, I'll kick you, I'll bite you, I'll kick you in the balls, I'll do anything to you—you'd better leave me alone." The prank was never attempted. When another Assemblyman made fun of TR's appearance across a tavern one night, Roosevelt walked right over and punched him in the face. When the man arose, Roosevelt knocked him to the floor a second time. Finally TR helped him up and said, "Now you go over there and wash yourself. When you are in the presence of gentlemen, conduct yourself like a gentleman," and ordered the man a beer. This was in keeping with the advice of his father, as TR would recall: "He certainly gave me the feeling that I was always to be both decent and manly, and that if I were manly nobody would laugh at my being decent."

Then the bold freshman Assemblyman dropped a real bombshell: in the first weeks of 1882, he announced his intention to formally investigate Judge Theodore Westbrook, generally recognized as prepatory to moving articles of impeachment. TR had discovered that Westbrook granted outrageous favors to elevated railway lines in New York—setting values, harming competitors, and defrauding investors—that benefited financier Jay Gould. In fact, before his rulings, the judge met with Gould in the latter's hotel suite. Now the press and statewide electorate, and not only fellow legislators, took notice of Theodore Roosevelt, and for substantial reasons.

Young TR did his homework. He conducted hearings, orchestrated a release of information to newspapers, and navigated the waters of Assembly procedures. However, he was a pilot without sufficient experience, and his efforts were thwarted twice, with bribes to Assemblymen, parliamentary maneuvers, and other methods even more sinister. A wealthy friend of his father's generation privately advised TR to "go along" with the

system, now that he had made his "splash." (TR later cited this as his first personal introduction to the invisible collusion between corrupt politicians and malefactors of great
wealth.) Then, one night in Albany, a woman fainted on the sidewalk in front of him.
Ever the gentleman, Roosevelt hailed a cab and took the woman to her address. When
she insisted he take her to her rooms, he grew suspicious. After leaving her at the door,
he had the house watched, and discovered that men were waiting there to frame and
"expose" him in an affair for the ultimate purpose of blackmail. Every attack, and even
his highly publicized hearings on Judge Westbrook, taught TR how to carry on the fight
for reform. (Westbrook was found dead in his rooms, a possible suicide, several weeks
after he "survived" the investigation.)

TR stood so squarely in the public eye after only one term that his caucus nominated
him for Speaker of the Assembly. As Republicans were in the minority, his election was
unlikely, but the process resulted in his becoming Minority Leader. He took on more
duties, researching legislation, managing his caucus, and pushing reform measures. He
spent the long, busy weekdays in Albany, and commuted by train to Manhattan for
weekends with Alice; she seldom joined him in the relatively backwater state capital.
Through it all, he wrote articles for magazines and maintained a proper and very busy
social life. A staunch Republican, he nevertheless publicly cooperated with the new
reform-minded Democrat governor Grover Cleveland. They were brothers under the
skin: Cleveland, former sheriff of Erie County and mayor of Buffalo, was called "ugly
honest," and was once praised with the greatest compliment a reformer can receive:
"We love him for the enemies he has made!"

Now that Roosevelt's reputation was extending beyond his district, city, and even
New York State, he also attracted the notice of cartoonists. Then, as now, cartoons
provided a barometer of a politician's public standing. Though still young and wiry,
Roosevelt's distinctive features were the stuff of caricature—moustache, *pince-nez*, and the
look of fierce determination. *Puck*, America's first successful cartoon magazine, featured
TR in front-page and center-page cartoons. Thomas Nast, the "Father of American

Thomas Nast, the Dean of American political cartoonists, drew some of the first nationally published cartoons of Theodore Roosevelt. Some featured the unknown young reformer with the new governor of New York, also a young and unheralded reformer, Grover Cleveland. The two men cooperated on legislation that impressed people of both parties, as well as crusading cartoonists. From *Harper's Weekly.*

political cartooning," whom Abraham Lincoln had dubbed "the North's best recruiting sergeant" for his pro-Union drawings, and whose cartoons in *Harper's Weekly* had brought down the Tweed Ring and assisted in the defeat of Horace Greeley in the presidential election of 1872, unknowingly heralded two future reform-minded presidents when he pictured Roosevelt and Governor Cleveland cooperating on reform measures.

Meanwhile, the young politician was learning that there were institutional evils that threatened republican government and the economic system itself. And the problem ran deep, because tainted officials like Westbrook allowed graft or sanctioned the ruin of honest competitors from a sincere motive: to maintain the "greater good" (at least in their view) at all costs. Wealthy members of TR's class sincerely regarded oppression and manipulations as necessary, minor evils. Their philosophy in the face of obvious corruption tended to be, "Don't rock the boat." This did not sit well with TR. He began to realize that coarse and corrupt petty politicians were no worse threats to a republican democracy than were refined and corrupt prominent men of influence. This came as no surprise to a young man whose father had accorded the same respect to an orphaned newsboy as he did the moguls with whom he discussed numerous charity projects. The Roosevelts understood that honesty and integrity demanded respect, no matter a person's social standing, while wrongdoing should incur blame, regardless of one's high reputation or status.

A tour of cigar-making shops in lower Manhattan really opened Roosevelt's eyes to the social problems that were rampant at the time. (He was invited to witness the conditions first-hand by Samuel Gompers, four years previous to Gompers' founding of the American Federation of labor.) The shops were located in neighborhoods teeming with overcrowded tenements and sweat-shops. New Yorkers were well aware of these ghettos; TR himself had accompanied his father on visits to missions in their streets. Yet few citizens actually climbed their stairs, and fewer were outraged by the social, health, and economic ills prevalent there. Visiting the dark rooms where large families slept, ate, and rolled cigars or sewed shirtwaists eighteen hours a day obliged TR to open his eyes. His concern was quickened by the fact that some families in his social set uptown profited from the businesses whose goods were made in those tenements. Additionally, anarchists and socialists were increasingly active in the neighborhoods, attempting to recruit adherents.

TR determined to reform those conditions—the system behind them, if it could be done—in the name of justice; this became a thematic preoccupation of his career: not reaction, not revolution, but realizable reform. His was a conservative impulse that might resort to radical means. He set to work immediately, holding hearings and introducing legislation to alleviate conditions in the slums and reform the bureaucratic corruption that allowed for countless violations of law and regulation.

When Roosevelt began his third term in the Assembly in 1884, the Republicans were in control, the beneficiaries of the gathering tide of reform across the country. The Pendleton Civil Service Act, a mild but significant reform expanding the percentage of merit appointments in federal government jobs, had become the law of the land. In Albany, TR did not receive the nomination for Speaker of the New York Assembly. While his colleagues were willing to make him Minority Leader, they were not quite ready to elect him Speaker. TR was, understandably, disappointed. He bitterly regretted doing scant spadework on his campaign (he had taken the attitude that the office would find the man) and the unreliable assurances of his colleagues that the Speakership would be his. He later wrote, "I rose like a rocket and then came an awful cropper, and had to learn from bitter experience the lesson that I was not all-important." But he would never forget this crash course in practical politics, and the primacy of nitty-gritty organization. The routine but tedious work of identifying allies and opponents, "counting noses," and other such everyday political activities thenceforth became second nature. In fact TR grew to enjoy the nuts-and-bolts of politics, and in later years he stoutly defended the "practical" side of politics.

Always resilient, TR spent little time licking his wounds before plunging back into his work, doing what he could, with what he had, where he was. Whether as consolation prize or by merit, he was named chairman of the powerful Cities Affairs committee, and he undertook a task more daunting than any he had previously set before himself: to restructure the entire municipal government of New York City. The most practical means to effect reform of that corrupt system, he believed, was to transfer power from the non-elected Board of Aldermen (most of them beholden to party machines) to the office of the currently powerless but popularly elected—and accountable—mayor of the city of New York.

As he prepared for this gargantuan task, two other matters also absorbed his attention. First, TR was determined to play a role on behalf of reforming the GOP at the Republican

National Convention in several months. He wanted to see a "pure" standard-bearer nominated.

The other matter was less prosaic, but it fairly blotted out any other concerns about political defeats or crusades. Alice was pregnant. TR was bursting with joy at the prospect of being a father. Now he could emulate his own father, who had fulfilled Proverbs 22:6, "Train up a child in the way he should go, and when he is old, he will not depart from it." Roosevelt was eager to establish his own family in the same manner.

While he was at work in the Assembly on February 13, 1884, word reached Roosevelt that Alice was delivering their child, and in distress. An unusually heavy snowstorm raging between Albany and Manhattan made travel excruciatingly slow. When TR finally arrived at the family home on 57th Street, he was met at the door by his brother Elliott, who told him: "Alice is dying. Mother is dying too. There is a curse upon this house."

Indeed, both ladies were fevered and insensible. Alice had given birth to a healthy baby girl, but was dying of Bright's Disease, a kidney ailment. Mittie was dying of typhoid fever. She had always been a virtual germophobe—one of her eccentricities—but this dread disease appeared suddenly, despite all her precautions, and now threatened to claim her life. Theodore spent the night going up and down the stairs, from bedside to bedside. His mother died first. He trudged upstairs once more and held Alice's hand and mopped her fevered brow in the hours until she also died.

Roosevelt was inconsolable. His diary entry on the occasion was nothing but a large X and the legend, "The light has gone out of my life."

At the double funeral, attended by throngs of mourners, nearly everyone, including the pastor conducting the service at the Fifth Avenue Presbyterian Church, was sobbing. But not Theodore, who simply sat as if in a daze in the front pew; witnesses said he seemed insensible to the events of the funeral and the double burial at Greenwood Cemetery in Brooklyn, resting place of many prominent New Yorkers.

Afterwards he summoned the emotional strength to publish a memorial for close family and friends. He wrote about Alice:

*She was beautiful in face and form, and lovelier still in spirit; as a flower she grew, and as a fair young flower she died. Her life had been always in the sunshine; there had never come to her a single sorrow; and none ever knew her who did not love and revere her for the bright, sunny temper and her saintly unselfishness. Fair, pure, and joyous as a maiden; loving, tender, and happy as a young wife; when she had just become a mother, when her life seemed to be just begun, and when the years seemed so bright before her—then, by a strange and terrible fate, death came to her. And when my heart's dearest died, the light went from my life forever.*

Theodore composed himself sooner than most souls could, and returned to the legislature two days after the funeral. He explained grimly, "I shall come back to my work at once; there is now nothing left for me except to try to so live as not to dishonor the memory of those I loved who have gone before me." Assemblymen of both parties, including enemies and Tammany men, paid tribute to their colleague and his departed darlings; again, there were few dry eyes in the chamber. Then the Assembly adjourned in mourning, a gesture usually reserved for actual members who died.

Now TR worked like a dynamo, at a faster and more intense pace than he ever had before on any project. He drafted many reform bills, all complex and formidable. He held hearings in Albany and extensive hearings in Manhattan, even on weekends. He wrote out the bills longhand, making numerous corrections; and when opponents attempted subterfuge by manipulating deadlines for reporting and voting, he worked through the nights and even sent the bills page by page to the Assembly printer. At the end of the whirlwind, nine bills were reported from committee, and seven were passed by the full Assembly. The sheer work involved was an astonishing achievement, a testimony to Roosevelt's energy and his ability to create public pressure through publicity and the press, a gift he learned to cultivate with increasing cleverness and effectiveness. In three short terms in the New York Assembly, TR was responsible for a host of reform legislation, from civil service corrections (informally called the Roosevelt-Cleveland Law) to workplace safety (the Cigar Bill) to reforms of New York City utilities, operations, and charter.

When the Assembly adjourned in April of 1884, TR "relaxed" by throwing himself into work preparatory to the Republican National Convention. He wanted to see the nation's rising tide of reform float the GOP's boat. In recent elections, the major Republican factions, Half-Breeds and Stalwarts, had proven equally corrupt. So it appeared that James G. Blaine, a senator from Maine who was a magnetic leader, a capable politician, and a political hero, had a good chance at the nomination. As it turned out, though, he had feet of clay. Through the years, going back to his days as a congressman and Speaker of the House, Blaine's record was littered with incidents—and incriminating documents— of soliciting money for legislation, peddling influence, and even destroying evidence. Nevertheless, after seeking the presidency in 1876 and 1880, it seemed to be his time in 1884. Garfield was dead; Grant was close to death; Conkling was off the stage; and President Arthur, who desired renomination, was a lightweight foe.

Reform-minded Republicans were aghast at the possibility of Blaine's nomination. Roosevelt and a new friend, Henry Cabot Lodge of Massachusetts, late member of his state's lower house and Lecturer at Harvard during TR's student days, mobilized themselves on behalf of a candidate they believed could serve the cause of reform, Senator George F. Edmunds of Vermont. They worked tirelessly to gather delegates' commitments, and to persuade others to withhold their commitments until the actual convention balloting. They conferred with dark-horse and favorite-son figures on the national scene. In their efforts they formed a phalanx of prominent reform-minded Republicans, including George William Curtis, editor of *Harper's Weekly*, and Carl Schurz, the German immigrant who had fought in the Civil War and led the "Liberal Republican" revolt against President Grant's reelection back in 1872.

Significantly, TR never even considered supporting President Arthur's renomination. Although Chester Alan Arthur had changed his spots when he assumed the presidency and surprised many citizens with decent if unspectacular support of civil-service reform, TR must have found it nearly impossible to think of him as anything other than the corrupt Collector of the New York Customs House, whose refusal to vacate his office had so humiliated TR's father a few years earlier. Although TR's surviving letters and the memoirs of his associates reveal no evidence of resentment or revenge, it is difficult to believe that Roosevelt would have been able to countenance Arthur's renomination, much less his reelection.

Roosevelt was elected co-chair of the New York State delegation, by virtue of his position in the state party and his vaunted accomplishments in the Assembly, as well as a deadlock between the convention forces of Arthur and his opponents. At the convention, TR assiduously worked the aisles and back-rooms on behalf of a reform platform and

## BELSHAZZAR'S FEAST

"The Royal Feast of Belshazzar Blaine and the Money Kings" referred to a dinner given to Blaine at Delmonico's restaurant by leading financiers a few nights before the election. The cartoon was printed in *The New York World* and distributed widely, especially to the clichéd poor folks in the lower left. It was a collaboration between Walt McDougall and Valerian Gribedayeff (who drew likenesses better than McDougall).

reform candidate. His first speech on the national stage was the emotional nomination of John R. Lynch to be convention chairman. Lynch, a former slave, late Speaker of the Mississippi House, and now a U.S. congressman, was elected chairman after TR's speech. In the end, "Blaine, Blaine, James G. Blaine, the continental liar from the state of Maine" was nominated for president. But Theodore Roosevelt, just twenty-five years old, was one of the most conspicuous and influential figures in the convention.

With Blaine as the party's nominee, Roosevelt was deeply conflicted during the canvass. Many of his confreres in the reform movement bolted from the party rather than support Blaine. This decision was easy to understand, especially when the Democrats obligingly nominated the paragon of reform, TR's sometime ally Grover Cleveland, Governor of New York State. But Roosevelt and Lodge decided to stay and work within the Republican party. They admired Cleveland to a point, but they could not abide the Democrats' passel of sectionalism, incipient corruption, and assortment of municipal machine bosses. Roosevelt and Lodge were vilified for their decision by their former allies and independent publications. Many cartoons had welcomed TR to the national stage in 1884; now, many more skewered him for "deserting" the forces of reform.

The intensity of the Assembly, his daughter's birth, the deaths of Mittie and Alice, and the hyperactivity of the convention work had all taken their toll on Roosevelt. Longing for solace and a change of scene after months of turmoil in both his public and his private life, he decided to retreat from it all. He left his young daughter, Baby Alice, in the care of his sister Bamie, and set his sights on an area that had previously beckoned: the Badlands of the Dakota Territory, far from politics and memories, newspaper reporters and cartoonists. He had already been there for hunting trips in the past, and he was intrigued by the bizarre landscape and compelling environment; now he decided to return for a spell.

# THE APOTHEOSIS AND FALL
# OF ROSCOE CONKLING

THIS IS NOT THE NEW YORK STOCK EXCHANGE, IT IS THE PATRONAGE EXCHANGE, CALLED U. S. SENATE.

The political faction that humiliated Theodore Roosevelt's father was immediately triumphant, and even more in the next couple years. Political hack Chester Arthur was, of all things, vice president of the United States and—as this J. A. Wales cartoon from *Puck* illustrates—still taking orders from Boss Conkling. The setting is the U.S. Senate, which was not far removed from the influence-peddling marketplace that Wales pictured. A center spread from 1881. Thomas C. Platt, later GOP Boss of New York, is depicted here as the little fellow at Conkling's side.

A cartoon that would have pleased TR's late father. Joseph Keppler of *Puck* depicted the haughty resignation of the Stalwart boss of the Senate, Roscoe Conkling. After winning a showdown with President Hayes (in which the elder Roosevelt was a pawn), Conkling lost a similar showdown with the new president, James A. Garfield. He and the junior senator from New York resigned, expecting to be vindicated by the Albany legislature and reappointed as senators. To the surprise—and humiliation—of the two men, the state legislature did not comply. Fellow senators in Washington, at least in Keppler's cartoon, were similarly dismissive of the overblown Conkling. The sputtering little balloon is junior Senator Platt, who slowly rose again to prominence to become TR's uneasy fellow leader in state and national politics.

A HARMLESS EXPLOSION.

# NEW YORK ASSEMBLY

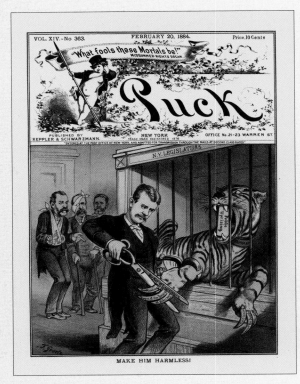

MAKE HIM HARMLESS!

MADE HARMLESS AT LAST!

Some of the very earliest political cartoons featuring Theodore Roosevelt were on the front covers of the greatest showcases he could have desired, and they were laudatory, not critical. *Puck* was well known as a crusading, reform-oriented publication, and in 1884 it was to score its big successes in the presidential campaign, contending against James G. Blaine. Naturally, Tammany Hall, the nation's hothouse of political corruption, was always a target. Roosevelt had made real progress in the Assembly, exposing the Democrat machine, drafting legislation, and pushing a complete overhaul of the city's charter, so as to curtail Tammany's virtual oligarchy. The first cartoon was published a week after TR's wife and mother died. It depicts Roosevelt toward the end of his work, while former NYC mayors, bloodied from their own unsuccessful fights, look on.

In the cartoon a month later, Governor Cleveland has joined Roosevelt, and the wounded and temporarily harmless Tammany tiger wears the face of its boss, John Kelly. The cartoonist was Friederich Grätz, an Austrian who was on *Puck*'s staff for three years.

# THE 1884 CAMPAIGN

THE NATIONAL DIME-MUSEUM—WILL BE RUN DURING THE PRESIDENTIAL CAMPAIGN.

*Puck* magazine opened its 1884 presidential campaign season with a center-spread cartoon of "the National Dime Museum," a sideshow of all the personalities and issues in contemporary politics. An unintended consequence of Bernard Gillam's cartoon was the depiction of James G. Blaine as a tattooed man, his many political sins and indiscretions apparent to all—and indelible. The depiction created a sensation, and *Puck* continued with Blaine's image so festooned throughout the campaign, to enormous public attention. The "Tattooed Man" cartoons were viewed as major factors in candidate Blaine's subsequent defeat, and they put *Puck* firmly

on the map. As influential cartoons, this series is on a par with Nast's Tweed Ring series in *Harper's Weekly* in 1871.

The other notable aspect of Gillam's cartoon is the sideshow's display of a stuffed Tammany tiger, prominently in the center of the drawing, "killed by Roosevelt." The label, like reports of Mark Twain's death, was greatly exaggerated, but TR's work in the Assembly had wounded the political machine in the extreme, and this cartoon confirmed the public's perception of the young reformer.

One of the most effective—and most famous—political cartoons in American history, and Roosevelt is at the center of it. Of course James G. Blaine, the Tattooed Man, is the subject. But as he is revealed by Whitelaw Reid, editor of the Republican party's chief organ *The New York Tribune*, the tribunal needs to be convinced. In Gillam's cartoon, the national GOP leaders are variously dismissive, shocked, or troubled. TR is the thoughtful young man (barely twenty-five, surrounded by veterans and graybeards of the establishment) in the front row. To his left are Carl Schurz, seasoned reformer; Senator William Evarts; and *Harper's Weekly* editor George W. Curtis. Above Roosevelt is Senator John Sherman with a white beard; and, pointing, General John A. Logan, who would be Blaine's running mate. The cartoon was modeled after a famous painting by Jean-Léon Gérôme, *Phryne Before the Areopagus*. Gillam's caricatures are masterful; he forsook labels in this cartoon. No one could fail to recognize Blaine, even though most of his face is obscured.

MEN MAY COME, AND MEN MAY GO; BUT THE WORK OF REFORM SHALL GO ON FOREVER.

Immediately after Cleveland's election in 1884 (and possibly pre-drawn in the case of his defeat, a practice cartoonists of the day employed because of advanced deadlines), Joseph Keppler of *Puck* celebrated the surge of Reform in America. Among the movement's leaders he depicted the figure of Puck, and the magazine's symbol of the Independent New Party, a putative third-party option if the Democrats were to disappoint.

# CHAPTER 4

# 1885~1888

# "BLACK CARE RARELY SITS BEHIND A RIDER WHOSE PACE IS FAST ENOUGH"

heodore Roosevelt was not exactly certain what he would do with his life. He had risen "like a rocket" in the New York State legislature, nominated by his party for Speaker in his second term. As co-chairman of the state's delegation to the presidential nominating convention, he became a major force in that convention and in the ensuing national campaign. Now, with the presidential campaign barely over, the twenty-six-year-old Roosevelt considered his political career—and more importantly, his political future—in shambles. To a man accustomed to doing several things concurrently—reading Thucydides and riding the range, writing history books and hunting elusive white-tailed deer, engaging in raw political fights and visiting chapels in the Newsboys' Lodging-House—it was a rare thing for TR to feel at a loss over what to do.

The young Roosevelt had gained a different perspective on politics, if not a career in public service, by the end of 1884. He had learned from mistakes, both of hubris and immature political calculations, in the legislature—but the lessons learned couldn't change the fact that mistakes had been made. Veteran politicians, whether sworn enemies or wary allies, have long memories. TR had been a hero of reform elements and independents, both of which he bitterly disappointed when he chose to remain in the Republican party and support James G. Blaine in his run for president. TR had learned that these types in politics, "professional do-gooders," could be as vicious as the political bosses they despised. They were willing to sacrifice progress in the name of abstract purity. And the Republican establishment was not wildly enthusiastic about embracing its prodigal son: the upstart had made it clear that he was a maverick unwilling to play by the rules; worse, he was obviously impatient to establish his own rules. He didn't know his place.

In many ways, his personal life at this time seemed as bleak as his professional life. The death of Alice remained a hole in his heart. It was her death, and his mother's only hours earlier, that largely drove him to forsake another term in the legislature. The dilemmas he faced—including the fates of his healthy, bright baby Alice, and the half-built grand home in Oyster Bay—contributed to the inchoate decisions he made in 1885. His sister Bamie would raise Baby Alice for the time being, and the house could sit, half-finished, until he sorted out his life. In the meantime, he needed an income, whatever decisions he made. An Assemblyman's stipend would not suffice. In characteristic fashion, he settled on something rugged, adventurous, and highly unusual. His decision to move to the Badlands in the Dakota Territory and live the life of a rancher greatly surprised his friends and family.

He invested a large portion of his patrimony in two ranches in the Dakota Territory. He hired from two pools: local men he met and trusted on sight, and Maine hunting-guides (friends from occasional hunts in the North Woods) whom he vetted with similar rigor. Dakota cowboys also joined the teams. TR bought thousands of head of Texas longhorn cattle, which a few years earlier had been found particularly suited to the rough terrain, short grass, and harsh weather of the Badlands. Because these cattle could thrive on the peculiar grass of the Badlands, cattle drives from Texas were no longer essential to the beef industry. Newly invented refrigerated railroad cars allowed cattle to be

slaughtered and processed locally and sent to Chicago, ensuring efficiency and higher profits. Indeed, this enterprise was more than a romantic whim for him; Roosevelt intended to become a businessman, not just a cowboy, in the West. More precisely, although he did the work of cowboys, he was a rancher–responsible for his cowboys, and for an enterprise that he hoped would provide income for his family.

The wildness and the utter desolation of the Badlands held much of the attraction of this lifestyle for TR at this point in his life. A patrician from New York, he could easily have led the life of a dilettante, making occasional hunting trips to the Dakotas and remaining an absentee investor, focusing his attention on the business opportunities becoming so readily available in the West. Instead, he chose to establish his ranches in that portion of the West known as the Badlands.

The Badlands were named for the other-worldly landscape of strange ravines, sulfur-steaming buttes, and bizarre vegetation. Legends say that early French trappers called the territory "a bad land to travel through." It was also a land full of bad men. The town near Roosevelt's ranches, Medora, was not far from Deadwood, whose legend exaggerates little. Some men populated the Badlands because they wanted to forget things—TR fairly can be added to that category; some inhabited the place in hopes that others (for instance, the law) would forget them. Even "frontier" justice was a scarce commodity. Drinking was rife; accounts were settled (as were some minor grudges) with guns; survival in its many forms was a daily challenge. The *Dickinson Press* in 1884 wrote about attempts to tame Billings County: "If there is any place along the line that needs a criminal court and jail it is Medora." Caricatures (like the drawing by J. H. Smith in *Judge's Library* on the previous page) fit the popular conception of the cowboy, then and now, and they were not too far off the mark.

Roosevelt in the outfit of a Badlands hunter. Woodcut from his book *Hunting Trips of a Ranchman* (1885).

TR didn't just settle for this environment, however; he chose it. Neither did the supposedly frail "dude" from New York avoid its rougher aspects. In saloons he didn't drink liquor and generally kept to himself. On one occasion, however, a drunken bully claimed that "four eyes" would pay for everyone's drinks. Roosevelt later remembered that he joined in the laughter, but the bully only grew more surly. TR noted that the cowboy stood with his feet close together, and, drawing on early boxing lessons, he delivered a one-two punch that felled the bully and left him unconscious. Not only did the town's estimation of the "dude" rise, but the humiliated cowboy left town. In another incident that impressed those who spread the tale, one of TR's cowboys brought the calf of a rival ranchman to Roosevelt during a roundup. He showed how the calf's brand could be altered to resemble one of TR's own herds'. TR fired the cowboy on the spot. When the cowboy protested that he was only looking out for Roosevelt's interests, TR savagely replied: "Any man who will cheat *for* me will cheat *from* me." Morality met practicality in the Badlands.

There were stories, too, that were less about specific events and more about TR's personality and pastimes—stories sometimes told in whispers, because here was a man whose type was not common, even in those rough lands and rough times. He frequently rode the plains alone, often at night, sometimes for days. We can suppose that lamentations for Alice and ruminations about his career rode with him. He wrote that "black care" was his constant companion, though he pointed out that "black care rarely sits behind a rider whose pace is fast enough." The very statement indicates a conflict between the presence or the escape from melancholia. Although he was clearly the boss of his ranches—his closest friends and employees in the Badlands always addressed him as "Mr. Roosevelt"—he invariably joined the roundups and drives. Frequently he rode a day and a half, without sleep, often in bad weather. Occasionally thrown from his horse or caught in a stampede, he rode through pain and sometimes with broken bones, never complaining. In one memorable cattle drive, he was in the saddle for forty hours straight, helping stop a stampede toward the end of the stretch. Many are the accounts of his outlasting seasoned cowboys or outpacing veteran hunting guides…usually to their astonishment, as well as their exhaustion.

Once a river scow of Roosevelt's was stolen. Bandits took it down the icy Little Missouri River. TR called two of his men, built a new boat, and headed out in pursuit.

His cowboys tried to dissuade Roosevelt, arguing that the difficulty of chase and recovery outweighed the value of the scow. But TR wanted justice. On the third day out, having fought snow and icy waters, they located the robbers, who were surprised that anyone would have pursued them seriously. They also expected to be shot, which would have been routine frontier justice. As the nearest sheriff was in Mandan, at least two weeks distant, Roosevelt pointed the party to Dickinson, where there was a justice of the peace. The group fought icy waters for seven more days, then went overland for another two days. He and his impromptu posse took turns sleeping, covering the thieves with rifles. When they had run through their slim rations (bread made of flour and water so dirty that the bread was brown), TR dispatched one of his men to scout for a "cow camp" from which they might ask for victuals. Eventually the party arrived at the Stark County Court-house in Dickinson. The justice of the peace who filed the complaint (and was astonished that TR had not simply shot the thieves on the spot) bore the unlikely but colorfully appropriate name of Western Starr. Roosevelt stayed until the thieves were tried the next day, and then he returned—this time by train—to Medora, thence to his ranch thirty-five miles north. The entire episode was an investment in righteousness for the untamed region, and it lasted about three weeks. And at odd moments—very odd moments—during the escapade, Roosevelt read a book he brought with him: Tolstoy's *Anna Karenina.*

The West carved new facets to TR's personality and his growing legend. The story of the outlaws, for instance, was spread far and wide. An astonished local even wrote a letter to *The New York Times* about "meeting a gentleman of his standing on the frontier, masquerading in the character of an impromptu Sheriff. But only such men, men of courage and energy, can hope to succeed in this new, beautiful, yet undeveloped country." The writer noted an important distinction: TR was rough-and-tumble, but still a gentleman. He did not abandon his essential habits and breeding. When he and his men built and furnished the ranch houses—one was 60 by 30 feet, with eight rooms—there were shelves for many books, and quiet spaces to study and write. In the Badlands, between cattle drives and roundups, TR wrote two books—a collection of his ranching experiences, and

"A Shot from the Verandah," a woodcut from TR's book *The Wilderness Hunter* (1893).

a biography of the old Jacksonian stalwart, Senator Thomas Hart Benton. He mailed requests for some research materials to his sisters and to Henry Cabot Lodge, but otherwise the creditable biography was written from his memory of history and his reading.

TR, always an agent of civilization and reform, also had ambitions for his adopted region. Loathing the West's lawless character, he organized the Little Missouri Stockmen's Association, which addressed business affairs, cooperative action, the establishment of more places of justice and worship, and eventual statehood for the territory. (He declined suggestions that he run for office or represent the territory in Washington.)

As he had made occasional hunting trips to the West during his Assembly days, now TR made occasional trips back East to see his daughter and maintain contact with his affairs and friends. During one visit, he accidentally bumped into his childhood friend Edith Carow at his sister's house. Edith had been the sweetheart of his youth; in fact, many people had assumed they would marry, but then Alice happened. It is lost to history whether there had been a lover's quarrel between Theodore and Edith, or why. Likewise shrouded in mystery is what transpired after the chance encounter at Bamie's house; but evidently there were discreet meetings and exchanges of correspondence. Working his way through the guilt related to Alice's relatively recent death and Victorian customs that discouraged early (or any) remarriage, Theodore proposed to Edith. She accepted, and they managed to keep the engagement secret for a year.

Roosevelt now set his compass back toward New York City. He could accommodate the rough-hewn life on the frontier, but Edith never could. He would reclaim little Alice (a tough separation for both Bamie and her ward) and finish work on the home in Oyster Bay, which he renamed Sagamore Hill after the ancient Indian chief, instead of Leeholm in honor of his first wife (Alice Lee Roosevelt). When New York heard that Roosevelt was returning, the Republican Party persuaded him to run for mayor of the city where his ancestors had landed, settled, and prospered.

The nomination to run for mayor in 1886, however, given the local circumstances, was a relatively empty gesture, because the socialist Henry George was running on the Single-Tax platform and receiving unexpectedly widespread support. The Democrats nominated Abram S. Hewitt, a dignified industrialist, son-in-law of inventor and entrepreneur Peter Cooper, and no friend to Tammany Hall. In another year, young Roosevelt might have won the election, for his reputation as a reformer was still high. But he was a sacrificial lamb, and he knew it: the city's conservative element was so afraid of George's possible victory that many Republicans quietly voted for Hewitt. (Ironically, among Hewitt's investments were cattle ranches in the Dakota Territory, but the whitebeard was an absentee, and certainly no cowboy.)

Foregone conclusion or no, TR hardly ruminated over his loss. Within days of the election, he and Edith sailed for London, where they married. The best man was a junior diplomat met on the Atlantic cruise, Cecil Spring-Rice. He became a lifelong friend of

Theodore and Edith and served as British Ambassador to the United States during TR's presidency.

In what was virtually a cosmic affirmation of TR's new life-detours, in the winter of 1886–87 the Dakota Territory sustained a blizzard whose severity seldom has been matched. Four-fifths of the local herds died, many frozen where they stood, and surviving cattle were emaciated. People literally were trapped in their cabins. Settlers' food supplies and firewood dwindled. Desperation reigned, and when spring returned, the Badlands were more desolate than ever. Even old residents moved away; churches and saloons alike closed; newspapers ceased publication; and the Medora meat-processing building was abandoned. Roosevelt's partners returned to their previous pursuits, his Maine comrades (and their families) moving back East. TR himself lost a fortune—a large portion of his inheritance, but perhaps more importantly his dreams—but it was time, for a variety of reasons, to move on.

Although frequently sentimental, TR was never a sentimentalist. He realized other, more lasting factors had heralded the end of the brief period of open ranges and cowboys. The blizzard might have damaged business prospects of ranchers, but barbed-wire fences and the influx of family farmers ended the lifestyle and romance, such as they were, of the cowboy. "The cattle-men," TR wrote in *Hunting Trips of a Ranchman* (1885), "keep herds and build houses on the land; yet I would not for a moment debar settlers from the right of entry to the cattle country, though their coming in means in the end the destruction of us and our industry. For we ourselves, and the life that we lead, will shortly pass away from the plains as completely as the red and white hunters who have vanished from before our herds." While he occasionally made hunting trips to the Badlands after this period, he fully divested himself of his ranches around the turn of the century and never returned to ranching for any extended time.

He was now a husband again, settling into a new Long Island estate with his wife and daughter and, in 1887, a son on the way. He commenced writing a biography of Gouverneur

Morris of the American Revolution, as well as a monumental history of American expansion, *The Winning of the West*. The work eventually ran to four volumes, and is still regarded as an essential study of social and political history.

Again, politics beckoned. The national issues included a rising tide of labor unrest and urban violence, and a federal budget surplus which President Cleveland termed a national moral crisis, tantamount to theft from the citizenry (a situation perhaps unintelligible to modern readers). Cartoonists captured the public's fears of a French-style revolution and the budget problem (not a deficit like the budget problems we face today, but a real issue nonetheless). Roosevelt addressed both these topics, and others like them. Ultimately, however, TR's heart was not in his 1888 speeches, made on behalf of Indiana Republican Senator Benjamin Harrison.

Throughout this time, TR was busy, as always, especially with his writing. He did not expend much energy in pursuit of his own ambition. This was partly because friends like Henry Cabot Lodge were ambitious for him. Lodge, now a congressman from Massachusetts, was rising in the GOP, and began a decade's work of arranging higher and higher positions for his friend Theodore, who he believed was destined for great things. Benjamin Harrison won the presidency, and Lodge immediately advocated for TR to be a part of the administration. Thus the literary life of a Long Island patrician proved to be a short way-station for TR between cattle ranches and the nation's capital.

# RUNNING FOR MAYOR OF NEW YORK

"AGE BEFORE BEAUTY!"

In a race for mayor of New York City, the white-bearded industrialist Abram S. Hewitt defeated Theodore Roosevelt, who turned twenty-eight a week before the election. In between them (not shown in this C. J. Taylor cartoon in *Puck*) was the single-tax theorist Henry George. The safe and sane Hewitt, who was the son-in-law of inventor Peter Cooper, received votes from Republicans alarmed at the prospect of George's labor supporters coming to power.

# TR: FUTURE HOPE OF THE GOP?

A remarkable cartoon in a national publication, "Little Roosevelt! The Grand Old Party Must Be Hard Up!" (1887) *Puck* had pictured TR before, usually with favor; and it was less than a year since Roosevelt had run for mayor of New York City. Nevertheless it was a compliment, even if a backhanded one, to the 28-year-old Roosevelt. In this image, the national Republican hierarchy of the day, including his friend Henry Cabot Lodge, is gathered around TR.

*Puck* ridiculed TR in its editorial: "Mr. Roosevelt, be happy while you may.... Bright visions float before your eyes of what the Party can and may do for you. We wish you a gradual and gentle awakening. We feel the Party cannot do much for you.... You are not the timber of which presidents are made."

In fifteen years, of course, Roosevelt would be not just timber, but president.

CHAPTER 5

# 1889~1897

# REFORM: "HE SEEN HIS DUTY AND HE DONE IT!"

**H**enry Cabot Lodge had served one mere term in the U.S. House of Representatives by the time Benjamin Harrison was inaugurated president in March of 1889. He was a rising star in the Republican party due to the force of his personality, the pedigree of his ancestry and Harvard connections, and his important friendships. In his second term, Lodge co-sponsored the Federal Elections Bill, a landmark bit of civil-rights legislation. It protected voting rights of blacks in the South; Democrat opponents called it a "Force Bill." Lodge had vigorously campaigned for Harrison, the diminutive former senator from Indiana and grandson of President William Henry Harrison.

"Old Tippecanoe," as the elder Harrison was called, was the shortest-serving president in history, dying just a month after his inauguration. His grandson Benjamin possibly became the shortest-*looking* president, thanks to cartoonists like Joseph Keppler of *Puck*, who emphasized Harrison's modest height by depicting him under an enormous hat ("Grandfather's hat," implying that the only item on his résumé was his lineage). Indeed, Harrison had been a compromise candidate at the 1888 Republican convention. Several colorless hopefuls deadlocked in the convention, and in the end the former one-term senator Harrison was chosen.

Despite the general lack of enthusiasm over Harrison's nomination, Lodge canvassed for Harrison fervently, and he persuaded his friend Theodore Roosevelt to do the same. For Lodge, this type of canvassing and working for one's party was the natural activity of a professional politician. Although he had been branded a Reformer from the 1884 convention, "working from within the party" was what he proposed and lived out. In the future he was to become the Dean of the Senate, the first to hold the post of Majority Leader, and a major influence in foreign policy in the 1920s. Now, however, he was tending to his young career...and that of TR.

Lodge and Roosevelt were contemporaries, the former only eight years senior, and they developed a close and occasionally complicated friendship. Their politics were almost always synchronous, although Lodge was less conservative, and TR often more so, than history has portrayed them. Lodge and his wife Nannie—and their son George, a brilliant poet who died young—were intellectual companions of Theodore and Edith. Lodge's political ambitions were finite: he knew his limitations and frankly enjoyed living within them. His ambitions for Theodore, however, were without limit. He counseled and cajoled; he schemed and made appointments on TR's behalf; he lobbied Edith to persuade her husband to "climb the ladder" until Roosevelt might achieve the position Lodge (and others) always pictured for him: the presidency.

In 1888 TR was beginning to settle into the life of a literary gentleman in Oyster Bay, writing books of history and biography (three of the latter were arranged by Lodge). His heart was not in the efforts to stump for Harrison. They were up against incumbent Grover Cleveland, the Democrat candidate, who had made some progress with Civil Service reform during his first term. Cleveland won the popular vote but narrowly lost the electoral vote, thanks to brazen fraud in Harrison's home state of Indiana. (Pennsylvania Senator Matthew S. Quay later said that Harrison would never know "how close a number of men were compelled to approach...the penitentiary to make him President.")

Despite his lack of zeal, TR did campaign for Harrison in New York, in Lodge's Massachusetts, and in the West, where he was already a folk hero for his cowboy life. His books on ranch life and hunting trails, and cowboy articles he wrote for many magazines including the children's literary monthly *St. Nicholas*, cemented his persona in the public's mind.

After Harrison won the election, Lodge was a frequent caller at the White House, not on his own behalf, but seeking an appointment for Roosevelt in the new administration. Harrison proposed an appointment for him as chairman of the U.S. Civil Service Commission. This was the perfect window-dressing for a president who frankly was indifferent to reforming the federal bureaucracy. TR possibly was the most prominent Republican agitator against corruption and in favor of reform; his appointment, attended by meager support from the White House, would give Harrison cover.

Before long, the president likely felt that he needed cover from Roosevelt himself. True to form, TR made a splash, doing what he could with what he had. The Civil Service Commission, with Roosevelt as its chairman, actually tended to the business, even minute business, of government jobs. It extended the merit system and lobbied Congress to legislate further extensions. TR mediated disputes and reviewed claims of unfair dismissal. He engaged in public disputes with Post Master General John Wanamaker and other prominent Republicans. He frequently called on Harrison at the White House (at that time, even the general public could enter the building and request a meeting with the president), making his case both for reform and for more substantial endorsement of his own reform efforts. Thanks in large part to cartoonists who enjoyed caricaturing the ebullient crusader, as well as the political dust he raised, TR found himself increasingly featured in national cartoons and thus increasingly familiar to the public.

In some ways, the Civil Service Commission years were a golden interlude for TR. He served from 1889 to 1892 under Harrison, and then until 1895 under Grover Cleveland, who asked Roosevelt to remain on the Commission. This meant TR at times had to live apart from his family. He was economically comfortable, but not wealthy enough to move his growing family to Washington. Baby Alice had been joined by siblings

Theodore Jr., Kermit, Ethel, and Archie. (Another boy, Quentin, was born subsequent to TR's chairmanship of the Commission.) Roosevelt rented homes for himself in the capital, always in the social and neighborhood orbits of the Lodges. Edith often visited and sometimes stayed for stretches, variously alone or with combinations of the children. Mostly, though, she remained at Sagamore Hill, to which Theodore repaired as often as practical, considering it was six hours away by train.

When he was not working, TR's life was a heady time of intellectual stimulation and social bling. He dined out almost every evening, invited by prominent households of literary, governmental, and diplomatic figures. He was a member—usually at the vital center—of cultural salons. And he belonged to the District's most prestigious private clubs, including the Metropolitan Club and the Cosmos Club. John Hay, who had been President Lincoln's private secretary and a friend of TR's father (and would later serve as TR's Secretary of State), frequently hosted gatherings of colorful personalities and stimulating conversation, and TR was a fixture at these events. TR had a harder time cracking the social circle of the brilliant recluse Henry Adams, whose Lafayette Square townhouse across from the White House adjoined the Hays'—but he managed it eventually, and the two became good friends.

Adams was the scion of John and John Quincy Adams, and a respected historian and former diplomat. The invariably icy Adams cast aspersions on Roosevelt's equally eternal ebul-

In a cartoon brilliant in its simplicity, Joseph Keppler of *Puck* has Uncle Sam looking into the "grandfather's hat" of President Harrison and asking, "Where is he?"

lience, but he also respected the young man. He once remarked that TR possessed a characteristic Medieval philosophers ascribed to God Himself—"pure act." The author of the monumental books *Mount St-Michel and Chartres* and *The Education of Henry Adams* emerged into the sunshine to call on the White House when Roosevelt's term expired in 1909, and said, with tears in his eyes, "I shall miss you very much," and then returned to his townhouse. As with his best friend Hay, Adams maintained an open door to TR at his own salons. Other regulars in the movable feasts of clever conversation and intellectual exchanges of the era were Henry Cabot Lodge, Speaker of the House Thomas Brackett Reed of Maine, British diplomat Cecil Spring-Rice, and German diplomat Speck von Sternberg. British author Rudyard Kipling, who made the Cosmos Club his *pied-à-terre* on his visits to America, painted a fair portrait of the salons, and of the role TR played in the Washington scene despite his relatively minor status in government at the time: "[TR] would come and pour out projects, discussions of men and politics, criticisms of books, in a swift and full-volumed stream, tremendously emphatic and enlivened by bursts of humor.... I curled up on the seat opposite and listened and wondered, until the universe seemed to be spinning 'round, and Theodore was the spinner."

During his six years at the Commission, TR made headway against the hydra-headed spoils system, despite the glacial size and glacial speed of reform efforts. His severest critics, ironically, were not just the entrenched interests of corruption, but also his fellow impatient reformers. The latter included publishers and "professional goo-goos," a shorthand for "good-government" theorists who never got their hands dirty in the actual work of reform. These putative but unreliable allies were the bane of Roosevelt's battles throughout his career. He dubbed them "the lunatic fringe."

Cartoonists, whose attitude to Civil-Service reform was generally supportive, even if they drew for fiercely partisan journals, further raised Roosevelt's public profile as they depicted his challenges and actions. The most cynical comments against TR were that Harrison would allow him to reform the civil service just *so* much. Indeed, that was Harrison's intention, but TR was prone to wriggle free of the presidential leash.

The cartoonists and the public alike relished the dust-ups surrounding the independent-minded Roosevelt.

Somehow during these years, TR continued to find time to write articles and books. He completed a monumental four-volume history *The Winning of the West*. He also wrote *The Wilderness Hunter*, a companion to his earlier *Hunting Trips of a Ranchman* and *Ranch Life and the Hunting Trail*. He co-authored a book with Henry Cabot Lodge entitled *Hero Tales from American History*, and he wrote *New York*, a history of his birthplace and his family's ancestral city.

In 1894, Roosevelt returned to New York City to join in reform efforts that had begun under newly elected mayor, Republican William L. Strong. Strong was elected on a Fusion ticket, as another of the periodic reform waves washed over the city. He had an ambitious agenda to improve the city, which was preparing to merge with Brooklyn to become Greater New York. To address the improvements in the quality of life, he appointed Colonel George Waring as Streets Commissioner. Waring, who had directed the drainage of Central Park for its designer Frederick Law Olmstead and had helped invent the modern toilet device, organized military-style battalions of "white wings"—uniformed sanitation workers who maintained the city streets, garbage removal, and sewer systems.

Along with sanitation, Strong focused on reforming the public safety of New York City. He persuaded Theodore Roosevelt to join the Police Board. TR became the board's president with the goal of cleaning out the Mulberry Street Police Department headquarters. In many ways TR's task was more daunting than the challenges of the federal civil service. Corruption in police ranks was ubiquitous; the public had become resigned if not inured to the system of payoffs, paybacks, and extortion. The corruption of the police force demoralized some officers, but it attracted others. Recruits were largely drawn from the city's population of impoverished Irish immigrants. It was an open secret how much money recruits were expected to cough up in order to be accepted into the police academy, and, further up the line, how much money it cost to receive promotions. Merchants paid policemen for protection, and police "supervised" local elections, especially when

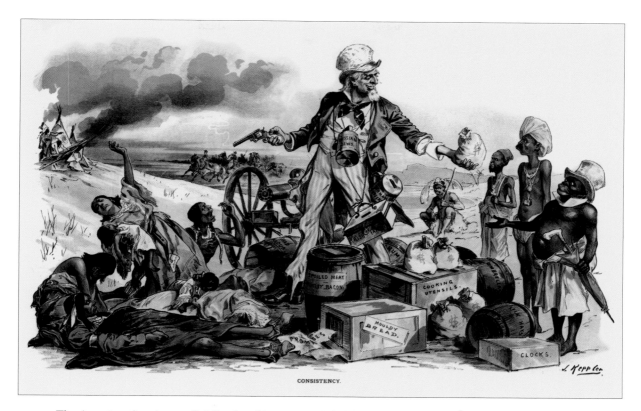

CONSISTENCY.

The American frontier unofficially closed between 1889's Oklahoma Land Rush and 1893, when historian Frederick Jackson Turner declared it so, and analyzed the role of the frontier on America's psyche. One ongoing aspect was the "Indian problem," depicted by Joseph Keppler as one of savage inconsistency (*Puck*, 1890). Indian wars were virtually the only activity of the Army between the Civil War and the Spanish-American War.

Tammany Hall needed votes. Police were the bagmen for politicians, and in many cases protected those who broke the law. For instance, rather than enforce Sunday "closing laws," they actually protected saloons that operated on Sundays in contravention of statutes.

Such was Roosevelt's challenge, or rather the challenging tip of the iceberg. Policemen and the civic establishment both resisted any "reform" of the status quo. Most of the city's press was likewise hostile to any changes, invariably pandering both to merchants and the immigrant class. In addition, newspapers themselves profited from a cozy system of protection: there were more than a dozen newspapers in New York at the time, and vital distribution was carried out by newsboys and newsstands, whose livelihoods were achieved and maintained by strong-arm tactics and the collusion of cops. Finally, the four-member police board consisted of one weak ally of TR and two invariably hostile opponents.

TR refused to be checkmated, however, and went above the heads of the establishment to the people. He enlisted the aid of newspaper reporters and cartoonists, preaching from the "bully pulpit" of his circumstance. This tactic of circumventing the establishment altogether would become a hallmark of TR's career in politics, a strategy begun in Assembly years that he would perfect during his presidency.

During this time, TR developed what would become a lifelong friendship with Jacob Riis, a Danish immigrant who recently had written an exposé of poverty in Lower Manhattan, *How the Other Half Lives*. In this book, Riis drew the public's attention to the same conditions TR had discovered and acted upon in his early Assembly days. There was now an entire class of reporters who took interest in the problems of the urban poor. Some sought simply to fill their sensationalist newspapers, others hoped to write books, still others to turn to "Naturalist" fiction. Among these writers were Lincoln Steffens, Stephen Crane, and Edward W. Townsend. Roosevelt, providing exclusive leads and colorful copy along the way, was featured as a hero in many of their reports.

TR began to roam the streets surreptitiously at night, acquiring the nickname "Haroun al-Roosevelt." He wanted to check for himself that cops were not sleeping or grafting on the beat. The nickname was inspired by Harun al-Rashid, the pasha of ancient Persia in *1001 Nights* who, according to legend, wandered the streets of Baghdad at night disguised as a merchant in order to observe his subjects' activities. More than once the Commissioner was trailed by paid detectives, hoping to discover Roosevelt in a compromising situation. "What? And me going home to my bunnies?" TR asked when he learned of these futile blackmail attempts.

His major battles were over enforcement of the Sunday closing laws. Saloons were closed on Sundays, which disappointed many immigrants who worked laborious six-day weeks and embraced Sunday as their only day of relaxation. TR insisted that he was not leading a prohibitionist crusade. He pointed to laws that were on the books, and suggested that anyone who objected to closing saloons on the Sabbath should talk to their legislators, not the police whose sworn duty it was to enforce the law. There were upwards of fifteen thousand saloons and restaurants and even bawdy houses in New York at the time, and many flouted the closing laws—a convenient situation all around for a system that thrived on bribery and corruption. What made the entire issue sticky was that pious legislators also compelled the closure of museums and art galleries on the Sabbath. Commissioner Roosevelt became the target of people whose wrath should have been directed at those who drafted the laws he was sworn to enforce.

An interesting incident of Roosevelt's tenure as Police Commissioner was his handling of a rally organized by a notorious European anti-Semite named Hermann Ahlwardt. Visiting New York City, Ahlwardt planned a speech designed to incite antagonism against Jews, and he requested police protection. There were contrary appeals to the Commissioner to prevent the rallies. "Of course I told them I could not—that the right of free speech must be maintained unless he incited them to riot," Roosevelt later wrote. "On thinking it over, however, it occurred to me that there was one way in which I could undo most of the mischief he was trying to do." Roosevelt detailed a Jewish police sergeant and "a score or two" of Jewish policemen to the event. To avoid making the demagogue a martyr, TR "made him look ridiculous."

As the months wore on, TR's corrupt opponents and some of the city's newspapers, particularly Joseph Pulitzer's *World* and James Gordon Bennett's *Herald*, made battling for reform increasingly onerous. But Roosevelt had the personal satisfaction of knowing his was good work well done. Besides, he enjoyed other, palpable forms of satisfaction as well. For one thing, there was an increase in applicants to the police force. Within the ranks, honest cops, previously harassed, personally thanked the Commissioner for imposing higher standards. Roosevelt was personally involved in almost every case of dereliction or corruption in the police force; even the bad apples appreciated their chief delivering harsh sermons, or offering personalized counsel, as he saw the need, case by case. Speaking as a doting parent would, TR later filled his autobiography's pertinent chapter with story after story of individual cops who were recognized, awarded, or redeemed, and some who earned the Commissioner's devotion despite political pressures.

The 1896 quadrennial campaign presented another diversion. Lodge did not need to persuade Roosevelt to enlist in this presidential canvass. Much of the brooding unrest in the nation, incipient revolts that he sought to forestall by reform proposals, boiled over in 1896. The immediate causes of unrest included the crippling Depression of 1893–1894, and attendant veterans' marches and labor strikes. Several of these labor actions, including the Homestead and Pullman actions, were bloody. One "leg" of the stool that represented labor unrest was the economic woes of farmers, which dated back to the formation of the Grange and the Greenback movement of the 1870s. Many western farmers had come to see Wall Street as their enemy. The bloody Haymarket riot that followed an incendiary protest by community organizers of Chicago in 1886 further polarized society. And in the early '90s, these protests coalesced, loosely but in great aggregate numbers, in the formation of the People's Party—the Populists. The party fielded a presidential ticket that polled considerable support in 1892, led by a ragtag corps of radicals from anarchist sympathizers to urban socialists to agrarian reformers. Mary Ellen Lease of Kansas provided one of the movement's memorable slogans: "We need to raise less corn and more hell!" A national economic depression in 1893 further exacerbated the radicalization of lower classes and working groups.

Many malcontents gathered under the Democrat umbrella, although the Populists still hoped to be a viable third party. The Democrat Party's embrace of the issue of free coinage of silver, to be an additional medium of exchange at a fixed rate against gold (a latter-day Greenback movement to inflate the currency and thereby ease farmers' debts) sparked a veritable revolution in American politics. Republicans and Democrats had never been divided on strict party lines over the issue of silver. But now a congressman, barely old enough to serve as president according to the Constitution, delivered an electrifying speech to the 1896 Democrat convention. William Jennings Bryan, of stentorian voice and arresting manner, the "Boy Orator of the Platte," was a prairie David aiming at the Wall Street Goliath. He seemed to summarize every complaint and irritation of a generation's immigrants, factory hands, mine workers, and poor farmers. He finished his powerful speech with these famous words:

> There are two ideas of government. There are those who believe that if you just legislate to make the well-to-do prosperous, that their prosperity will leak through on those below. The Democratic idea has been that if you legislate to make the masses prosperous their prosperity will find its way up and through every class that rests upon it.
>
> You come to us and tell us that the great cities are in favor of the gold standard. I tell you that the great cities rest upon these broad and fertile prairies. Burn down your cities and leave our farms, and your cities will spring up again as if by magic. But destroy our farms and the grass will grow in the streets of every city in the country.
>
> If they dare to come out in the open field and defend the gold standard as a good thing, we shall fight them to the uttermost, having behind us the producing masses of the nation and the world. Having behind us the commercial interests and the laboring interests and all the toiling masses, we shall answer their demands for a gold standard by saying to them, you shall not press down upon the brow of labor this crown of thorns. You shall not crucify mankind upon a cross of gold!

Bryan was nominated in a frenzy, and a platform was adopted that contained many propositions that are standard today, but were widely seen as dangerously radical at the time, such as a federal income tax. The Populists endorsed Bryan, and then withered and died as a third-party movement. Most major Democrat newspapers, and many major Democrat office-holders including the incumbent President Cleveland, refused to endorse Bryan. Cartoonists led the charge in forcefully opposing Bryan, drawing countless images of revolutionary crowds, bloody vandals, red flags of communism, and riots, all led by a young Bryan with a crazed expression, under invariably stormy skies. The normally Democrat cartoonists of *Puck, Life, The New York World,* and *The New York Herald* changed sides and attacked Bryan.

The subtext of Roosevelt's career from its earliest battles—that reform is a righteous necessity in many areas, but also an antidote to revolution—was now proven in reality. Always the champion of order, TR saw Bryanism, with its purported tendency to outright revolution, as a threat, not a platform. He offered his services to the Republican National Committee. His name already excited interest in sections of America itching for reform, such as New York and Boston, and especially in the West, which considered him one of its own. Besides, the exuberant TR made scores of appearances, sometimes even in front of hostile, radical crowds. This served to augment the "front porch" campaign of GOP nominee William McKinley, who waited for potential voters to travel to the front lawn of his Canton, Ohio, home, to see him. Roosevelt's method made its mark.

By November, not enough of the nation was persuaded to accept Bryan's theses and march into the unknown with him. The Republicans scored a historic victory, despite their genuine insecurity during the campaign. Within a few months, prosperity roared back, probably the result of normal economic cycles, but possibly kick-started by an authentic sense of stability that followed the elections. The American people felt that political demons had been exorcised from the body politic. President-elect McKinley trumpeted the gold standard (about which, ironically, he had been agnostic earlier in the decade), high tariffs, and traditional Republican dogma. The nation breathed a sigh of relief, and even many Democrat journals and cartoonists were happy to celebrate a long honeymoon with the GOP.

One Republican, however, was still anxious, contacting the president-elect constantly. Henry Cabot Lodge was concerned for the career of his friend and protégé Theodore Roosevelt. Lodge was now a Massachusetts senator, with more heft behind his importuning. TR was eager, too, for the right position in the new administration, but deferred to Lodge's lobbying. But McKinley was not forthcoming with a position. During TR's Civil Service Commission days, which had overlapped McKinley's congressional tenure (when McKinley sponsored the controversial, eponymous tariff act), the two men had not been particularly cordial. It did not help matters that McKinley's mentor, Ohio businessman Mark Hanna, had a thinly concealed contempt for TR. And if TR's behavior in his earlier position under President Harrison was any indication of what McKinley could expect, perhaps the new president thought it best not to go there.

Eventually, though, Roosevelt did receive an appointment: Assistant Secretary of the Navy, to serve under John Davis Long, former governor of Massachusetts. It is likely that Roosevelt was appointed for his knowledge of all things naval–his first national recognition had been for his classic study, *The Naval War of 1812.* Besides, he maintained an interest in, if not an obsession with, the American seaborne military. TR and Admiral Alfred Thayer Mahan were mutual admirers. The admiral's book, *The Influence of Sea Power on History*, had already affected several countries' strategic planning, and Roosevelt hoped to see similar effects in the United States Navy as well. But he received a hint along with his appointment: he was to be the *assistant* secretary, serving under Secretary Long; and McKinley would be the president. TR's tendency to enact reforms (as well as nearly anything else) with gusto preceded him.

He accepted the appointment and dove into the job with—naturally—more enthusiasm than was required or, probably, expected. Just as other men hum a tune or check their watches, Assistant Secretary Roosevelt was constantly active; he brought research materials to his desk and took charts and graphs home for evening study. He brainstormed with countless experts about ships and armaments and naval technology and international politics. He mapped out innumerable contingency plans—what to do in the event of war with Spain, Germany, England, or Japan; the effect the lack of an isthmian canal had on merchant commerce or military necessities; the lessons of history, and the possibilities for the coming American century—all, roughly, during his first week on the job.

Never busy enough, while he sank his teeth into his new job and managed the exigencies of a growing family—his sixth and last child, Quentin, was born in 1897—Roosevelt also published one more book. It was titled *American Ideals*, a collection of his articles and speeches about various topics, united by the theme of practical idealism. *American Ideals* is notable in that material he reprinted from the early 1880s differed little from his strong opinions of 1897, which were identical to positions held at the end of his life. Roosevelt was the picture of consistency, an organic thinker. "It is not difficult to be virtuous in a cloistered and negative way," he wrote in the preface. "Neither is it difficult to succeed, after a fashion, in active life, if one is content to disregard the considerations which bind honorable and upright men. But it is by no means easy to combine honesty and efficiency; and yet it is absolutely necessary, in order to do any work really worth doing." That was his credo.

Roosevelt was made to understand that his work in the Navy Department should be limited to his position as assistant, but the rising star was already proving himself capable of much more. Theodore Roosevelt had a vision for America's future that was clear and confident. And—as he demonstrated through his writings—it was a vision he could share forcefully and articulately with the American people.

# THE POWER OF MONOPOLISTS

THE BOSSES OF THE SENATE.

The nexus of America's booming Industrial Revolution was the government's policy of "protecting infant industries" through tariffs and other favors. The system also nurtured a crony culture of corporate "donations" to legislators. At the time, the Constitution mandated the election of senators by pliable state legislatures. Here the monopolies ("trusts") are depicted in the gallery overlooking the United States Senate. Joseph Keppler, *Puck*, 1889.

---

# CIVIL SERVICE REFORM

*Puck* cynically predicted that President Harrison (in his "grand-father's hat" at rear) would let his young Civil Service Commissioner go only so far in his reform crusades. Cartoon by Louis Dalrymple, 1889.

Almost exactly ten years after his father's humiliating treatment as a pawn in New York's political wars, TR was named United States Civil Service Commissioner. Over the course of that decade, matters of political corruption had marginally improved. President Cleveland had been a creditable fighter for reform of the civil service and honesty in government. Incoming President Benjamin Harrison desired at least to be seen as an advocate of civil-service reform, even if he wasn't all that devoted to the cause in actuality.

So the nomination of Theodore Roosevelt seemed like a perfect political move. Harrison ought to have realized, however, even so early in Roosevelt's career, that he had added a determined, headstrong crusader to his administration. TR found himself embroiled in many fights with members of Harrison's very cabinet. John Wanamaker, the famous dry-goods merchant and pious Sunday school teacher, was Postmaster General, and he pursued an aggressive policy of firing Democrats and giving jobs to "deserving" Republicans. Harrison's Commissioner of Pensions, Corporal James Tanner, practically raided the federal treasury to dispense jobs and largesse to members of the Grand Army of the Republic, the veteran's group. Roosevelt held interminable hearings and traveled around America to interview aggrieved officeholders and mediate conflicts. He drew up new regulations and then had to fight the inertia of congressional traditions to see them enacted. And he fought bogus charges against his own integrity all the while.

DRAW YOUR OWN CONCLUSIONS

When Stanley carried the first steamboat up the Congo, the natives ran along the banks, yelling with rage, and striving to check his progress by throwing stones and other missiles. Mr. Stanely got there, just the same.

Stories of *New York Herald* reporter Henry Stanley in "darkest Africa" were enthralling the public. Louis Dalrymple of *Puck* cast Roosevelt as Stanley, and recalled the story of the first steamship that natives on the shorelines ever witnessed. In the image, various politicians—mostly Republicans—are scattering on the shore at the sight of an ironclad. And the young Civil Service Commissioner, Theodore Roosevelt, is depicted on board, "getting there just the same."

Roosevelt appeared in three major cartoons in *Puck*, in 1889, during the very first months of the new Harrison administration. He was obviously creating a stir from a relatively minor post in government, and reform publications like *Puck* noticed. It is noteworthy, too, that TR's fellow commissioners are clad in frock coats and top hats—probably his actual wardrobe too—while TR is depicted in cowboy hat and boots. His reputation as a rancher and cowboy preceded him.

It never hurts a public figure to come ready-made, so to speak, with one's own icons. President Harrison is the flippant figure atop the elephant. Cartoonist Dalrymple shows the "Republican Press" as muzzled because Harrison appointed many publishers and editors to government and diplomatic posts.

# AMERICA IN THE GAY NINETIES

In the late 1880s and early 1890s, a rising middle class moved from urban areas to suburbs and "rural" areas like Brooklyn and northern New Jersey, undertaking the lifestyles immortalized by cartoonists like F. Opper in *Puck*. His "Suburban Resident" series ran sporadically for years. This example is from 1891. These gentle comments resonated with readers, but there was more empathy than ridicule: Opper moved to the suburbs, as did two authors of the Nineties known for their suburban themes: H. C. Bunner (*The Runaway Browns*) and Frank Stockton (*Rudder Grange*).

America's move to suburban towns—whence exurbs would commute to cities—or fashionable but often inconvenient rural getaways in summer months, were hallmarks of the Nineties.

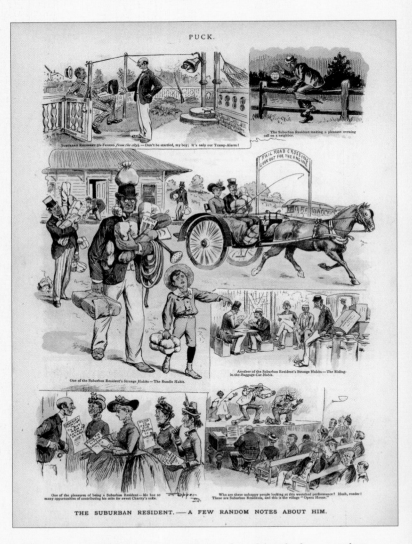

Another cartoon by Frederick Burr Opper about lifestyle disparities between urban and rural Americans. From *Puck*.

DRAWN FOR THE INTER OCEAN BY THOMAS NAST.

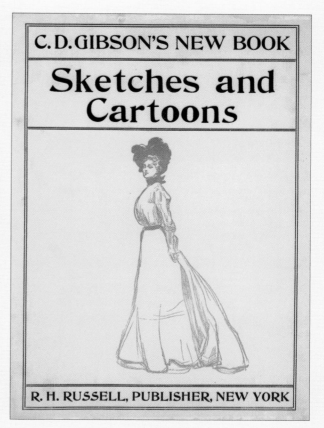

The Chicago World's Fair—technically, the World's Columbian Exposition, marking the 500th anniversary of Columbus' voyage—was an astounding event. Its many visitors saw national displays, technological marvels, and a virtual city of snow-white architectural elegance reflecting the artistic trends of the day. They saw the naughty Little Egypt dance, and a pavilion built by *Puck* magazine, with artists working and presses rolling, right before the public's eyes. The leading local newspaper, the Chicago *Inter-Ocean*, introduced the novelty of color newspaper printing to the industry. One of their artists was Thomas Nast, cartooning icon of the 1870s, pioneer of a new phase in cartoon history.

"The Gibson Girl" was the creation of cartoonist Charles Dana Gibson in *Life* magazine. A spokeswomen for her era, she was independent, assertive, beautiful, and fashionable. American women wanted to look like her, and American men wanted to look like the square-jawed, clean-shaven, toned Gibson man. The Gibson Girl inspired plays, songs, prints, ceramic ware, and reprint books. Above, a poster for a Gibson book of the prestigious art publisher Robert Howard Russell.

# HOW THE OTHER HALF LIVED

The old clo'e's man—in the Jewish quarters

The open door

Two illustrations from Jacob Riis's seminal *How the Other Half Lives*, based on hundreds of photographs Riis took in New York's slums and ghettos.

The Danish-born Riis first took his camera to poverty-stricken areas of Manhattan's Lower East Side, like the Jewish ghetto of Chatham Square, and dangerous neighborhoods like Five Corners, in order to illustrate his points in lectures at churches, and in magazine articles. As his photographs attracted attention, they became the basis also of books. Riis became a founding father of photo-journalism. In his book, because reproduction of photographs was still in its infancy, many shots were re-drawn by illustrators. One of them, Thomas Fogarty, was a teacher of Norman Rockwell.

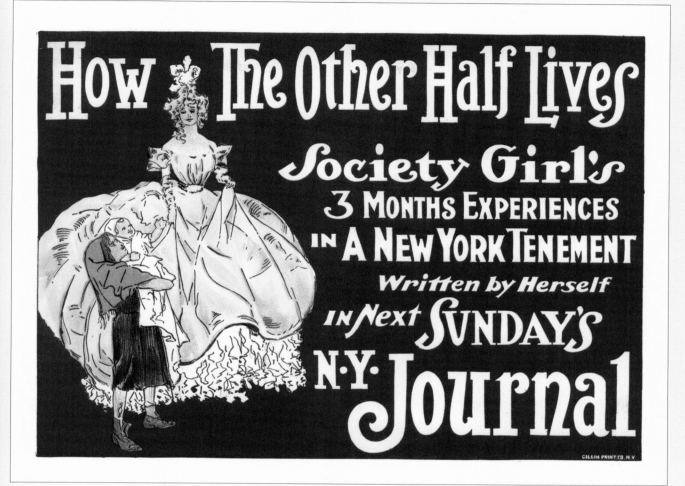

A poster for a Nellie Bly-type series of articles of William Randolph Hearst's *New York Journal*, ca. 1900. This was not Jacob Riis's own series, but the appropriation of his title illustrates how open the public was to previously taboo subjects like urban poverty and social injustice.

Sensationalist or "yellow" journalism appealed to the curious, sympathetic, and possibly the prurient among readers, and was engaged in primarily to sell newspapers. But it cannot be denied that yellow journalism, like Naturalism in literature or Expressionism in art, helped to awaken the public's conscience to many social ills.

# POLICE COMMISSIONER

A RATIONAL LAW, OR ---- TAMMANY.
TAMMANY. – Goin' to wait till dem reformers repeal dat law, are yer?
Put me back and you won't need no repeal! See?

The dilemma of tavern owners, pictured by Charles Jay Taylor in *Puck*, 1895.
The owners were caught between the forces of families looking for Sunday
relaxation, the liquor trade, the temperance movement, politicians and some
policemen engaging in extortion on the one hand, and Police Commissioner
Roosevelt, determined to enforce the law, on the other.

1 Parkhurst and Roosevelt will have to take strong measures to keep before the public eye. Here is a suggestion.

2 A "turn" at the music halls might help to make them prominent.

3. Or a flying leap from the bridge.

4 They might start a Raines law saloon and give drinks free to any one who would listen to them.

5. There is a big chance for them also in the circus line.

6. If they did this all the papers would print their names in big type.

7. An experiment of this kind would force the newspapers to issue extras.

8. Here is a better suggestion still.

9. But the very brightest idea would be for them to row across the Atlantic in an open boat at the beginning of the equinoctial gale season.

Opponents of municipal reform, such as Pulitzer's *New York World*, often attacked TR as being a publicity hound rather than a dedicated crusader. In this 1896 cartoon he is paired with fellow reformer and clergyman Dr. Charles Parkhurst. The image was drawn by cartoonist Carl Anderson who, decades later, created the cartoon icon *Henry*.

## WHY OFFICER HOULIHAN DIDN'T WAIT FOR THE END OF THE PERFORMANCE.

Policeman (After an hour's watching the flashlight advertisement)—Well, I'll stay and watch a few dozen more. It ain't meself that's afraid of Roostervelt—

But he didn't stay.

*LEFT:* In the 1890s, advertisements were projected by "magic lanterns" onto the sides of city buildings. Here a visual pun plays upon TR's already familiar glasses and toothy grin. The cop on his night beat runs because Commissioner Roosevelt was famous for hitting the streets at night, checking on patrolmen.

The cartoonist was Charles Saalburg, creator of the pioneer comic-strip characters the Ting-Ling kids.

*RIGHT:* Despite frequent attacks on Commissioner Roosevelt's enforcement of closing laws, *The New York Herald* paid tribute to TR at the end of his term. This cartoon shows Mayor William Strong engraving a message of gratitude on the Commissioner's statue. (300 Mulberry Street was the headquarters of the Police Department, near the infamous Five Corners in lower Manhattan.)

The cartoonist was Charles Green Bush, regarded at this time as the Dean of newspaper cartoonists but, sadly, forgotten today.

FIFTH SECTION. **THE NEW YORK HERALD.** PAGES 1 TO 4.

NEW YORK, SUNDAY, FEBRUARY 2, 1896. PRICE FIVE CENTS.

300 MULBERRY ST

"HE SEEN HIS DUTY AND HE DONE IT."

TEDDY

SCULPTOR STRONG'S GIFT TO THE METROPOLIS.

# POPULISM AND THE 1896 CAMPAIGN

ON TO THE ABYSS.

Marxian theories were frequently promoted in America after the Civil War. From fringe "Utopian" and "Communistic" experimental communities, to economic theorists like Henry George and Ignatius Donnelly, from radical immigrant groups to Socialist farmer and labor movements, the Populist Party in the early 1890s seemed to provide an umbrella for all the disaffected and the visionaries. This *Puck* cartoon by J. S. Pughe labeled the will-o'-the-wisp, appropriately, "Paternalism." Slight changes to the banners and fashions of the crowd Pughe depicts, and this cartoon would be pertinent today.

Cartoonist Frederick Burr Opper aimed wide with this satirical forecast of the Supreme Court under a Populist United States. Rubes and hayseeds on the bench represent the Populist base, and the youngster arguing his case represents William Jennings Bryan, who was barely over the constitutional minimum age when he ran for president. Opper (1857–1937) produced cartoon masterpieces of this caliber for more than half a century; this, for *Puck*, 1896.

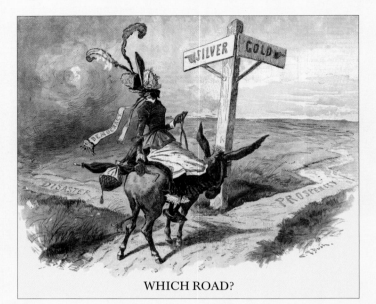

WHICH ROAD?

The fork in the road confronts the Democrat Party in this C. G. Bush cartoon from *The New York Herald*, 1895. In truth, however, the "silver agitation"—to put America on a two-metal economy instead of the (now long abandoned) gold standard—was a national, not a strict party, issue. The "Gold Standard Nominee" in 1896, Republican William McKinley, had flirted with the free coinage of silver a few years previously.

There were few cartoons of William Jennings Bryan in the 1896 campaign that did not feature flames of anarchy, storm clouds, or menacing mobs. This Grant Hamilton portrait of the young Bryan graced a front cover of *Judge*.

"THE BOY STANDS ON THE BURNING DECK, WHENCE ALL BUT HIM HAVE FLED."

CHAPTER 6

# 1897~1898

# THE SPLENDID LITTLE WAR

**W**. A. Rogers, a news sketch artist who drew cartoons, story illustrations, and news drawings for *Harper's Weekly*, visited Washington in February 1898. The United States Navy was embroiled in a crisis in the aftermath of the February 15 explosion of the U.S. battleship *Maine* in the harbor of Havana, Cuba, where it had been dispatched to protect Americans during upheavals in that city. Two hundred sixty-six sailors had been killed in the blast. Assistant Secretary of the Navy Roosevelt, true to his character, had become heavily involved in the U.S. response to this disaster. Rogers sketched TR leaning against his desk, deep in thought and reading a dispatch, amidst diplomatic reports and visitors. It is likely that Rogers' scene depicts one of the few quieter moments in that office in the first months of 1898.

To this day, the cause of the *Maine*'s explosion is a matter of dispute; but at that time, many Americans assumed the Spaniards had provoked and committed the act. The Spanish monarchy had suppressed many revolutions and stifled widespread discontent throughout its four-century rule of Cuba. The oppression often caught the attention and

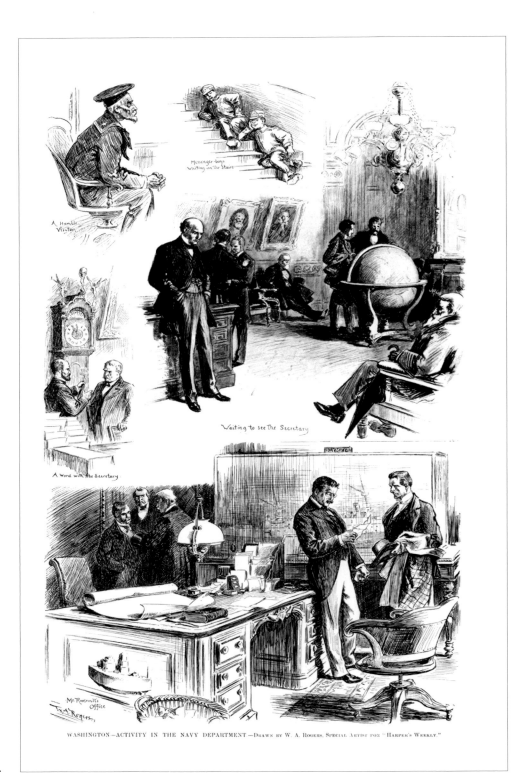

WASHINGTON—ACTIVITY IN THE NAVY DEPARTMENT—Drawn by W. A. Rogers, Special Artist for "Harper's Weekly."

the sympathy of Americans, some of whom envisioned the annexation of Cuba, while others were sincerely moved to urge humanitarian intervention. Spain's empire had begun to creak from old age and poverty, and its policies—for instance, herding numerous subjects of its colonies into "reconcentration camps"—grew more brutal.

In earlier decades, some Americans had had particular reason to keep their eyes on Cuba. The antebellum South, for instance, sought new slave states. Likewise, agricultural trusts and monopolies had a particular interest in the island. Meanwhile, Cuban revolutionaries grew ever bolder, provoking major Spanish military intervention every decade since the 1860s.

Assistant Secretary Roosevelt's office, while it was always a lively center of activity (especially when Secretary of the Navy John D. Long was away—which was often), was particularly busy on the day W. A. Rogers came to sketch it. TR's office was also the nerve-center of the "war party" in Washington, comprised of those who thought that Cuba should be liberated from Spanish rule. They believed that it was the duty of the United States to become a world power, sweeping away the mossy vestige of European colonialism from the hemisphere, and expanding America's real estate.

COL. THEODORE ROOSEVELT IN THE ROUGH RIDER UNIFORM.

Many newspapers and magazines covered America's shortest war exhaustively. This portrait of Colonel Roosevelt is from a book published by the Chicago *Record-Herald*. *The New York Journal* published a long part-series. Reporters Edward Marshall and Burr McIntosh wrote illustrated histories of the little war. Roosevelt, who fought there, and Henry Cabot Lodge, who remained in the Senate, wrote books. Folio volumes overflowing with personal accounts, drawings, paintings, and photographs, were issued by the magazines *Harper's Weekly*, *Leslie's*, and *Collier's*.

Since the Civil War, the ranks of America's armed forces had been at meager levels, and the state of armaments and naval forces were in frightening disarray. This was the view of perfervid disciples of Manifest Destiny like Assistant Secretary of the Navy Roosevelt, Admiral Mahan, and senators Albert Beveridge and Henry Cabot Lodge. Among the other proponents of expansion, or at least the adventure promised by a swift, short war (which a war with Spain would be, by general consensus) were sensationalist newspaper publishers William Randolph Hearst and Joseph Pulitzer, whose flagship papers were, respectively, the *Journal* and the *World* in New York City.

Big Business was against a war, however. And so was President McKinley, for the same reason: the uncertainties of war could disrupt the economic recovery, which was robust after years of depression and the recent scare of the Populist revolt. A panoply of anti-expansionists, pacifists, and nativists joined ranks to oppose militarism and the conquest of foreign lands and alien peoples. Even the destruction of the *Maine* had not turned public opinion entirely in favor of war.

Theodore Roosevelt saw war as a legitimate instrument of foreign policy and national purpose—even as a means to inculcate "manly virtues" in a new generation—and his position was well known. His was not an uncommon attitude at that time. TR always frankly discussed war as routine in the life of nations—something that strenuous diplomacy should work to make unnecessary, but a reality that a virile republic should never avoid. The belief was woven into his first major book (*The Naval War of 1812*), magazine articles, and even his recent address to the Naval War College. As with many of his policies, the codification, "If I must choose between peace and righteousness, I choose righteousness," was TR's consistent, lifelong credo, not an evolving ideal. So McKinley's nervousness in appointing TR had been reasonable, given the common impression of Roosevelt.

Behind the scenes, TR worked on an initiative that would strengthen the American offensive, should war against Spain become a reality. He recalled the strength a group of his manly cowboys were willing to wield against the Haymarket rioters and bombers in Chicago in 1886. He had envisioned such volunteer action at the time. What if he were to gather those same men into a "democratic posse" of cowboys from the west and brave patriots from the east, to take part in the Cuban struggle? This was an idea he had revived more than once since 1886, under presidents Harrison and Cleveland, despite the fact that war was never a remote possibility in those years. The presidents never had to do more than take Roosevelt's offer under advisement. TR would continue to bring up the idea even after the Spanish-American War and his own presidency, even petitioning President Wilson, unsuccessfully, at the height of his political opposition. Now, at the outset of war with Spain, TR contacted countless willing warriors, drafted organizational charts, and so forth. Significantly, he had never raised such a band of brothers, or proposed doing so, during all the years when the Army was preoccupied with battling American Indians. It was unrest on foreign soil that stirred his martial spirit.

Drawn by W. Frazee Strunz.

ROOSEVELT.     MARSHALL.               R. H. DAVIS.     WOOD.

*Lieut.-Col. Roosevelt Examining the Severed Wire just before the Battle of Las Guasimas.*

A scene from the battlefield—Roosevelt as detective. He discovers freshly cut barbed wire and concludes that Spanish troops have recently passed. From *The Record-Herald.*

From his office, and as wide as he was able extend its influence, Assistant Secretary of the Navy Roosevelt grappled with the possible requirements and contingencies to the nation if war came. Exercising enormous sagacity and brilliant military strategy, TR ordered Commodore George Dewey to move the fleet to Manila, in the Philippines. It is plausible that by doing this he exceeded his authority; he was not authorized to issue such orders, except in the technicality-based provision of the Secretary's incapacity or absence. Secretary of the Navy Long, though not in the office on the day TR cabled Dewey issuing this order, was neither sick nor unreachable; he was merely taking a day of rest. Long chided Roosevelt for this action upon his return to the office, but the deed had been done; Long did not rescind the order.

While TR continued active in his civilian capacity as Assistant Secretary in the Department of the Navy, he was equally busy building his cowboy regiment as a part of the Army. Since the War of 1812, the states had been allowed, even encouraged, to raise volunteer corps. The practice served to mobilize (and democratize) public support of war, which arguably was more important than the supplementation of the regular Army. The volunteer troops also were politically important, allowing prominent politicians and citizens to carry their states' flags, and accommodating the quick integration, and later demobilization, of state guard units. Roosevelt astutely arranged for the First United States Volunteer Cavalry, thereby not restricted to one state. He recognized that this must be a national effort. And he was confident enough to take on a leadership position within his volunteer corps, despite his lack of military experience. The most experience he could boast–besides reading military history and tactics—was service in the New York National Guard, which he had joined on August 1, 1882, commissioned a 2nd Lieutenant of B Company, 8th Regiment. He was eventually promoted to Captain, and he resigned his commission in 1886. All rather too minor, even TR realized, to be relevant to the upcoming duties. TR declined the highest rank of the First U.S. Volunteer Cavalry—Colonel— recommending his friend Leonard Wood for the position. Wood was an Army surgeon who served as personal physician to presidents Cleveland and McKinley; his previous service was in American Indian campaigns, during which he had been awarded the Medal of Honor.

The greatest obstacle Roosevelt faced in preparing for service in Cuba, however, was the serious illness of Edith. Diagnosed as near death in the spring of 1898, Edith was recovering at an alarmingly slow pace after an operation following the birth of their last child, Quentin. But recover she did, so TR determined to participate in the war he had advocated for so strongly—to "pay with his body for his soul's desire," if need be.

There were two months between the *Maine* disaster and the actual declaration of war (an Alphonse-Gaston situation where both sides eventually declared that a state of war "already existed"). Spain was

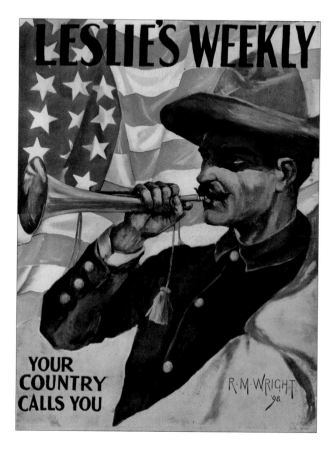

decrepit and in no condition to defend its colonies. President McKinley sincerely wished to avoid war, and exhausted all means of diplomacy and patience in his attempts to do so. TR was quoted during this time, characterizing his commander-in-chief as "having the backbone of a chocolate éclair." Still, in the interim, Roosevelt was able to see to all arrangements for his volunteer regiment. He filtered through thousands of applications, as newspapermen and cartoonists helped spread the word. He ordered custom uniforms for himself from Brooks Brothers, and dozens of extra spectacles. Finally, he resigned as Assistant Secretary of the Navy, in order to take on his new duties as Lieutenant Colonel of the First U.S. Volunteer Cavalry. Secretary of the Navy Long told him frankly that besides being a fool and courting death, he was throwing away a promising career in public service. In his diary entry for April 28, 1898, Long wrote of TR: "He thinks he is following his highest ideal, whereas, in fact, as without exception every one of his friends advises him, he is acting like a fool. And, yet, how absurd all this will sound if, by some turn of fortune, he should accomplish some great thing and strike a very high mark."

The public was quickly warming to the thrill of an American military adventure, and TR's regiment of patriotic citizen-soldiers—comprised of cowboys and playboys, cattle drivers and polo players, men of shady résumés and blueblood pedigrees, "Half-Breeds" and WASPs, from every part of the land—gained almost instant celebrity. Although Leonard Wood was the colonel of this popular regiment and TR only the lieutenant colonel, it was TR who stood out in the public mind. Reporters, cartoonists, and plain folks dubbed the unit "Roosevelt's Rough Riders," and their affection matched their awe. The Rough Riders were the stuff of legend before they ever set foot in Cuba.

Getting to Cuba proved no small feat, since boats were scarce and logistics chaotic. First, they would need to go to San Antonio, Texas, to train, to become a disciplined fighting force virtually overnight.

TR was acutely aware that this war might be over before he could get his men into it. Straining against this possibility, he managed a whirlwind of contacts, preparations, and personal arrangements at home, for Edith's recovery was fragile. The Rough Riders needed only minimal training in riding and shooting—these men were among the best riders and the best shots in the nation—but they needed to learn discipline, and a strict understanding

Even the Yellow Kid joined the war fever. This sketch appeared in *The New York Journal.* Cartoonist R. F. Outcault illustrated a book about the Rough Riders written by the wounded war correspondent Edward Marshall. Outcault's *Yellow Kid* is regarded as the first comic strip.

of the democratic nature of their regiment, where all would be equal in what was offered and expected. Colonel Wood handled the military drills, while Lieutenant Colonel Roosevelt addressed the group ethos and camaraderie. And of course, newspapermen and cartoonists kept the Rough Riders' activities squarely in the public eye.

In fact, the press corps flocked to Roosevelt and his Rough Riders. It was the Rough Riders' congenital circumvention of red tape that provided part of its appeal. To the public, the Rough Riders embodied a youthful free spirit that seemed to mirror the American eagle spreading its wings. To the press corps, TR provided reliably good copy, as well as a "friend in court" if they needed favors to do their work, landing scoops or obtaining interviews. Two of the newspapers reliably opposed to Roosevelt and his policies in New York were the *Journal* and the *World*; but they were his allies in beating the drums for war. Not every newspaper in America was bellicose—remember, traditional Republicans, business interests, and many Democrats were against a war—but Hearst and Pulitzer eclipsed the other New York papers. War fever (as well as an array of "yellow journalism" features like the popular Yellow Kid cartoon) served to push the circulation of the *Journal* and the *World* past a million copies a day. The idea of chasing Spain from the Western hemisphere was beginning to excite American youth *and* sell newspapers. When war was finally declared, the *Journal*'s headline type was almost as tall as the newsboys who hawked as many as fifteen editions a day on street corners.

Among the reporters and artists who flocked to publicize the activities of the Rough Riders were Richard Harding Davis, Stephen Crane, Edward Marshall, James Creelman, and Burr McIntosh. The pioneer movie-makers J. Stuart Blackton and Albert E. Smith covered the war with primitive motion-picture cameras. The illustrators included news artists like T. Dart Walker and Thure de Thulstrup; military artists like H. A. Ogden and Henry Reuterdahl; society artist Howard Chandler Christy; and, importantly, Frederic Remington.

Remington, the quintessential pictorial chronicler of the American cowboy, was itching for America to wage war in Cuba. After the wild west, the setting and potential action stirred the artist's narrative urges. The illustrator's career had virtually begun with

Theodore Roosevelt's cowboy stories. Remington produced almost a hundred drawings for TR's *Ranch Life and Hunting Trail*, serialized in *Century* magazine a decade earlier, and the two men were good friends. Waiting impatiently for the war to start, Remington went so far as to produce incendiary drawings (for example, images of humiliated women being strip-searched by Spanish officials), in order to fuel war fever in America. He bemoaned the lack of action to his publisher of the moment, Hearst, who cabled back (at least in legend): "You provide the pictures; I'll provide the war."

When war came, many of its memorable images—including thrilling and romantic, if not romanticized, iconic paintings of the Rough Riders in action—were provided by Frederic Remington.

LANDING HORSES FROM THE GUSSIE OFF THE COAST OF CUBA.

What romantic elements there were in the victory over Spain came with much effort and deadly determination, even before combat began. When the Rough Riders arrived in Tampa for transport to Cuba, there was virtual anarchy—no schedule of what troops would leave, or when, or how. TR and his men displaced other soldiers in their scramble for spaces aboard a troop transport ship, all in their effort just to *get* to Cuba. Once off Cuban waters, there were no logistics for speedy, practical, or orderly disembarkation. Men jumped and managed to swim with heavy packs; provisions were dumped, and much was lost; horses were pushed, and many drowned. Roosevelt was so angered that he was heard to utter the word "damn" one of the only times in his life. Once they finally got to shore, there was further confusion regarding assignments for camps and plans for the soldiers.

Cuba proved a difficult adjustment for the Americans. Their woolen uniforms were ancient or of ancient design, and not at all suited for tropical weather. This was due to poor tactical considerations from quartermasters back in Washington, who should have been aware of Cuba's heat and humidity. Soldiers also had to contend with yellow fever and rancid canned beef in Army rations. (After the war, the "embalmed beef" scandal would tear through the War Department.) Once soldiers penetrated the dense tropical vegetation, they became the targets of sharpshooting snipers; soldiers were as exposed in the forests as on the open field. Another problem was weaponry. The Spanish were equipped with new German Mausers, repeating rifles that used smokeless gunpowder, a recent invention. American soldiers often had older weapons and old-fashioned gunpowder, which made it impossible for a U.S. soldier to keep his position hidden.

The Rough Riders landed—or rather splashed, trudged, or swam ashore—with troops of the regular Army. Many of the professional soldiers resented the presence, and the notoriety, of these temporary soldiers in hastily assembled volunteer units. On June 22, the Americans gathered in Daiquiri, which was fifteen miles from the Army's main objective, Santiago (on the southern coast of Cuba, west of Guantánamo). Many Spanish troops and the majority of the Spanish fleet were in Santiago and its harbor, a good defensive location due to the harbor's narrow entrance. The Americans marched quickly over roads and hacked through jungle growth to the town of Siboney, where the American base was established. On June 24, they fought their first major battle, at La Guásimas. It was a bloody frontal assault by the Americans, from which the Spanish eventually withdrew toward Santiago. One of the colorful anecdotes of the war arose from this battle. The American general Joe Wheeler had been a Confederate general in the Civil War; his leadership position in the Spanish-American War was a sign that healing was finally beginning from that old fissure in America's national life. Whether old "Fightin' Joe" was nostalgic or just dotty, he yelled as the Spanish retreated, "Come on, boys! We've got the Yankees on the run!"

Many of the American troops in the early action were the Rough Riders under Colonel Wood and Lieutenant Colonel Roosevelt; and many of the casualties were theirs also. Indeed, when the war was over, the Rough Riders sustained the highest percentage of loss of any cavalry unit in Cuba. At La Guásimas, Roosevelt's men were joined by the 1st U.S. Regular Cavalry, and the 10th U.S. Regular Cavalry, a unit of black troops nicknamed the Buffalo Soldiers. The performance of the Rough Riders was such in the next few days, and with Generals Wheeler and Young being incapacitated by yellow fever,

that Colonel Wood and Lieutenant Colonel Roosevelt received field promotions to Brigadier General and Colonel respectively.

While the United States Navy maneuvered to either bottle the Spanish fleet in Santiago Harbor with a scuttled ship or pick it off if it tried to escape, the U.S. Army advanced on the city of Santiago itself. By July 1, the last major obstacles the Americans faced were fortified blockhouses set atop hills overlooking Santiago, known as the San Juan Heights.

What happened in these campaigns is the stuff of legend. Because war correspondents and artists were attracted to Roosevelt like ants to honey, the representatives of the great newspapers and magazines witnessed, and generously chronicled, the action of the Rough Riders at the San Juan Heights. Despite the inevitable embellishment by many of the writers and artists, the glory of the Rough Riders' fighting defied exaggeration: their success was genuine and singular. The written and pictorial embellishments were civilian artists' meager attempts to describe the intangible qualities of bravery and heroism to people back home, and to succeeding generations. The Battle of San Juan Hill was fought from July 1 to 3, just before America's Independence Day in 1898, as if to confirm the battle as a seminal event in American history, not just in the life of Theodore Roosevelt.

At the base of Kettle Hill, which was in front of and to the right of San Juan Hill, TR comprehended the necessity to capture the promontory, and either kill or rout the Spaniards within the hacienda. The enemy was within its fortification, while the Rough Riders were exposed in open field. Because of the problems with transporting troops, disembarkation, and impassable jungles, the Rough Riders had few horses, though Colonel Roosevelt still had his horse, Little Texas. He initially charged up Kettle Hill atop Little Texas, but was impeded by a wire fence. At that point, he let Little Texas free and continued on foot to lead the successful charge of the Rough Riders and other regiments up Kettle Hill. After securing Kettle Hill, Roosevelt saw that those attacking San Juan Hill needed help. He called "Charge!" and began to run down Kettle Hill. Unfortunately, due to the cacophony of gunfire and yelling, only five of his men had heard his order and charged alongside him. After about a hundred yards, he realized that the rest of the troops remained atop Kettle Hill, so he instructed the five with him to stay where they were and he ran back to get the others. After some coaxing and yelling on the Colonel's part, the Rough Riders and the rest of the brigade atop Kettle Hill quickly fell in and charged the San Juan Heights. Only the last-minute scramble of routed Spanish troops from the summit of the San Juan Hill prevented hand-to-hand combat in the blockhouse.

For the rest of his life, Theodore Roosevelt called the charges up these two hills his "crowded hour." The actions taken by the Rough Riders and the other regiments went by so fast that they even tested Roosevelt's fantastic ability to recall minute details. In his book *The Rough Riders*, Roosevelt writes that he killed a Spanish soldier from only ten yards away during his charge up San Juan Hill. Yet, in letters written to both Edith and Henry Cabot Lodge only days after the conflict, Roosevelt wrote that this event happened during the initial charge up Kettle Hill.

In fact, the Rough Riders were not alone as they scaled the San Juan Heights. A glorious slice of America—truly the picture of the new nation—comprised the wave of men. Lieutenant John J. Pershing ("Black Jack"), the leader of the Buffalo Soldiers, later wrote: "[T]he entire command moved forward as coolly as though the buzzing of bullets was the humming of bees. White regiments, black regiments, regulars and Rough Riders, representing the young manhood of the North and the South, fought shoulder to shoulder, unmindful of race or color, unmindful of whether commanded by ex-Confederates or not, and mindful of only their common duty as Americans."

In a few short hours, American soldiers swarmed over the top of San Juan Hill, occupying a piece of land that was to enter the annals of the war, and of American history writ large. The Rough Riders posed for a photograph under the American flag at the top of the hill, a proud, beaming Colonel Roosevelt in the center amidst his comrades, pistol in holster, wearing a sweat-stained shirt and trademark dotted neckerchief, hands on hips, chest out, beaming.

Following this victory, Secretary of the Navy Long would add a post script to his April 28, 1898, diary entry. "Roosevelt was right," he wrote, "and we his friends were all wrong."

TR had molded this unit, from conception on paper to assembling men from across the nation, training, and virtually commandeering by squatter's rights a place for them on troop transports. He "pulled no rank," eating and sleeping with his men, and suffering the same privations, of which there were many. He pulled the Rough Riders together on shore, pushed them through jungles, facing enemy soldiers in the field and snipers in the trees. Sometimes following orders with liberal interpretation, he inspired his men in battle and led the assaults up San Juan Hill and Kettle Hill.

"OUR FLAG."
ONE GRAND WAVE OF PATRIOTISM ANSWERS UNCLE SAM'S CALL TO ARMS.

After the victories of San Juan Heights, the Americans had to decide whether or not to attack Santiago. The troops encamped to regroup, and leaders considered the Navy's role. It had unsuccessfully scuttled the USS *Merrimac* in order to block the harbor entrance…a blessing in disguise for those who sought a more glorious armed victory rather than a siege. After a long standoff, the Spanish fleet made a break for open seas, but was demolished by the awaiting American ships, which sustained only minimal damage.

TR charged up San Juan Hill during those steamy July days in Cuba, not to indulge ambition, but because he considered the American cause one worth fighting and even dying for. In his view, risking all, sacrificing for a cause, and acting on one's convictions, were simply the marks of a man with integrity, and of a nation with character. Through his actions, he intended to do his forebears proud, and to inspire future generations. He attracted and molded the Rough Riders to act in the same way. The Riders' honor roll was lengthy and grim, and as democratic as the regiment itself. Two of its earliest casualties were the Eastern blueblood Hamilton Fish Jr., grandson and namesake of President Grant's Secretary of State, and the charismatic bronco-buster and Arizona sheriff "Bucky" O'Neill, who, moments after telling his comrades that a "Spanish bullet was not made that could kill" him, was felled by a whizzing Mauser bullet through his neck. Another casualty was *The New York Journal* correspondent Edward Marshall, who was shot in the back and subsequently partially paralyzed. In a display of the camaraderie that prevailed in the Rough Rider "family," soldiers and non-combatants, correspondents from rival papers wrote or sent Marshall's dispatches for him, shared "scoops," and generally saved his professional, not just his physical, life.

The Rough Riders were like family, and they would remain so until the last member died decades later. In Roosevelt's political campaigns, veterans would assemble in parades. At his inaugurations, they formed honor guards. A popular song of the day, "A Hot Time in the Old Town Tonight," somehow became associated with the Rough Riders and therefore Roosevelt; this became a theme song at TR's political rallies for the rest of his life.

Once the Americans had won the Cuban campaign, they naturally wanted to go home. The soldiers were sweltering in the tropical haze. The tainted canned beef supplied by the Army was making them sick, and many were starting to contract yellow fever. More soldiers died of yellow fever, malaria, and dysentery than had died in combat in Cuba. Military professionals in Cuba wanted their men to be allowed to return home, but military bureaucrats in Washington dragged their feet. Now, TR's "temporary" military status proved an asset to the commissioned officers; he implicitly became a sacrificial lamb. At their instigation, TR executed a "round robin" letter, which was dispatched to the Secretary of War, requesting that troops return to American soil. The letter embarrassed the

THE FLOWER THAT SPRUNG FROM THE "MAINE" SAILORS' GRAVE.

Department when made public. Though written in a committee format, no one was fooled as to its authorship—TR had already been quite vocal on the issue. He got his way—the troops left Cuba. But Army brass were rankled, and TR did not receive the Medal of Honor that he, and millions of American citizens, thought he deserved. The Medal was finally awarded posthumously at a White House ceremony in 2001, making Theodore Roosevelt the only president to receive both the highest American military honor and

Colonel Theodore Roosevelt's portrait in U.S. Volunteer Cavalry Uniform was everywhere. By Charles Dana Gibson.

the world's highest recognition to a peacemaker, the Nobel Peace Prize.

The soldiers returned to U.S. soil. After a month of quarantine at Camp Wickoff, on Montauk Point at the top of Long Island, the soldiers were mustered out. The public—including Edith, now fully recovered—was allowed in . . . with press and cartoonists, of course. Even President McKinley traveled up from Washington and all the way to the eastern point of Long Island to honor the Rough Riders. The biggest honors, however, were exchanged between TR and his men. As the Rough Riders assembled one last time, they made speeches in tribute to their Colonel, and they presented him with a bronze sculpture by Frederic Remington, "The Bronco Buster."

TR thanked them:

*I am proud of this regiment beyond measure. I am proud of it because it is a typical American regiment. The foundation of the regiment was the cowpuncher. No gift could have been so appropriate. The men of the West and Southwest—horseman, rideman, and the herders of cattle—have been the backbone of this regiment, which demonstrates that Uncle Sam has another reserve of fighting men to call upon if necessity arises. Outside of my own immediate family, I shall never show as strong ties as I do toward you. I am more than pleased that you feel the same for me. Boys, I am going to stand here, and I shall esteem it a privilege if each of you will come up here. I want to shake your hands, I want to say goodbye to each of you in person.*

Before that happened—few dry eyes among the troops—TR stopped to pay tribute to the black soldiers of the 9th and 10th "Colored cavalry" regiments who were also present. "The Spaniards called them 'smoked Yankees,' but we found them to be a very excellent breed of Yankee indeed!" And then, for hours, Rough Riders passed by in file, each one exchanging good-byes and thanks.

After San Juan Hill, John Hay, TR's father's old friend who would sign the peace accords with Spain as Secretary of State, wrote to TR: "It has been a splendid little war, begun with the highest motives, carried on with magnificent intelligence and spirit, favored by that Fortune which loves the brave." If wars can be splendid, this one certainly was for America. In concert with many other aspects of expansion—population, prosperity, culture, invention—America was on the verge of a splendid new era. It would be called The American Century.

And Theodore Roosevelt was poised to lead *that* charge, too.

# THE GOLDEN AGE OF YELLOW JOURNALISM

CAPTURED BY THE YELLOW KID.

"While William Hemment photographed the wreck I scanned the shore for Spaniards, and finally saw some score of figures huddled together in one corner of the beach. We shouted to them and made a demonstration with our firearms, and the poor, cowed fellows, with great alacrity, waved a white handkerchief or shirt in token of surrender.

"I sent our small boat for the ship's launch, first having landed Mr. Hemmett and his assistant. We three stood guard over our wretched Spaniards until the launch arrived."

—*Telegram in N. Y. Journal, from W. R. Hearst at Santiago.*

Because an early pawn in their circulation wars was R. F. Outcault's cartoon character the Yellow Kid, for years Pulitzer and Hearst were referred to, and depicted, by detractors as yellow kids in nightshirts. (The character is generally believed to have given rise to the term "yellow journalism.") Some of those critical cartoons were drawn by Leon Barritt for the short-lived color cartoon paper *Vim*.

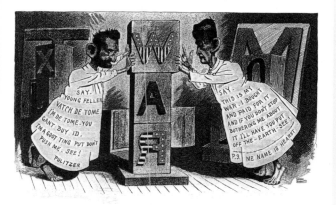

**LEFT**: Even today this would be a startling newspaper headline. But in the staid nineteenth century, when color and artwork were new things in newspapers, headlines such as this attracted readers like never before. Hearst's *Journal* sometimes printed sixteen editions a day (most of the changes being updates in the front pages, and bulletins), with newsboys hawking, "Extra! Extra! Read all about it!"

**BELOW**: In addition to screaming headlines and screaming newsboys, the *Journal* delivered news in two other unique ways: at night it projected war headlines onto the sides of buildings by magic lanterns. This method had been used by papers on election nights since the 1880s, but during the Cuban War fever, as this illustration shows, Hearst devised an enormous frame on the front of his Park Row headquarters, opposite City Hall, and put a cartoonist on scaffolding. He lettered the latest news, and made drawings, portraits, and cartoons of breaking news. Huge crowds gathered to watch.

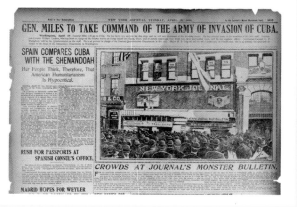

A provocative cover cartoon by Grant Hamilton that appeared a week after the Rough Riders' charge up San Juan Hill.

# AMERICA AND CUBA

The cover of *Judge* magazine from March 26, 1898, a relic of the days when, some might say, Uncle Sam was capable of outrage over human rights violations in Cuba and slights against the American flag. The cartoonist was Eugene Zimmerman ("Zim").

T.R.'s military celebrity changed the flavor of national politics. Grant Hamilton's commentary in *Judge*, 1898.

# THE ROMANTIC ROUGH RIDERS

A war likely to be of short duration, a nation hungry for dashing heroes, a colorful adventurer like Theodore Roosevelt, and a press corps of writers and artists happy to attract readers with instant legends. The combination resulted in countless images of the romantic Rough Riders. Below, in *The New York Herald*; above right, *The New York World*; opposite below, a painting by W. G. Read that graced many posters and postcards.

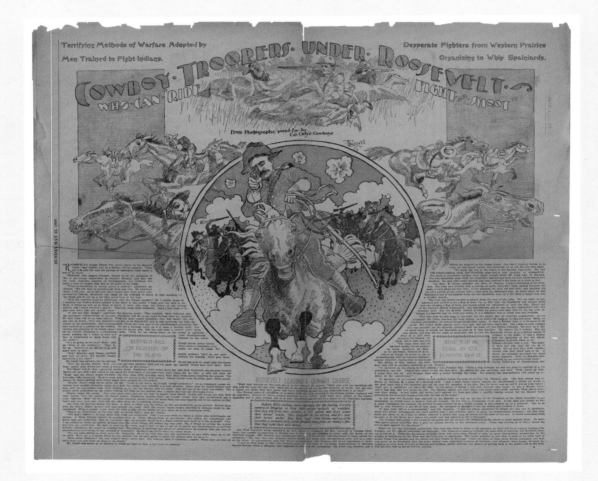

# THE REALISTIC ROUGH RIDERS

THE STORMING OF SAN JUAN—THE HEAD OF THE CHARGE—SANTIAGO DE CUBA, JULY 1.
Drawn by Frederic Remington, Special Artist for "Harper's Weekly" with General Shafter's Army.

Not a dashing cavalry charge, but the brilliant Frederick Remington managed to make a desperate scramble up a hardscrabble hill seem romantic. It seems a forgotten fact that Remington drew and painted a great number of Army subjects, mostly in the American West. It was natural that he depicted Rough Rider Roosevelt's exploits, and helped create a popular legend. Some of his first work was illustrating TR's cowboy articles and books. This painting appeared in *Harper's Weekly*.

## The Supreme Moment Before Santiago.
The 71st, Rough Riders and Regulars Routing the Spaniards at the Block House at San Juan.

Howard Chandler Christy's painting from *Truth* magazine. It is ironic that Christy, an illustrator famous for high-society themes and glamorous women, would depict the war in such paintings. Not, that is, that he covered the war—it seemed that every illustrator, cartoonist, and reporter in America had gone to Cuba—but that he eschewed the glamorous aspect of the war and captured the nitty-gritty.

# THE END OF THE SPANISH~AMERICAN WAR

On the day the battle for San Juan Hill commenced, *Judge* opined that Uncle Sam had learned his lesson about preparedness. A large part of the Cuban campaign was fought and won by volunteer regiments (with disproportionately heavy casualties). Fifteen years later, despite the lesson reinforced in Grant Hamilton's cartoon, America again wrestled with questions of inadequate military readiness.

TEDDY TO THE RESCUE OF REPUBLICANISM!

Not every cartoonist was reverential about the Spanish-American War, or its hero Roosevelt. Horace Taylor drew this for the short-lived *Verdict* magazine, which was opposed to the war and anti-imperialist.

CHAPTER 7

# 1898~1901

# FROM SAN JUAN HILL
# TO CAPITOL HILL

mong the many visitors to Camp Wickoff for the joyous homecoming of the conquering hero was a man who quietly waited his turn behind hordes of family and friends, newspapermen and cartoonists, common well-wishers and even the president of the United States. This man bore the memorable name Lemuel Ely Quigg, and he represented Republican Senator Thomas Collier Platt of New York, ostensibly to say "welcome home." Quigg was known as Boss Platt's fixer, a reliable political operative. Platt himself, almost two decades earlier, had been a similar lackey to Senator Roscoe Conkling, the scourge of TR's father in the Collector of the Port of New York episode. Conkling and Platt had both been opponents of young TR in his Assembly days and at the 1884 convention.

Platt was known in those early days, derisively, as "Me Too Platt," so dubbed by cartoonists after his protector Conkling had maneuvered a U.S. Senate seat for him. In 1881, President Garfield had asserted his independence from the Stalwarts, as Rutherford Hayes

VOLUME XXXII. NEW YORK, AUGUST 4, 1898. NUMBER 817.

TEDDY THE TERROR.

had attempted to do during his presidency, and ironically over the same patronage issue: the appointment of a Customs Collector for the Port of New York. Conkling, in an attempt to establish his party influence over President Garfield, resigned his Senate seat over the issue, thinking he would be returned triumphantly to his position. (At the time, U.S. senators were elected by state legislatures, not by popular vote.) Platt, the compliant junior senator, followed suit. It was a bold political gambit by Conkling, but the legislature decided it had had enough. In a surprise move, it elected two replacements to the U.S. Senate.

Conkling was, of course, disgraced. His public career was over. Still, he continued to exercise residual power behind the scenes, and he gained a quick fortune as a trial lawyer. When his old henchman "Chet" Arthur became president, he nominated Conkling to a Supreme Court vacancy, but Conkling declined. This awkward situation helped seal Arthur's fate both as a politician, and as president.

Meanwhile, Thomas C. Platt patiently rebuilt his career from the ground up. He eventually became a Republican boss of New York State more powerful, and certainly more savvy, than his former chief. By 1898 he had been appointed senator for the second time. Now, as Boss and senator of the Empire State, Platt approached Theodore Roosevelt in the person of his liaison, Lemuel Ely Quigg.

Elections were a few months away. The Republicans had an incumbent governor, Frank Black, a man in the pocket of Platt, a mesmerizing speaker, but suffering widespread opprobrium for presiding over a scandal-ridden administration. New York Central Railroad president Chauncey Depew, the GOP candidate for the U.S. Senate, told Platt in frustration that the best defense of the governor he could mount, when asked on the campaign circuit, was that "only" a million dollars of the infamous Canal Frauds could be pinned on Black. If the Republicans were to retain control of state government—no certain thing—they needed to jettison Black and find a popular replacement. Theodore Roosevelt, born in Manhattan, scion of New York aristocracy, former state Assemblyman and candidate for New York City mayor, had a sterling résumé. Of TR's *bona fides*, however, the most important to Platt was his popularity. (In politics, this translates to "Electability.") So Platt sent Quigg to TR in his tent at Montauk, offering the party's nomination.

Roosevelt was "dee-lighted" (his trademark pronunciation), but there were flies in the ointment. First, Independent reformers, many of TR's longtime allies in assorted municipal battles, were in one of their quadrennial danders, determined in 1898 to spurn both Democrats and Republicans and

Even before Roosevelt was elected governor, speculation was rife of his presidential possibilities. (McKinley was often depicted by cartoonists as Napoleon because of his facial resemblance.)

elect one of their own to the governor's chair. The feelers came from the editorial columns of *The New York Evening Post* and *The Nation* magazine, and various clergymen and reformers. They anointed Theodore Roosevelt, though they never fully secured his assent. TR was not comfortable spinning off from his main party to run on an Independent ticket.

He knew well enough that a division of Republican (or anti-Democrat) ranks would assure a Democrat victory. This was a time in the pendulum-swings of New York politics when the worst Tammany Hall elements controlled the state Democrat party. Roosevelt declined the Independents' overture with thanks and offered assurances that he was "one of them" as always; that his administration would be as honest and reform-oriented as they could wish. Their response was common to "purists" in politics, in contrast to "practical reformers," as TR termed himself: they rejected him vehemently. Political hell hath no fury like a "Goo Goo" (good-government zealot) scorned.

Roosevelt's relationship with Boss Platt, a particular worry of the Goo Goos, was the other fly in the ointment. In the political dance that opened with Quigg's visit, TR made it clear that he would demand independence; Platt required obeisance. Ultimately, Roosevelt accepted the nomination of the regular party and promised to consult Platt on all matters of state business and appointments. As it turned out, after he was elected, TR even stroked Platt further by having weekly breakfasts in the famous "Amen Corner" of the senator's Manhattan hotel, for all the public to see. The drawback for Platt in all those consultations and breakfasts was a particularly Rooseveltian combination of consistency, integrity, and obstinacy. In his autobiography, Platt recalled that TR "religiously fulfilled this pledge [to consult]…although he frequently did just what he pleased."

THE PARTING OF THE WAYS.

F. T. Richards of *Life* recognized that Platt must have wondered just who was the "Boss" after all. Note that he drew the White House at the end of the path TR was choosing.

Before any of this, of course, there was the election. A brief scare about TR's eligibility (he had paid taxes in the District of Columbia during his work in the Navy Department) was resolved by Republican super-lawyer Elihu Root, one of the original backers of young Roosevelt's first political campaign. Then there was the matter of uniting factions loyal to the tainted Governor Black and the spurned suitors from the Good Government societies. Roosevelt left those details to the "Easy Boss" Platt. Meanwhile, he embarked on an astonishing whirlwind campaign around the state talking directly to the people. On trains and by coach, TR traveled everywhere and was seen by everyone, or so it seemed—and if not, it wasn't due to lack of effort by brass bands and the ubiquitous Rough Riders, many of whom stepped in to help. It was indeed a hot time in the old town.

The Democrats were united behind Judge Augustus van Wyck. The two Dutchmen fought it out—TR's popularity against van Wyck's strong argument that beneath the popular Roosevelt were the rotted floorboards of a corrupt party. In the November election, more than 1.3 million votes were cast; Theodore Roosevelt, just turned forty, was elected governor by a margin of 17,786. It had been quite a year for TR. He had gone from being a minor government official in the McKinley administration, to a genuine war hero, to the governor of the most powerful state in the Union.

The Roosevelt family moved to Albany, a provincial city in the eyes of Manhattanites, and not much changed from when young TR lived in rooming houses there during his years in the Assembly. Now his home would be the Executive Mansion, and he had a large family to fill it. Alice, almost fifteen, already portrayed the free spirit that would characterize her very public persona for decades to come. She disliked the lack of excitement and glamour in Albany. At times she paid long visits to her maternal grandparents in Chestnut Hill, or to her beloved "Auntie Bye" or "Bamie," TR's sister Anna. Theodore and Edith hoped that Bye might be a palliative to Alice's obstreperous tendencies. She wasn't. But the rest of the children—Theodore (born in 1887), Kermit (1889), Ethel

(1891), Archibald (1894), and Quentin (1897)—were happy: they had a governor's mansion through which to romp.

The governor, meanwhile, found his own places to romp. He "romped" through precedents, political propriety, the "old way of doing things," and, especially, the prerogatives of Boss Platt. He endorsed Platt's slate of nominees when he approved of them, but he frequently, in some very public clashes, appointed his own people. The newspapermen and cartoonists, as always, were eager to report on TR's activities, and their news reports and cartoons helped him proceed with confidence. He had already learned the tactic of going over the heads of the political establishment, straight to the people. The ebullient character depicted by cartoonists—flashing teeth, bright spectacles, constant motion, and the frequent exclamation of the approving phrase "Bully!"—had become a figure of both familiarity and curiosity to the public.

Probably the most spectacular contretemps with Platt came when the governor supported legislation placing a tax on the franchises of public utilities. Roosevelt believed this to be a proper source of revenue, as operators were granted, in effect, monopoly status, and were profiting from common, public domains, paying no taxes in return. Sometimes, when no monopolies but only subsidies were at play, these entities stifled honest competitors. Growing out of a dispute involving street-car fares in Buffalo, a bill to tax public franchises—"common sense" in the governor's words—was twice defeated in the legislature; Roosevelt supported it more fervently, however, instead of retreating from it. In New York, the governor was entitled to submit bills on his own, and out of order on the legislative calendar. TR took full advantage of this to push his bill. This action signaled his clear priority. Besides his believing it to be good common sense, TR also gave the bill his support because he realized that the system of public works and economic efficiency—theoretically, capitalism at its best—had calcified into a network of schemes. Monopolies were protected and were gouging the public with arbitrary rate hikes; interlocking groups of cronies sat on boards and court benches and legislative seats, and favors

A Predatory Bit from the rehearsal of the Extravaganza "An AIR APPARENT"

*Second Violin:* YOU, OF COURSE, KNOW, SIR, THIS IS NOT MY REGULAR INSTRUMENT.
*The Director:* I WAS TOLD IT WAS, WHEN YOU WERE HIRED.
"NO, SIR. THE LOCAL MANAGER, MR. PLATT, WHO GOT ME THE JOB, SAID THAT, SIR—I PLAY THE SNARE-DRUM, CYMBALS, THE BASS-DRUM, AND FIFE, SIR—OR NOTHING."

As cartoonists predicted and Boss Mark Hanna (center) had feared, "What to do with Roosevelt?" was the question of the day after the new administration took office in March of 1901. Perhaps the question would be resolved in the fall, because Congress took off for all spring and summer, leaving politics too on a bit of a vacation…. A cartoon by Albert Levering in *Life*, 1901.

were exchanged for campaign donations—or bald-faced bribes. Some businessmen even intimated that the taxes would double what they were already paying to politicians and judges for protection from this sort of thing. But with reform of a corrupt system as the wind in his sails, Roosevelt prevailed.

Senator Platt was fairly beside himself, wondering whether he had created a Franken-stein's monster in securing the governorship for Roosevelt. The breakfasts with the governor were producing little more than heartburn. He wrote TR a letter, a severe scolding sandwiched between the diplomatic niceties:

*When the subject of your nomination was under consideration, there was one matter that gave me real anxiety. I think you will have no trouble in appreciating the fact that it was not the matter of your independence. I think we have got far enough along in our political acquaintance for you to see that my support in a convention does not imply subsequent "demands," nor any other relation that may not reasonably exist for the welfare of the party.... The thing that did bother me was this: I had heard from a good many sources that you were a little loose on the relations of capital and labor, on trusts and combinations, and, indeed, on those numerous questions which have recently arisen in politics affecting the security of earnings and the right of a man to run his own business in his own way, with due respect of course to the Ten Commandments and the Penal Code. Or, to get at it even more clearly, I understood from a number of business men, and among them many of your own personal friends, that you entertained various altruistic ideas, all very well in their way, but which before they could safely be put into law needed very profound consideration.... [T]o my very great surprise, you did a thing which has caused the business community of New York to wonder how far the notions of Populism, as laid down in Kansas and Nebraska, have taken hold upon the Republican party of the State of New York.*

Similar criticisms would be leveled at Theodore Roosevelt time and time again in the years to come. But his response was as old as his first public statements, and consistent with his lifelong view that the best way to preserve capitalism, and the Republic itself, was to reform them when necessary. As he said in many ways and places, he could no more tolerate wrong committed in the name of property than wrong committed against property. Platt did not yield, however, claiming that the governor was flirting with socialism and communism for supporting a tax on public franchises like street lines and water companies.

TR's reply to Platt included a firm rejection of the senator's lecture:

*I knew that you had just the feelings that you describe; that is, apart from my "impulsive-ness," you felt that there was a justifiable anxiety among men of means, and especially men representing large corporate interests, lest I might feel too strongly on what you term the "altruistic" side in matters of labor and capital and as regards the relations of the State to great corporations.... I know that when parties divide on such issues...the tendency is to force everybody into one of two camps, and to throw out entirely men like myself, who are as strongly opposed to Populism in every stage as the greatest representative of corporate wealth, but who also feel strongly that many of these representatives of enormous corporate wealth have themselves been responsible for a portion of the conditions against which Bryanism is in ignorant revolt.*

"THE PARTY'S DARLING.'

Charles Nelan in *The New York Herald*.

*I do not believe that it is wise or safe for us as a party to take refuge in mere negation and to say that there are no evils to be corrected. It seems to me that our attitude should be one of correcting the evils and thereby showing that, whereas the Populists, Socialists, and others really do not correct the evils at all, or else only do so at the expense of producing others in aggravated form, on the contrary we Republicans hold the just balance and set ourselves as resolutely against improper corporate influence on the one hand as against demagogy and mob rule on the other.*

*[Party leaders] urged upon me that I personally could not afford to take this action, for under no circumstances could I ever again be nominated for any public office, as no corporation would subscribe to a campaign fund if I was on the ticket, and that they would subscribe most heavily to beat me.... Under all these circumstances, it seemed to me there was no alternative but to do what I could to secure the passage of the bill.*

As the time for Roosevelt's renomination approached, Platt found himself confronted with the irony of his 1898 dilemma with Governor Black, this time turned on its head: he had a Republican incumbent now, wildly popular with the public, but loathed by the entrenched political classes. He saw his way out of the situation in Washington, D.C.

President McKinley's renomination was secure, and most likely also his reelection in 1900. But the vice presidency was open, as McKinley's vice president Garret A. Hobart, a New Jersey party functionary and pioneer baseball entrepreneur, had died in office. In those days, the presidential candidate did not have a role in the selection of a running-mate, that being the prerogative of delegates. Platt jumped at the opening and urged the selection of Roosevelt to be McKinley's vice-presidential candidate.

For years—in fact, since his childhood—TR's family, friends, and acquaintances had predicted he would one day be president of the United States. He was flattered, of course, but he also would fiercely rebuke such talk: no friend of his, TR said, should plant such dreams in his head; he did not want to be tempted to tailor his actions in calculation toward that ambition. In this instance, looking to 1900, however, Thomas C. Platt was not necessarily a friend; and, besides, it was the vice presidency Platt urged for TR, not the presidency.

Many of TR's vicariously ambitious friends saw the vice presidency as a dead end on his road to the White House. Roosevelt himself dreaded the prospect of presiding over the Senate, the lone duty ascribed the vice president by the Constitution. He considered the Senate a turgid debating society, and the vice president was proscribed from even joining the debate. The nation's first vice president, John Adams, had called the office the "most insignificant office that ever the invention of man contrived or his imagination conceived." A later vice president, John

Farmer William Jennings Bryan, in the cartoon from *The St. Louis Globe-Democrat*, says, "Hi there, you're ruining my crop!"

Nance Garner, famously described his office as "not worth a bucket of warm spit," or words to that effect. TR was less than enthusiastic about consigning himself to oblivion. Henry Cabot Lodge, the same friend who had worked on TR's behalf for the earlier Civil Service and Navy Department posts, was the only friend who now encouraged Roosevelt to accept a spot on the ticket if offered. "The only way to make a precedent is to break one," said Lodge.

At first Roosevelt told Platt that he would rather be a professor of history somewhere than be vice president; besides, he had work to finish as governor. There were Republican leaders opposed to the idea as well, such as Senator Marcus Alonzo Hanna, Chairman of the Republican National Committee, and McKinley's longtime *éminence grise*. Mark Hanna had muscled past other veteran GOP bosses in national councils thanks to his friendship with McKinley, and was therefore an object of jealousy among members of the Republican party. So when Hanna counseled against TR's selection—"Don't any of you realize there would be just one life between that madman and the White House?"—even more local Republican bosses joined Platt's crusade, eager to frustrate Hanna.

But there was no need for backroom machinations, Platt's desperation and Roosevelt's disinclinations notwithstanding. There was a national groundswell of support for Theodore Roosevelt, arguably by now the most popular man in the country. Rank-and-file Republicans lauded him as an "eastern man with western ideas" (when "western" referred not just to his cowboy days but to the region's flirtation with Populist reforms), and even southerners appreciated his mother's plantation background. He was the Coming Man, the personification of the emergent, confident, vital America. TR attended the Republican convention in Philadelphia wearing a broad-brim hat, which delegates instantly dubbed a "campaign hat," thinking it signaled TR's willingness to join the ticket. In fact he chose the hat to conceal an ugly, shaven head wound, sustained in a rock-climbing romp with his children a week earlier. Still, even if he had shown up in his union suit, delegates would have interpreted it as a sign of his availability as a candidate.

Despite the widespread supposition that Platt "put Roosevelt on the shelf" with the vice-presidential nomination (with other rivals to Hanna, like Senators Quay of Pennsylvania and Foraker of Ohio, trumping the GOP Boss), TR faced down Platt before the convention. He let the "Easy Boss" know that he desired to continue as governor, and would fight to the finish to continue in office. Platt relented. It was the true groundswell of enthusiasm from Republicans across the nation that persuaded Roosevelt during the convention that his larger duty was to join the national ticket.

J. Campbell Cory in *The New York World* envisioned Vice President Roosevelt presiding: "Gentlemen! The Senate will come to order!"

President McKinley reprised his "front porch campaign," literally greeting small groups on his small front yard in Canton, Ohio. In contrast, TR offered himself "to the hilt," just requesting of Chairman Hanna that his voice not be taxed, so that he might close the campaign with speeches in his own city. Roosevelt was indeed worked to the hilt, his special assignment being the heartland of America, between the Alleghenies and the Rockies. This included the home turf of William Jennings Bryan, again the Democrat candidate. Despite Bryan's scramble for a Nebraska colonelcy in the Spanish-American War, he had added fervent anti-imperialism to the 1900 platform, giving TR an extra reason to peg away at the Democrats.

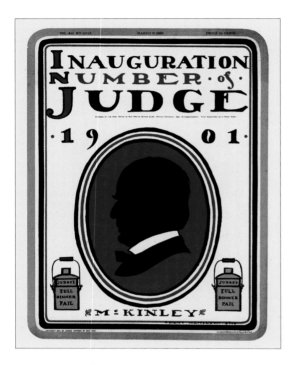

McKinley and Roosevelt won an unprecented victory in 1900. *Judge* Magazine claimed partial credit, having popularized the GOP's cartoon icons of "Full Dinner Pails" of prosperity.

"Mr Dooley," the Irish-dialect alter-ego of humorist Finley Peter Dunne, a popular and sagacious commentator on current events, observed, "'Tis Tiddy alone that's runnin'. And he ain't r-runnin'…he's gallopin'!" Accompanied again by Rough Riders, with brass bands playing "Hot Time in the Old Town" at every whistle-stop, TR criss-crossed the continent. By some reports, he traveled more than 20,000 miles. Sometimes he delivered a dozen speeches a day, attracting audiences totaling more than 3 million people.

To Republicans still nervous about the economy, Roosevelt was of sound-money, gold-standard, high-tariff orthodoxy. To citizens squeezed by railroad monopolies or agricultural trusts, he had credentials as a reformer. Social conservatives were well aware of his stands against labor unrest and immigrant radicals. Patricians knew him as one of their own; so did ranchers and farmers, cowboys and hunters, scholars and sportsmen. In none of these roles did TR pander; in all—and more—he was in sympathy with these groups. Not since the 1884 presidential election had cartoons played such a role. *Judge* magazine invented an icon, the workingman's tin lunch pail, with a label indicating that prosperity and employment had returned: The Full Dinner Pail. The icon appeared hundreds of times in cartoons and on millions of GOP campaign handouts. In the Hearst press, cartoonist Homer Davenport (who later became TR's personal friend) drew vicious attacks, mostly on Roosevelt's hunting prowess—"Terrible Teddy, the Grizzly Killer." Davenport's attacks on TR matched his grim cartoon depictions of Mark Hanna as "Dollar Mark," whose foot invariably stood on the dried skull of

Labor. F. Opper of *Puck*, known as the "Mark Twain of cartooning," drew a long series of daily political cartoons based on McKinley and his running mate. "McKinley's Minstrels" depicted the president and his running mate in blackface; "Willie and His Papa" portrayed McKinley and Roosevelt as little boys in the care of a bloated father labeled "Trusts" and a nursemaid, Mark Hanna. Opper's cartoons were hilarious (often hitting the mark with depictions of little Teddy receiving more attention than Willie), and Edith kept a scrapbook of them. Reportedly Theodore also sought them out for his personal amusement.

The McKinley-Roosevelt ticket triumphed in November, winning the largest majorities for Republicans in a generation. The GOP's burgeoning constituencies were ecstatic, full of hope for the future. TR himself, however, was not particularly sanguine. He planned to take some law courses, to aid him when he presided over the Senate's debates. He knew that life in Washington had its agreeable aspects, and the family would manage to live on the $2,000-a-year annual reduction from the New York Governor's salary. Roosevelt's friends, Henry Cabot Lodge chief among them, were still confident that Theodore, being Theodore, would break the chains of erstwhile obscurity that had overtaken his vice-presidential predecessors. Theodore would find a way.

So would Fate.

# A WILLING GOVERNOR AND RELUCTANT VP

IS IT ONLY A SHADOW?

So popular was TR throughout America after the Rough Rider campaign, that cartoons began to appear about his presidential possibilities. This cartoon by Grant Hamilton in *Judge* appeared before Roosevelt had even been elected governor of New York.

THE UNEASY BOSS.

BAD BOY TEDDY

Few people (including Tom Platt, the "Easy Boss" of New York politics) believed
that Roosevelt would be a pliant governor. Cartoon by C. G. Bush in *The New
York Herald*, 1898.

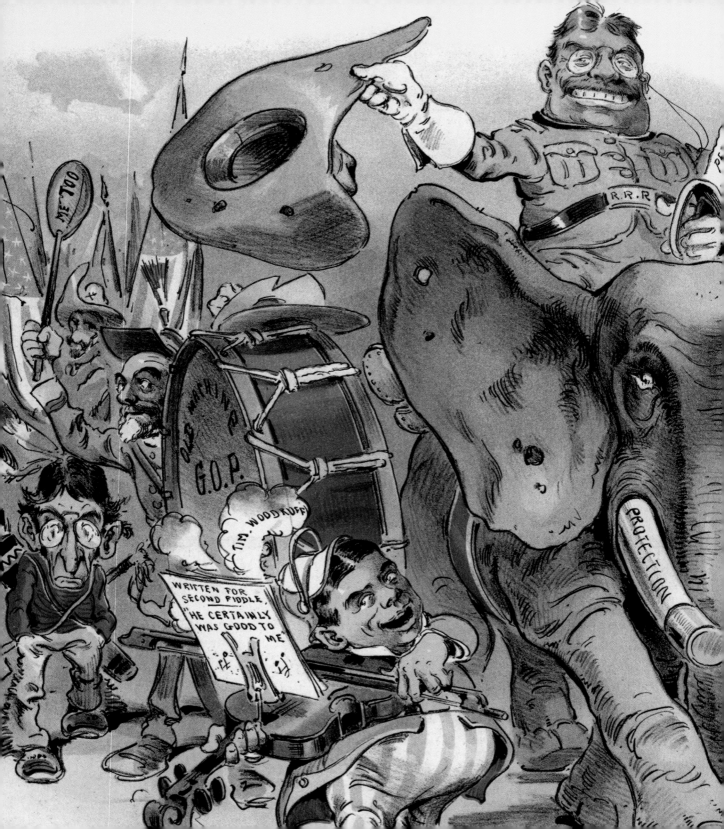

Even with the "good-government" reform crowd staying home and pouting, Roosevelt won the gubernatorial election in 1898. Representatives of GOP factions are united around him, and the field is scattered with vanquished Democrats. By Eugene Zimmerman in *Judge*, 1898.

The parties in the 1900 presidential election ran on slogans, as usual (Democrats, vestigial Populist complaints and imperialism, Republicans, the "Full Dinner Pail" of prosperity), but there were serious issues that carried implications for the new century. One was the "protective tariff," duties on imports, a burning issue for the previous generation. It generally existed to make foreign imports more expensive, not only to generate revenue but to encourage domestic industries. However, now that the U.S. was a robust economy, American industry and agriculture was interested in exporting. Other countries often retaliated with their tariffs against American goods. No major policy revisions were to take place for another decade.

The caption of this cartoon by J. S. Pughe in *Puck* was: "The Next Thing to Do." Uncle Sam says to himself, "By Jingo! That reminds me that I've got a wall like that;—I'd better take it down, myself, before other people do it for me."

# 1898-1901: Cartoon Portfolio

## WILLIE AND HIS PAPA.

"Now, Willie, we're off. But what is that awful howling back there?"

"It's Johnny Hay. He's afraid his portable bawth tub will be left behind, and he's lonesome without that Pauncefote boy."

Frederick Burr Opper was called by some "the Mark Twain of American Cartooning" when he left *Puck* magazine to draw for *The New York Herald* in 1898, and subsequently for William Randolph Hearst in 1900. Opper had illustrated books by Twain, Bill Nye, Eugene Field, H. C. Bunner, Edward Eggleston, Marrietta Holley, and other major humorists. When he joined Hearst he drew *Happy Hooligan, Alphonse and Gaston, Maud the Mule,* and many other strips.

Opper jumped into the 1900 campaign. *Willie and His Papa* was so popular that a reprint book was published in the United States and England; and the cartoons continued up to McKinley's assassination. Hearst syndicated the cartoons drawn during the presidential campaign to Democrat papers around the country.

## WILLIE AND HIS PAPA.

"Trouble again, Willie? Well, what now?"

"Teddy says this is the way he is going to arrange the Inaugural Parade."

"Now, Willie, we will rehearse our great railroad trip around the country. Nursie and I will act as ballast, Johnny Hay can be an English tourist in America, and Teddy, as you're not going, you can be the enthusiastic populace along the route."

*ABOVE*: For Democrat cartoonists, like Winsor McCay of *The Cincinnati Enquirer*, McKinley's second inauguration represented the triumph of big business and imperialism. Four years after this cartoon was drawn, McCay was in New York City, drawing the classic comic strip *Little Nemo in Slumberland.*

*LEFT*: A letter from Governor Roosevelt to the Republican cartoon magazine *Judge*. TR reportedly was a fan of political cartoons, even those at his expense. There are anecdotes of Edith keeping a scrapbook of cartoons about her husband (the critical ones prominently pasted to keep her husband's feet on the ground) but he reportedly was amused by F. Opper's cartoons in *Puck* and the Hearst press. *Judge* was a Republican organ that occasionally received subsidies from Republicans. The McKinley campaign's "Full Dinner Pail" slogan in 1900 was inspired by cartoons that began in *Judge* shortly after this letter was written.

# OVER THE HORIZON: SPECTRE OF ANARCHY

After the election of McKinley and Roosevelt (by a huge majority) and barely into the president's second term, he was assassinated by an anarchist (details, next chapter). Leon Czolgosz was the murderer, but many people placed ultimate blame on radicals in the mainstream of American life, like publisher William Randolph Hearst. His newspapers at the time espoused some radical ideas and solutions, but it specifically was a poem (supposedly written by Hearst staffer Ambrose Bierce) that predicted, more than outright advocated, that McKinley would be the victim of an assassin's bullet. The poem quoted over the amateurish cartoon on this contemporary postcard refers to the assassination of Kentucky governor Wilhelm J. Goebel.

The public perception lingered that the Hearst papers' radicalism in general, and virulent hostility to McKinley in particular, contributed to the president's assassination. It affected Hearst's own presidential ambitions. This cartoon of McKinley's ghost visiting Hearst is reproduced from the original artwork.

CHAPTER 8

# 1901~1908

# "NOW THAT DAMNED COWBOY IS PRESIDENT OF THE UNITED STATES!"

———————— ❦ ————————

Theodore Roosevelt and his family anticipated their first summer in Washington, D.C., as a sort of "calm before the calm." The locals abandoned the swampy city each summer for cooler vacation spots, so the season promised to be a quiet one. And then TR looked forward to an autumn of inactivity, in the enforced lassitude of the vice president's office. The new vice president had resigned himself to spending four years (at least) in sedentary obscurity, despite the opinions of a growing number of friends that TR was destined to be president some day. The vice-presidency, they were sure, was merely another unorthodox path in a very unorthodox political career journey.

The Roosevelt family settled its affairs. Alice was a young woman now, and ready to enter Society. Alice later remembered being excited that her formal début would be as a White House lady, but she was "humiliated" that her parents served punch instead of champagne, and that the event was a dance without a cotillion. On the other hand, she also confessed to knowing no other girl "more frivolous and inane, more scattered and self-centered" than she at that time. Ted had been packed off to Groton prep school, with his sights set on Harvard. Roosevelt set about bundling the rest of the family from Oyster Bay to Washington again. He arranged a reasonable rental of the small mansion owned by Ohio friends, the Bellamy Storers, as there was no official residence for the vice president in those days. TR presided over the Senate for a couple weeks after the March 4 inauguration, before Congress adjourned until November. Then he took advantage of the long break to go hunting in Colorado.

After two extremely hectic years, he also looked forward to spending more time with his children, planning trips and activities. Even when his schedule was busiest, however, TR never failed to make time for romps and stories and hikes and chats with his children. He even famously declined invitations to the White House when they conflicted with his

JUSTICE *VERSUS* PREJUDICE.

President Roosevelt.—Lincoln emancipated you, the people gave you citizenship and I'll protect your rights.

time with his "bunnies." During this half-year, TR inaugurated the first of what was intended to be a series of informal meetings with college students (the first group comprised of students from Harvard and Yale) to discuss programs of commitment and service to civic reform. He also arranged to receive tutoring in the law from, of all people, the Chief Justice of the Supreme Court. He officiated at the ceremonies opening the Pan-American Exposition in Buffalo. The list of his scheduled activities went on—to most people, a busy schedule, but for Roosevelt, a sedate interregnum. It was not destined to last.

Roosevelt's brief period of "rest" ended abruptly on September 6, 1901. President McKinley visited the Exposition in Buffalo himself and, while shaking hands with the public, was approached by a man whose hand was wrapped in a handkerchief, concealing a .32 caliber revolver. Leon Czolgosz, son of Polish immigrants and a disciple of anarchist Emma Goldman, shot the president twice in the abdomen, at point-blank range. Five weeks earlier, King Umberto I of Italy had been assassinated by an anarchist, an act that supposedly inspired Czolgosz. Seven weeks after murdering William McKinley, Czolgosz was arraigned, tried (he never entered a plea, nor cooperated with lawyers, nor spoke a word in self-defense), convicted, and executed. Similar swift justice had been meted out to President Garfield's assassin Charles Guiteau twenty years earlier, in an America very different from ours today.

TR rushed to the president's bedside in Buffalo, at the residence of the Milburn family, after the shooting. He left the city immediately upon making a brief visit. Doctors were optimistic about the president's recovery, and both Roosevelt and White House advisors considered it ghoulish to hover at the scene. Moreover, the public needed to be reassured of the president's prognosis. Convinced that all would be well, TR remained in New York, going off to hunt and hike in the Adirondacks. Shortly thereafter, a guide located the Roosevelt party in a remote and barely accessible portion of the mountains late one night and reported that the president had taken a turn for the worse. TR clambered down long, winding, muddy trails in the dark, and learned at a lodge where he stopped for further news that the president had died. He engaged a horse-drawn wagon and driver to take him the rest of the way down the mountain. In the moonless night, they descended seventeen miles of treacherous trails, TR frequently prodding the nervous driver to plunge the buckboard along the inky paths. "Push along! Hurry up! Go faster!"

It had been six months and two days since the inauguration of McKinley. Suddenly this young man Roosevelt (forty-two at the time, and the youngest man to date to serve as president), with young children still at home, was the leader of a country that had only recently reinvented itself by conquering a continent, winning a war, and gaining an empire. Theodore Roosevelt was president of the United States. America might have felt insecure about the upheaval and sudden change in government, except that the country *knew* TR. He had not come from nowhere. His splashy successes as governor of the largest state in the Union were well known; he was also a war hero and a familiar figure in the news, where he had been a highly visible reformer with two decades' worth of battle scars.

Moreover, America knew more about TR than his political and military résumé. He had written best-selling books in varied fields—history, civic affairs, and natural history. His exploits as a cowboy were famous, both from his own books and from the accounts of others. He wrote streams of articles for magazines, from popular monthlies and academic journals to children's magazines and Christian periodicals. When Theodore Roosevelt took the oath of office on September 14, 1901, in the parlor of the mansion of a Buffalo citizen named Wilcox, America needed no introduction to its new president, and few people were nervous about the future.

One man who *was* nervous, however, was William McKinley's best friend and political guide, Senator Mark Hanna—the man who as Chairman of the Republican National Committee had been adamantly opposed to Roosevelt's nomination to the vice-presidency, warning his fellow politicos: "Don't you realize there's only one life between that madman and the White House?" Now he cried to friends, "That damned cowboy is president of the United States!" What worried Mark Hanna was not the dust on

Roosevelt's boots before entering the White House, but the dust he would raise once he was there. Despite TR's sincere declaration that he would "continue, absolutely unbroken, the policies" of the McKinley administration, very few Americans doubted that their nation would be turning a page…maybe several pages.

After scrambling down the mountain, the "cowboy" Roosevelt borrowed formal wear from the ceremony's host Mr. Wilcox, and he met McKinley's assembled cabinet—*his* cabinet now, for he asked every member to stay on—to take the oath of office. Among the notable figures present for the oath-taking were Secretary of War Elihu Root—who had been one of TR's mentors when he ran for the Assembly two decades earlier—and Secretary of State John Hay, a personal friend of TR who had also been close to the elder Roosevelt a generation earlier.

TR's dinner guests on his first day as president were only family. The Roosevelts were a tight-knit clan, conscious of their heritage and mindful of their exceptional gifts. Theodore gathered the immediate family that evening for encouragement as he prepared to embark on this new, exciting, and challenging period of his life.

Anna, the eldest sibling, nicknamed Bamie and Auntie Bye, was by numerous accounts the most

LITTLE MISS MUFFET
SAT ON A TUFFET,
HER FEAR OF THE FUTURE WAS SMALL;
ALONG CAME A ROUGH RIDER,
WHO SAT DOWN BESIDE HER,
AND SHE WASN'T FRIGHTENED AT ALL.

The great cartoonist and illustrator James Montgomery Flagg expressed the feelings of many Americans, especially after an anarchist murdered the president, as the new century argued peril or promise.

remarkable of women, a brilliant conversationalist and intimate of the literary, diplomatic, and social elites of two continents. She had reared Alice for the first three years of her life, and received her again and again through the years, whenever a firmer hand than those provided by Theodore or Edith was required; Alice could be a handful. Alice, in her autobiography, stated that Auntie Bye could have risen to the American presidency herself, if the system had allowed—and if TR had not been on the scene. By the time of TR's elevation to the presidency, Bamie was Mrs. William Sheffield Cowles, wife of a sedentary admiral. One of her homes was in Washington, D.C., where she maintained a notable salon of the intellectual and power elites. She opened her home to the new First Family while Mrs. McKinley slowly vacated the White House. Through the years, Bamie, as much as Edith or Cabot Lodge, was one of Theodore's closest confidants and advisors.

The other Roosevelt sister, Corinne—Mrs. Douglas Robinson—was similar to Bamie in intelligence and wisdom. Her husband was in finance and advised Theodore in the realms of money that forever mystified him. Corinne became a poet of fair reputation. Both Corinne and Bamie were unwavering hero-worshipers of their brother, sublimating many prerogatives and personal goals on his behalf. This was, of course, in part because it was an age before women could assert themselves, but also largely in devotion to their exceptional brother.

One sibling was not there for the family dinner at the White House. Elliott (father of the future first lady Eleanor Roosevelt)—who had been a young man more dashing and daring, and certainly handsomer, than Theodore—had died almost a decade earlier. Elliot was a character not in keeping with the rest of his immediate family. Something of a playboy, he led the life of a sportsman and foreign hunter, growing increasingly dissolute. His drinking problems led to financial troubles. He was also sexually promiscuous, leading to a failed marriage. And he died in a cheap apartment in the arms of his mistress.

President Theodore Roosevelt's first dinner was appropriately private, a time for reflection, spiritual renewal, and inspiration. Family was always as close as TR's very heart, and as present as every horizon in his field of vision.

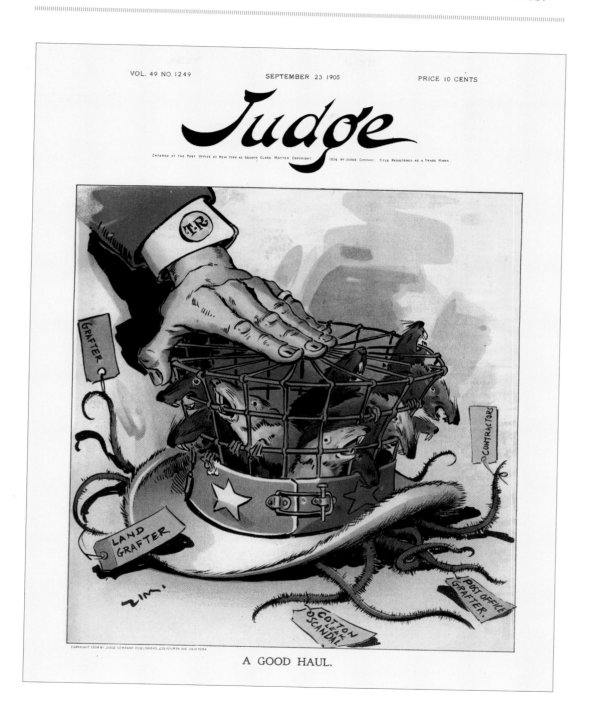

A GOOD HAUL.

Even his beloved father was "present" at that dinner in a certain way. TR noticed, for instance, that by sheer coincidence the flowers set on the table were his father's favorite variety. The day was also his father's birthday. Indeed, he felt his father's influence and presence very strongly as he began this most strenuous period of his public career. He would write, "I have realized it as I signed various papers all day long.... I feel as if my father's hand were on my shoulder, and as if there were a special blessing over the life I am to lead here." For all the distant and worthwhile goals that TR likely harbored, whether in the forefront of his mind or in inchoate ambition, he knew that he could travel farthest by staying close to his father's values and wisdom.

Neither introspection nor the multitude of new responsibilities averted TR from his form. As he noted, he signed many papers his first day. In his early days in the White House he also wrote many letters, received many visitors, and among his very first acts he invited the black educator Booker T. Washington to the White House, to discuss federal appointments and reform measures for blacks. White southerners (and many northerners) were outraged. The firestorm of opposition merely stiffened Roosevelt's resolution to let all citizens know that he was their president, regardless of their race. He also wanted to send a clear message that no one could dictate his course of action. As he took over the White House, while respecting McKinley's memory, TR did not refrain from sinking his teeth, and his spurs, into the presidency. He wrote Lodge that, although he had succeeded to the office by a dreadful circumstance, "It would be a far worse thing to be morbid about it." The fact was that he was obliged to go to work as president. From the start, he was busy. He met with congressional leaders and the diplomatic corps, issued policy statements, and drafted his State of the Union message.

The first week proved to be a microcosm of Theodore Roosevelt's entire presidency. Based on those early days, no one should have been surprised by TR's initiatives or accomplishments during his tenure. His policies evolved, certainly, but in line with the changing times. His views on social unrest, economic hardship, corporate greed, union abuses, conservation, national interest, righteousness, the "manly virtues," the sanctity of the family, military preparedness, and countless other issues, hardly changed at all over the course of his public life. TR's solutions and programs changed, of course, if only because the system's toleration of injustice sparked the public's intolerance of the status quo; and that shaped his view of the government's responsibilities. However, Roosevelt's basic views on the relationship between capital and labor, social and industrial justice, and the individual's role in society scarcely changed. The presidency merely gave Roosevelt an opportunity to focus his advocacies and to better achieve some of them.

The seeds of the issues he would make his own during his presidency had been planted during his days as New York Assemblyman, and later as governor of the state. His earlier efforts for better conditions in New York tenements, and his work to combat the evil collusion of big business, politics, and the courts, as well as his battles against railroad monopolies, coal mine owners, and meat packers, were the same issues he would strive for during his presidency, but now on a larger platform.

Roosevelt's abhorrence of political corruption likewise was a conviction he had developed early, certainly strengthened by his father's victimization in the brazen political mud-fight in New York back in 1877. "Without honesty," TR once said, "popular government is a repulsive farce." In his first week as president, he announced to a delegation of congressmen that if he could not find good Republicans to appoint, he had no problem with good Democrats. Soon thereafter he nominated an Alabamian Democrat to a federal judgeship.

His policies, then, had been on display for decades in countless speeches and articles. The only surprise as TR threw the society—or at least the government—into overdrive was that the American public offered little resistance. In fact, it seemed happy to be along for the ride. Times were ripe for change: that is undeniable. Yet much of the transformation of the culture's attitudes was due to the fact that TR preached reform, not revolution. And, as always, he was clear that reform was the antidote, not a mere substitute for (or postponement of) revolution. By these attitudes, Theodore Roosevelt proved himself to be at core a conservative. He claimed Lincoln as his model and described himself using terms like "sane radical" and "progressive conservative"—in a time before the words were made oxymoronic. To his bemusement, socialists, or at any rate social reformers, were often attracted to his policies. He ultimately would dismiss many of these followers as the "lunatic fringe."

There is another, easily missed reason why the public so quickly—and enthusiastically—embraced his policies: Theodore Roosevelt explained his positions well. He had a gift for persuasion and a talent for finding the perfect phrase to encapsulate a concept. Besides, his personality was magnetic, and people wanted to hear what he said and like what he liked. He was wise enough to accede to the hunger of cartoonists and reporters, and he knew the value of going over the heads of legislative opponents, straight to the people. The presidency afforded TR a virtual pulpit; "a *bully* pulpit," he frankly called it, in the jargon of street kids of the day ("bully" being more common in the mouths of cartoon gamins in magazines and newspapers than in presidential speech). The term has survived, but few presidents have exercised it so well, or used it so often, as did Theodore Roosevelt.

One charge often leveled against Roosevelt is that he expanded presidential powers during his time in office, often acting contrary to tradition, for instance, without counsel of his cabinet. He routinely bypassed secretaries to

FIRST IN WAR — FIRST IN PEACE — FIRST IN THE ARTS OF DIPLOMACY

TR, in the minds of his detractors a warmonger, established a substantial record of effective work on behalf of hemispheric and world peace, and was awarded the Nobel Prize for his actions.

consult with lower-echelon experts. As a result, his opponents frequently charged that he ignored time-honored practices, and even the Constitution itself. Roosevelt believed the president should be free to act in any manner that is not specifically prohibited. He once said that when he felt "certainly justified in morals," he was "therefore justified in law." If nothing else, this suggested that TR was as naïve in legal matters as he was in economics.

Another example of his view on the subject of presidential powers derives from a compliment he once paid to Senator Spooner, who desired to sit in the Cabinet instead of the Senate. Roosevelt told him, "What I need is a great Constitutional lawyer right at my side every minute."

Spooner replied that two of the country's best constitutional lawyers, Root and Taft, already served in the cabinet.

"I know it," TR admitted; "but they don't agree with me."

" IN TIME OF PEACE PREPARE FOR WAR."

A similar case concerns the Great White Fleet. As a contribution to worldwide peace, Roosevelt wanted to assemble the American fleet, paint it goodwill-white, and send it on a world tour of great nations. The purpose would be to assert America's presence as a great power and affirm her value as an ally. The mission would also serve as a warning to any potential adversary. A recalcitrant Congress refused to appropriate funds for the cruise. TR ordered the Great White Fleet to sail anyway, requiring Congress—if it wanted the Navy back in American waters—to appropriate funds needed for the project's budget.

Roosevelt recognized that sometimes the only way to get things done was to *do* them.

## THE COAL STRIKE

Early in his presidency, TR averted a potential national disaster. Coal miners in the anthracite fields of eastern Pennsylvania called a strike over grievances related to pay and safety of the workers. The maximum pay for miners at the time was $10 a week, and nearly 500 miners had died in safety-related accidents the previous year. Workers were bound to live in company towns, and there were no such things as workman's compensation provisions. The mine owners flatly refused to negotiate with the newly formed United Mine Workers, which called the strike in May 1902. By chilly autumn, the public was restive about prospects of no coal, or high-priced coal, during the upcoming winter. Already, schools were closing on particularly cold days.

TR directly intervened, the first time in U.S. history that a president attempted to arbitrate a labor dispute. The union chief, John Mitchell, offered to abide by the findings of an arbitration panel proposed by Roosevelt. The mine owners' representative, George F. Baer of the Philadelphia and Reading railway, refused to participate, and even lectured the president peremptorily. TR, who later confided that he could barely keep himself from bodily throwing Baer from the room, announced he would consider sending 10,000 U.S. soldiers to operate the mines in the name of a public emergency, to keep people from freezing over the winter. Cabinet member Elihu Root, a former Wall Street lawyer, met with J. P. Morgan in New York, asking him to persuade the mine owners to change their position.

Coal barons agreed to arbitration, but even then there were evident scales over the eyes of some businessmen. The arbitration panel was to be composed categorically by the backgrounds and credentials of its members. The size of the panel proved a sticking point, as did the owners' unwillingness to accept anyone suggested by the miners. They even vetoed in advance former president Grover Cleveland, whom Roosevelt had asked about serving. Roosevelt wanted to offset the owners' representatives with one who would advocate the laborers' point of view, creating a balanced panel. He proposed the Catholic Bishop John Spalding, who knew miners and their conditions, but the mine owners balked. Roosevelt realized that the only unfilled position on the panel was for an "eminent sociologist." He thereupon named Bishop Spalding, but called him an eminent sociologist. Surprisingly, the mine owners offered no objections.

"It dawned on me that they were not objecting to the thing, but to the name. I found that they did not mind my appointing any man, whether he was a labor man or not, so long as he was not appointed *as* a labor man, or *as* a representative of labor," Roosevelt later wrote. "I shall never forget the mixture of relief and amusement I felt when I thoroughly grasped the fact that while they would heroically submit to anarchy rather than have Tweedledum, yet if I would call it Tweedledee they would accept it with rapture: it gave me an illuminating glimpse into one corner of the mighty brains of these 'captains of industry.'"

Miners went back to work on October 16 when the commission was officially comprised. The public—a public exceedingly grateful to President Roosevelt—was spared a huge crisis.

## TRUST BUSTING

More than any other topic, Roosevelt's "attitude toward the relations between capital and labor" worried Republican leaders and Wall Street. No matter that the Sherman

Anti-Trust Act was passed under a Republican president by a Republican congress, written by a Republican icon (Ohio Senator John Sherman, later Secretary of State under McKinley, and a brother of the Civil War general William Tecumseh Sherman), who possessed about as orthodox a pedigree as conservative industrialists could wish. A consensus prevailed in the country that the evils of monopolies far outweighed any benefits they might bestow, and that, unchecked, abuses would multiply. Even conservative Republican journals, like the GOP-subsidized *Judge*, railed against trusts. Trusts and high tariffs were center-stage of every presidential campaign since the 1880s. President Cleveland even devoted his State of the Union message in 1888 exclusively to the "immoral" government budget surplus caused by policies related to trusts and high tariffs. Before or since, that was the only Annual Message ever devoted to one topic.

At the beginning of the twentieth century, most politicians at least paid lip-service to opposing interstate combinations such as the Sugar Trust, the Wheat Trust, the Steel Trust, and so forth. Even McKinley had said that the challenge of unchecked industrial combinations needed to be studied. William Jennings Bryan, more than most politicians, really seemed to believe his own radical proposals to break up and outlaw trusts. Wall Street, and its disciples in the Senate such as Mark Hanna, breathed a sigh of relief when TR devoted only a few lines of his first Annual Message to the issue.

Then, in February 1902, TR dropped a bombshell that startled even most cabinet members. The president instructed Attorney General Philander C. Knox to file suit against the newly formed Northern Securities Company. The $400 million holding company merged the railroads of titans Edward H. Harriman and James J. Hill, which would have resulted in a monopoly in the northwest quadrant of the United States. The architect of the merger was financier J. P. Morgan, in whose New York social set the Roosevelts were members. Morgan treated the issue as something that friends could settle over dinner. "If we have done anything wrong, send your man to my man and they can fix it up," Morgan wrote TR. He also asked whether the suit threatened any other interests or trusts.

Roosevelt's reply could not have been very reassuring to robber barons: "Not unless we find out…they have done something we regard as wrong."

The landmark anti-trust suit was successful. It was appealed, and the Supreme Court upheld the dissolution of Northern Securities in 1904. The Sherman Anti-Trust Act had finally grown teeth, and TR received one of his many nicknames—"The Trust-Buster."

Roosevelt did not believe he was pulling down the pillars of American capitalism in his crusade against trusts, but rather saving it from its excesses and corruption. TR believed that trusts were not to be opposed on account of their size. It was not bigness, but wrongdoing, that merited attention. He believed when small competitors were unfairly crushed, or when prices and rates were manipulated so as to cause consumer distress or violate standards of supply and demand in such cases it was incumbent upon the government to play referee. For instance, railroads often issued rebates to favored customers and hid those practices from the public, creating instability, inflating retail prices, and polluting the supply-and-demand mechanisms. As trusts were established across state lines, TR was convinced the national government should be responsible. In this as in many areas, Roosevelt adopted a national policy inherited from Hamilton, Clay, and Lincoln. This was not the Jeffersonian denial of evolutionary growth, which attitude viewed all trusts as evil (and which Roosevelt termed "rural Toryism"). Courts and legislative bodies were supposed to pursue justice and defend vulnerable entrepreneurs and consumers, but for decades judges and lawmakers had proven themselves willing tools of the trusts. The system had been rigged for far too long.

## "I AM NO LONGER A POLITICAL ACCIDENT"

TR's old nemesis Mark Hanna was still a senator from Ohio and still chairman of the Republican National Committee during Roosevelt's first term. When the time came for Roosevelt's renomination, the meager opposition within the party coalesced around

Hanna; a willing spokesman for Big Business, he attracted the "stand pat" element resistant to reform. But any potential run for the presidency by "Dollar Mark" was derailed by a perfect storm of political machinations by Ohio's junior senator Joseph B. Foraker who, though not particularly fond of TR, was a rival of Hanna. A full year before the convention, Senator Foraker engineered a motion that the Ohio party establishment endorse the policies and renomination of Roosevelt. Hanna tried to avoid the box by cabling TR that he would abstain from the resolution for reasons Roosevelt would approve "when you know all the facts." Roosevelt knew all the facts he needed. He publicly responded, "I have not asked any man for his support…inasmuch as it has been raised, of course those who favor my administration and my nomination will favor endorsing both, and those who do not will oppose." Match, set, and game.

Roosevelt set out on speaking tours to all parts of America. In Pittsfield, Massachusetts, on September 3, 1902, he narrowly escaped death and was seriously injured when an electric street car collided with the presidential carriage; this resulted in TR's confinement to a wheelchair for several weeks.

Despite his accident, Roosevelt never curtailed his travel and speaking schedule. He probably "hit the trail" more than any previous president. He enjoyed massive support from the public, not just for his policies but for his person.

Late in 1902, TR went bear hunting in Mississippi. After three days, and no bears spotted, a guide and his hunting dogs finally found an old bear. The dogs injured the bear, and guides tied it to a tree and called for the president. TR refused to shoot the bear, except to put the old fellow down, so old and infirm was the animal. The political cartoonist of the *Washington Post*, Clifford K. Berryman, memorialized the incident in cartoons. The first cartoon was a vignette in a larger group of cartoons of the week's events, and depicted TR refusing to shoot an old bear. A second, cleaner cartoon, drawn in response to public interest, showed the bear as a cowering cub. This cute bear cub began to appear in other Berryman cartoons. Eventually, this bear cub became Berryman's dingbat (a cartoonist's mascot). Roosevelt called it the Berryman Bear; Berryman called it the Roosevelt Bear; but everyone else called it the Teddy Bear. After this famous cartoon

DRAWING THE LINE IN MISSISSIPPI

appeared in the papers, a Brooklyn shopkeeper, Morris Michtom, took two stuffed toy bears his wife made and put them in his shop window. He called them Teddy Bears and found instant success. His store eventually became the Ideal Novelty and Toy Company. Other companies such as Germany's Steiff soon followed suit, and an eternal identification was born.

All across the continent, TR wanted to see the people, and the people wanted to see him. The Democrats briefly put William Jennings Bryan on the shelf and nominated the conservative New York judge Alton B. Parker. Because Roosevelt had attracted many proponents of reform and change to himself, the Democrats had nowhere else to turn but to old-line platform planks. In the 1904 election, TR won a smashing victory, even breaking the "Solid South" and carrying Missouri. Of all people, Roosevelt himself was most surprised. He said to Edith: "I am no longer a political accident."

VOL. LIII. No. 1376.

PUCK BUILDING, New York, July 15, 1903.
Copyright 1903 by Keppler & Schwarzmann.

PRICE TEN CENTS.

Entered at N. Y. P. O. as Second-class Mail Matter.

"What Fools these Mortals be!"

# Puck

SOLITAIRE.

As the 1904 election approached, for the Republicans "everything was coming up Rooses." A cartoon by J. S. Pughe in *Puck*.

On election night he made a public statement, however, that made Edith and friends like Cabot Lodge blanch. "Under no circumstances will I be a candidate for or accept another nomination." Whether his motivation was humility in gratitude, or simply signaling a desire to do other things with his life four years hence, it cemented his status as an instant lame duck, emboldening congressional reactionaries to oppose him. And the statement would seriously complicate matters later, when he sought a non-consecutive term in 1912.

President Roosevelt's inauguration was a predictable, glorious, red-white-and-blue circus. Secretary of State Hay presented the son of his old friend—now his chief—a ring with a locket containing Abraham Lincoln's hair (Hay had been Lincoln's secretary). TR was touched, and he wore the ring when he took the oath of office. In the inaugural parade, coal miners, cowboy friends, and (of course) many Rough Riders romped down Pennsylvania Avenue.

"How I wish father could have lived to see it too," TR wrote to an uncle.

## "SPEAK SOFTLY AND CARRY A BIG STICK"

Throughout his two presidential terms, TR maintained staunch, clear policies. Just as in domestic affairs no one doubted where he stood on any issue, so too in foreign policy he left no room for confusion. Besides his trademark no-nonsense approach (encapsulated in his use of the old West African proverb: "Speak softly and carry a big stick; you will go far"), Roosevelt had a real knack for diplomacy. Cartoonists seized upon TR's foreign policy aphorism of the big stick, and it quickly became an icon. In the end, though, the remarkable successes of Roosevelt's foreign policies had less to do with the decibel-levels of his speeches and the heft of his bludgeon, than with his pitch-perfect instincts and sagacity. He knew how and when to act. "Nine-tenths of wisdom," he once said, "is being wise at the right time."

In 1904, an American citizen, Ion Perdicaris, was kidnapped in Morocco. The Berber tribal chief Raisuli schemed to embarrass the nation's Sultan by demanding $70,000 in ransom, partly to reveal the national government as powerless. TR cared not a bit about the internal dynamics of North African tribal disputes. When John Hay forwarded the president's reaction in a cable—"Perdicaris alive, or Raisuli dead"—Americans were electrified. The American likely was released before the actual cable reached Morocco, but the results were the same; the world knew where the U.S. president stood while TR was in office—that much was abundantly clear. Bluffs and equivocations were not in his vocabulary.

Morocco, coincidentally, was the site of another foreign-policy triumph for Roosevelt as a proactive peacemaker, a year later. Many details of his diplomacy in this situation, which defused a flash-point between colonial powers and perhaps diverted a European war by a decade, were not publicized until fifty years later. Germany, an emerging world power, had few areas of the world in which to expand its commercial activities. Other countries entered into secret agreements to constrict Germany on the continent and on sea—most notably England, France, and Russia, who would secretly work to support each other's actions. The German Kaiser appealed to President Roosevelt to mediate a solution to a crisis in Morocco, a potential battlefield. Germany had been frozen out of political influence in the North African nation but at least wanted an international guarantee of an "open door," as had recently been established *vis à vis* China.

TR undertook the role of mediator, with no certain prospect of success. American troops, he insisted, would not become engaged. This was peacemaking. At the Algeciras (Spain) Conference he was represented by his trusted chief diplomat Henry White. All parties were pleased, or at least satisfied, as Germany gained minor concessions but major prestige. And the very real threat of war was averted.

Another largely thankless diplomatic challenge was undertaken by President Roosevelt in 1905. The world had grown concerned about a conflict between Russia and Japan. Begun over commercial prerogatives in Manchuria and northern China, disagreements had extended into seaport rights and territorial claims in the Pacific, and a host of other issues. War was declared after a surprise attack by the Imperial Japanese Navy on the Russian fleet at Port Arthur. For months the European powers looked on with dread for the future, disqualified as effective mediators because of entangling military relationships. No country besides the United States appeared to be an honest broker. When the combatants had finally bled themselves dry and acceded to mediation, TR assumed the responsibility to bring about an end to hostilities.

Roosevelt quickly realized that a large component of statecraft is personal persuasion. The Japanese and Russian representatives were suspicious, jealous, and vain, often more concerned with protocol than peace. TR countered these idiocies by clever means. Who would enter the conference room with the president, in which order? TR managed to engage everyone in lively conversation, passing through the doorway together, before any of the plenipotentiaries realized exactly how they had arrived. Who would sit where, in relation to the president and each other? TR anticipated that nonsensical concern by having the wardroom chairs on the presidential yacht, where the parties first convened, unbolted from the floor. Chairs were instead arranged in a more informal, collegial pattern.

Such inanities, catering to whims and sensibilities, are often as important as matters of territories or indemnities in the world of negotiations, and TR proved to be a perspicacious master of diplomacy. He proposed scenarios, and very secretly consulted with (and solicited pressure from) England and, especially, Germany at certain points. He insinuated himself in the discussions only as much as he thought most useful. When things had gotten further along, he moved the site of the negotiations to Portsmouth, New Hampshire.

It was exhausting work, and TR grew exasperated with both delegations–but especially the Russians, whose obsession with minor concerns and meaningless points confirmed the impression that the Czarist regime was adrift. At one point he released steam in a very unorthodox way. An experimental submarine, the *Plunger*, was ready for testing. TR descended for an hour into the waters of Long Island Sound, off Oyster Bay, to examine the submarine's technology, experience a thrill, and clear his head. He was rather roundly criticized for recklessness when the news was later made public, but this one of many "firsts" *did* clear TR's head. Soon afterward he secured a peace treaty between Russia and Japan. In summary, three weeks of intense negotiations resulted in Japan retaining Port Arthur and gaining a protectorate over Korea. Russia avoided indemnities and agreed to share the island of Sakhalin with Japan.

In the end, TR became the first American president to win the Nobel Peace Prize, among many other "firsts" in his presidency. It was an ironic honor for the war hero frequently caricatured by cartoonists in Rough Rider garb, guns in his holsters or his hands, challenging some foreign foe, or anyone in the neighborhood. But it was fitting, too, for the man whose credo was, "If I must choose between peace and righteousness, I choose righteousness," but believed that without righteousness peace was fleeting.

## "I TOOK THE ISTHMUS"

In many ways, the foreign-policy landmarks of the Roosevelt administration can be told through the same subtext as his domestic agenda: he averted crises due to his management and foresight. Much of the Old World, for instance, assumed that America would retain Cuba as a possession, yet straightforward initiatives to assist the island nation toward independence proceeded. Roosevelt believed that immediate independence would have disastrous consequences for the island, so he instated governors-general to oversee the establishment of civic structures. Yellow fever was attacked and virtually eliminated, under the direction of Dr. Walter Reed. TR, who had seen the effects of yellow fever firsthand, gave priority to this situation.

In the Caribbean basin, in Central and South America, there were local revolutions. This was nothing new, but European powers were being drawn into them, and this had previously unfamiliar aspects. Regional flash-points tempted Old World powers to test the mettle of the United States as an emerging world power. Also, Latin countries were growing ever more irresponsible in international trade, as many defaulted on debts and violated trade and customs rules with European powers, chiefly England and Germany. To promote statecraft in the hemisphere, and to keep European nations from fishing in troubled waters, TR established what came to be known as the Roosevelt Corollary to the Monroe Doctrine. This stated basically that America would intervene to schedule debt payments of rogue nations to outside powers, and would perform other such acts to promote regional order and national responsibility. Many people opposed Uncle Sam acting as a hemispheric policeman, especially dictators and military strongmen whose schemes were thus thwarted.

These interventions were uniformly bloodless, and accompanied by no-nonsense diplomacy explained with no ambiguities.

In the case of the Panama Canal, Theodore Roosevelt did not restrict himself to speaking softly; he spoke as required, acted as he saw the need, and took responsibility as he should. A canal through Panama, joining the Atlantic and Pacific Oceans, saving weeks and vast distances on the seas (some of them dangerous), had been dreamed of for centuries. The construction of a canal through the relatively narrow strip of land connecting North and South America had actually been attempted in the 1870s and abandoned by the French, after expenditure of a quarter-billion dollars and widespread death from yellow fever and malaria.

In the United States, the concept of an isthmian canal was not new. Before Roosevelt took office, the United States had negotiated with both Nicaragua and Colombia, and Congress had appropriated funds

SUGGESTION FOR A LIGHTING ARRANGEMENT AT THE ENTRANCE OF THE PANAMA CANAL.

for possible leases of land. Roosevelt needed no convincing. He realized the canal would be beneficial to commercial shipping, private sea travel, and the military. But he also felt that building an isthmian canal was an historical imperative. TR wrote that "building of the canal through Panama will rank in kind…with the Louisiana Purchase and the Annexation of Texas."

The region in which the canal was to be built was in a constant state of unrest. The countries were small, with often-shifting borders; they dealt with deadly rivalries, ethnic and tribal competition, corruption, uncountable government overthrows, revolutions, and counter-revolutions. Colombia (and Nicaragua before it, in similar fashion) frustrated U.S. diplomats, who felt that the Central Americans seldom negotiated in good faith, or continually solicited bribes. A faction within a province of Colombia rebelled once again, and declared independence as the Republic of Panama. The United States recognized the new republic, and immediately concluded a treaty to lease land and build a canal through the middle of the new country.

It is not clear whether TR was aware of back-channel machinations between Panamanians, French representatives of the previous leaseholders, and nation-building brokers working, in effect, on commission; or that many of the diplomatic details of Panama's independence occurred in a New York hotel room, not in the jungles of Central America. In any event these would have been nothing more than details to TR. And a Navy ship sent near Colombian waters, ostensibly to protect Americans in the Panamanian province, probably influenced events. What was important was that a new nation had achieved its independence, and America—indeed, the world—was to have a significantly important canal.

TR viewed the Panama Canal as the most important achievement of his administration. To naysayers of his actions and rationale, he was unapologetic: "I took the Isthmus, started the Canal, and then let Congress, not to debate the Canal, but to debate me."

An unprecedented achievement then took place: in less than a decade, the Americans cleared land and jungles and dug across a 50-mile wide swath of resistant land; they moved mechanical devices of mammoth proportions and set them in place; and they developed many important innovations in the process (as would happen in America's later space program). Cuba *redux*: deadly diseases traditionally considered incurable were attacked and conquered. Today the Canal Zone is virtually free from yellow fever and malaria. Roosevelt worked through a few false starts and consultations, enacting solutions that would ensure the construction's success. For instance, he decided on a system of locks instead of a sea-level approach, and he appointed directors with authority and competence, men like Colonel George W. Goethels of the Army Corps of Engineers, and doctors Walter Reed and William Gorgas.

The workers used massive bulldozers and cranes, dynamite and portable double-track railroad lines. They established workers' colonies with mosquito-netted buildings, social events, and even a newspaper. Construction proceeded, foot by grueling foot. Rusting equipment from previous failed endeavors littered the landscape where they worked, but the Panama Canal opened two years ahead of schedule. Ironically—or significantly (since military contingencies were important concerns to Roosevelt)—it commenced operations in August 1914, the same month that World War I began.

In 1906, Theodore Roosevelt became the first president ever to leave U.S. soil while in office. He sailed to Panama to inspect progress on his pet project. Of course, he was not content merely to observe the progress; ever the exuberant boy, TR was caught by photographers in the operator's seat of a gargantuan steam shovel.

Almost a million vessels have passed through the Panama Canal since it opened. In every respect it is one of the wonders of the world's mechanical age. As TR predicted, his decision to move forward in building the canal was debated while the project itself proceeded, but he held firm. This astounding personal achievement of Theodore Roosevelt's has never been sufficiently recognized. It is unlikely that many other presidents could have managed the events and overseen such a bold project. Under his oversight, the jungles of Panama were transformed, a mechanical marvel was realized, ahead of schedule, without corruption or scandal. At the same time, the Americans conquered diseases in the region, benefited maritime trade, and confirmed the primacy of the United States.

## CONSERVATION

Among TR's domestic policies, perhaps the one for which he is best remembered is his initiative to conserve natural resources. His work on behalf of the nation's fields, forests, and habitats was sweeping. He regarded as some of his most significant domestic accomplishments the protection of vast tracts of land and the creation of parks, monuments, game preserves, and bird sanctuaries. Of TR's myriad interests, the love of nature and the care of the environment were among his earliest and most passionate. Protecting America's natural treasures was no easy task, for Congress was populated by many men who owed their political lives to lumber, coal, and mineral trusts. Also, many citizens believed that the country's resources were endless, and that exploitation required no

reclamation. People did not recognize, nor did they care, that actions like deforestation and wanton animal slaughter would have serious national consequences. Roosevelt needed to educate just as much as he needed to initiate reform.

"In utilizing and conserving the natural resources of the Nation, the one characteristic more essential than any other is foresight," TR said. "The conservation of our natural resources and their proper use constitute the fundamental problem which underlies almost every other problem of our national life."

Many contemporary Americans cannot reconcile TR's love of hunting with his love of the natural world and his reverence for nature. Roosevelt's own accounts of camping, exploring, riding, hunting, of discoveries in the open spaces, and of contending and communing with nature should be sufficient to prove him a genuine naturalist. As a child he loved animals and birds. As an adult, he was a close associate and friend of many noted naturalists. TR was a world-class authority in many areas of natural history, contributing to the standard literature theories about mammalian affinities on different continents, and the protective coloration of fauna.

To understand Roosevelt's devotion to these issues, from a national and not a personal point of view, one must pay attention to his precise choice of words: "Conservation of Natural Resources." He enjoyed the outdoors, but his policies were not motivated by pleasure. While he valued the heritage of open ranges, he understood the importance of advances in civilization, with its farms and fences. And he was mindful of the responsibilities of God's children to nurture God's creation. On the other hand, he advocated the development of woodlands, coal fields, and waterways; a growing nation required these things. He always coupled any exploitation with management: conservation, regrowth, and reclamation. More than replanting trees, he foresaw a national policy that would divert or dam rivers, reclaim land, and irrigate deserts. (The Roosevelt Dam on the Salt River in Arizona, begun in 1905 and the first of America's grand hydroelectric dams, honors his foresight.)

TR firmly believed these factors of conservation and development were not mutually exclusive. We honor nature by enjoying it to the full, learning and nurturing along the way, and we should leave the environment somehow better off than when we first encountered it. Many of the most beautiful natural preserves in our nation today might not exist but for the actions of Theodore Roosevelt.

TR's environmental legacy includes academic papers and books, and extraordinary numbers of museum exhibits and dioramas. But his impact can be seen especially in the outdoors. Over the course of his presidency, Roosevelt was responsible for placing approximately 84,000 acres a day under public protection, for a total of 230 million acres.

Among these protected areas are 150 national forests, fifty-one federal bird reservations, four national game preserves, five national parks, eighteen national monuments, and twenty-four reclamation projects. In his last year in office, he convened a national conference to confront environmental issues. Governors of every state and territory were invited, as were cabinet secretaries, Supreme Court justices, scientists, and even William Jennings Bryan as leader of the loyal opposition. Among the results were position papers, and the creation of conservation commissions in thirty-eight states. (The annual National Governors Conference grew from this event.) Roosevelt's chief lieutenants in his conservation work were Interior Secretary James R. Garfield and Chief Forester Gifford Pinchot.

A few months after the first Governors Conference, TR appointed a Rural Life Commission to study environmental, economic, and quality-of-life issues. The Old Guard Senate, then in open revolt against any of TR's reforms, refused to print the commission's findings. The Spokane, Washington, Chamber of Commerce did so as a public service.

The conservation of natural resources was not completely original to Theodore Roosevelt; Presidents Cleveland and McKinley, for example, had set aside public lands for protection, and even some lumber companies were realizing that reforestation was long overdue on the American landscape. Roosevelt took the concept to vast new heights, and through his passion for the land, made a priceless and lasting bequest to the nation, preserving its heritage.

## THE AGE OF THE MUCKRAKERS

The last two years of Roosevelt's presidency might, after all, have been everything the old Establishment types feared when "that damned cowboy" made it to the White House. It was a period of increasingly radical reform measures and urgent proposals from the White House. A spate of legislation kept pace with regulatory proposals. In the mid-term elections of 1906, a brash new group of congressmen and senators arrived in Washington. Contrary to all patterns, the president's party did not lose, but substantially gained, seats.

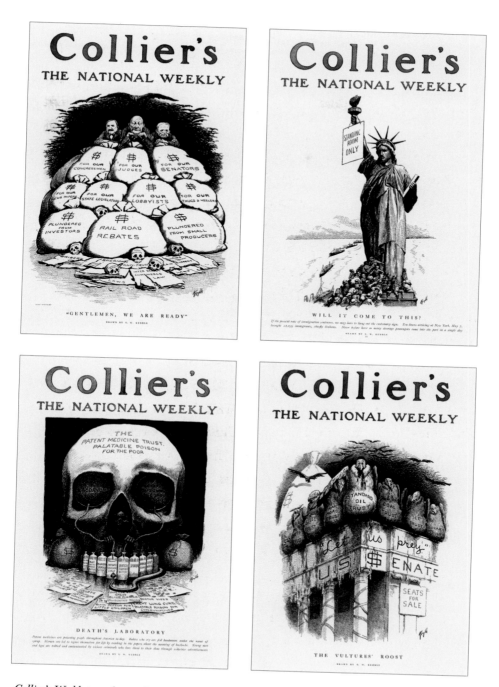

*Collier's Weekly* transformed itself from a family magazine like *The Saturday Evening Post* to a leading Muckraking journal during the Roosevelt years. Its covers, by E. W. Kemble, were as strong as anything Thomas Nast did in his heyday with *Harper's Weekly*.

And, significantly, most of those who swept in were ardent supporters of Roosevelt's policies. If anything, the new Congress prodded the president more than ever to agendas of reform.

Moreover, there was a new spirit in the land. Reform was the order of the day. Where before only a few periodicals touted reform measures (some of them, like Hearst and Pulitzer's newspapers, tinged with circulation-gathering sensationalism), now a legion of magazines regularly published exposés, revelations of corruption, shocking reports of lawbreaking in high places, exploitation of workers, scandals like squalid child-labor operations, and code violations in major industries.

Cartoonists in the newspapers and magazines largely took up and ran with the mode of cartoon-muckraking, with pictorial treatments of predatory businessmen, aggrieved consumers, and helpless citizens. Their pictures complemented the thousands of words of journalists.

Books of fiction and reportage on the same issues proliferated. In a sense, the genre was begun by TR's disciple Jacob Riis. The Danish immigrant was a pioneer of candid photography, and a newspaper reporter with a social conscience. Horrified by conditions he discovered in Lower East Side tenements, especially in New York City's infamous Five Points neighborhood, he threw himself into reform efforts. Throughout the 1880s he lectured with magic-lantern slides in churches. Riis also wrote extensively of these shocking conditions for *The New York Tribune*, *The Sun*, and for *Scribner's Monthly*. In 1890 his landmark book, *How the Other Half Lives*, was published. It became the model for exposés of the underbelly of American prosperity, pricking the consciences of those in a position to ameliorate such conditions, and inspiring other reformers to good works. Roosevelt had sought out Riis as a mentor during his days as Police Commissioner in New York. TR once said of Riis, "The countless evils which lurk in the dark corners of our civic institutions, which stalk abroad in the slums, and have their permanent abode in the crowded tenement houses, have met in Mr. Riis the most formidable opponent ever encountered by them in New York City." Riis returned TR's admiration. In 1904 he wrote the semi-official campaign biography, *Theodore Roosevelt, the Citizen.*

By the midpoint of Roosevelt's second term there were numerous magazines that heavily featured reform-oriented and investigative reporting, including *Everybody's, McClure's, Cosmopolitan, The American Magazine, Munsey's,* and even *Collier's Weekly* and *The Saturday Evening Post.* Roosevelt's old ally from Police Department days, Lincoln Steffens, wrote about urban corruption in *The Shame of the Cities.* Charles Edward Russell wrote about the Beef Trust. Samuel Hopkins Adams wrote about fraudulent medicines. Ida Tarbell and Henry Demarest Lloyd wrote about the Standard Oil Trust. Nellie Bly, the pioneering female journalist, frequently went undercover to expose various abuses. David Graham Phillips wrote about the culture of corruption in Congress in *The Treason of the Senate.* Burton J. Hendrick wrote about the insurance industry. Thomas W. Lawson wrote a series, "Frenzied Finance," about the stock market.

These were the Muckrakers. TR did not coin the term, though he applied it to these writers. He originally meant it as a caution, that some writers were more concerned with tearing down than reforming, and that they could spread cynicism by exaggerations and falsehoods. He once said:

> *You may recall the description of the man with the muck-rake [in John Bunyan's novel of Christian symbolism, The Pilgrim's Progress], the man who could look no way but downward with the muck-rake in his hands; who was offered a celestial crown for his muck-rake, but who would neither look up nor regard the crown he was offered, but continued to rake to himself the filth of the floor....*
>
> *There are, in the body politic, economic and social, many and grave evils, and there is urgent necessity for the sternest war upon them. There should be relentless exposure of and attack upon every evil man whether politician or business man, every evil practice, whether in politics, in business, or in social life. I hail as a benefactor every writer or*

*speaker, every man who, on the platform, or in book, magazine, or newspaper, with
merciless severity makes such attack, provided always that he in his turn remembers that
the attack is of use only if it is absolutely truthful.*

The term Muckraker stuck, but as an honorific title.

It is impossible to assess how much of the tidal wave of reform sentiment at this time
was inspired by Theodore Roosevelt, and how much he merely anticipated, to some
extent breaking the bronco and corralling it. No doubt he did a bit of both, for certainly
such movements would eventually have begun without him.

In Congress, however, a new generation of reformers, most of whom were frank
apostles of TR, immediately set a legislative agenda and did not hew to tradition in the
House and Senate. They introduced bills against the wishes of senior members. So it happened that, within a few years, House Insurgents even succeeded in stripping the Republican Speaker Joseph G. Cannon of autocratic powers. Among the laws passed near the close
of Roosevelt's term was the Hepburn Railroad Rate Act, to prevent railroads from dis-
criminating against smaller businesses and farmers. When he was a rancher, TR had seen
many such entrepreneurs, average Americans, squeezed out of business by collusion, favored
rebates, and false rate filings of the monopolies. The Pure Food and Drug Act was passed
at Roosevelt's urging, spurred on by muckraking articles and books like *The Jungle* by Upton
Sinclair, as well as revelations of serious health violations in the meat-packing industry.

Insurgents were to Congress what Muckrakers were to the press. Their era in Congress
(more active in the House) was between 1905 and 1913. They were Republican reformers
with agendas derived from Roosevelt: social and industrial justice. They were Nationalists,
once again in the Hamilton-Clay-Lincoln tradition, presuming that nationwide questions
required national solutions. They also saw problems within Congress itself, and their
targets were not Democrats as much as the hide-bound reactionary leaders of their own
party, the Old Guard. Angry town halls and local elections sent Insurgents to Washington

to change the way business was done on Capitol Hill. The Insurgents' era in Congress prefigured, in many ways, another generation's Tea Party grassroots revolt.

As the Insurgents felt their oats, the Old Guard dug in its heels. But history was not on the side of the Reactionaries. The Muckraking process was exposing congressional corruption old and new. In one case, Illinois senator William Lorimer was revealed to have paid bribes for his seat, and the furor was another nail in the coffin of senatorial elections by state legislators. Insurgents often held the balance of power in the House, and some Democrats joined their votes to achieve institutional reforms, such as stripping the Speaker of his simultaneous control of the Rules Committee.

Of course, the Republican Establishment in Congress (or the Old Guard, or Stand-Patters, or Reactionaries, as the nicknames evolved) were the same types of enemies of reform that TR had faced throughout his career, only with new names and different frock coats. "The opposition to reform is generally well led by skilled parliamentarians," he wrote of them. "[T]hey fight with the vindictiveness natural to men who see a chance of striking at the institution which has baffled their greed. These men have a gift at office-mongering, just as other men have a peculiar knack at picking pockets; and they are joined by all the honest dull men, who vote wrongly out of pure ignorance; and by a very few sincere and intelligent, but wholly misguided people."

# THE MOST INTERESTING AMERICAN

Besides his foreign and domestic policies, his many reform measures, and his countless other actions as president, Roosevelt has gone down in history as a fascinating individual in his own right. He captured the public's imagination even before entering the White House. Once there, he continued to inspire a certain level of awe, not only in the American people, but throughout the world. Whatever their feelings towards his policies, people could not help but be enamored of Roosevelt the man.

*The Most Interesting American* is the title of a book published at the nadir of TR's popularity, in 1915. While Americans might have waxed and waned in their support of Theodore Roosevelt the politician, they never lost their fascination with the man. The old naturalist John Burroughs observed that TR was a "many-sided man, and every side was like an electric battery. Such versatility, such vitality, such thoroughness, such copiousness, have rarely been united in one man." An opponent once said, "You have to hate the Colonel an awful lot to keep from loving him."

The man Roosevelt personified many admirable traits, and the public recognized and responded to his stellar example. He was a physical marvel, known for his advocacy of the strenuous life. He was also a man of impressive learning, more well-read than any other president, and known for his own prolific writing. TR endeared himself to the public as a family man, his loved ones—especially his children—always paramount. More than anything else, and uniting, solidifying, and supporting all the other facets of the man Theodore Roosevelt, TR possessed a staunch Christian faith. All these traits combined to make Roosevelt the most interesting American the world had ever seen, before or since.

## THE STRENUOUS LIFE

The public identified with Theodore Roosevelt in many ways, but especially with his athleticism, exercise, physical regimen, sports activities, and advocacy of fitness. His conquest of childhood debilities was a story well known; his exploits as cowboy and Rough Rider would, today, be the stuff of movies, graphic novels, and television mini-series. He had been a boxer in his Harvard days (a sport he later gave up when he came to disapprove of big-money prize fights), and he befriended the champion John L. Sullivan, who became a temperance crusader after, he said, TR led him to quit drinking. In the White House, Roosevelt learned the sport of jiu-jitsu. And, as he had since college days, TR regularly boxed. He was blinded in one eye by a young naval officer, who struck TR in the temple during a match. The public never learned of it, first because Roosevelt did not want to upset the man, but also because he did not want potential attackers to know they could approach him from a "blind side."

TR encouraged college football, saving it from bans by major schools; the National Collegiate Athletic Association (NCAA) was formed in 1906, largely due to his support. Today, the Theodore Roosevelt Award is the highest honor the NCAA confers, awarded to outstanding athletes who distinguish themselves likewise in the outside world.

While other presidents had "kitchen cabinets" of social and policy insiders, TR had his "Tennis Cabinet." He could not countenance golf, and advised his successor Taft never to be photographed on the links.

Also famous were Roosevelt's "point-to-point walks." Whether around Sagamore Hill or in Washington's Rock Creek Park, TR led children, friends, cabinet members, and diplomats on obstacle-hikes, the main rule of which was "never around, but over or through" after setting out in one direction. That meant a lot of climbing and jumping and wading. In one famous episode, the French ambassador Jules Jusserand followed his friend Theodore on an obstacle-hike, stripping down to nothing but his kid gloves in order to wade through a deep stream. When asked why he kept his gloves on, he replied, "In case we meet ze ladies!" More than once the president himself was

"I have no sympathy whatever with the overwrought sentimentality which would keep a young man [coddled]. Don't flinch! Don't foul! And *hit the line hard*!"—Theodore Roosevelt's Harvard address, 1907. Cartoon by Billy Ireland, *The Columbus Dispatch*.

seen by visitors to the park, stripped to the buff or skinned and bloodied after a challenging point-to-point.

Two months before his second term ended, President Roosevelt received heavy criticism from Congress and some in the military about his order that Army and Navy officers be required either to ride 100 miles or walk 50 miles over three consecutive days. The 50-year-old TR decided to answer the critics by riding the regimen in one day. Was it an unreasonable rule? He would find out for himself. He ordered horse relays between the White House and Warrenton, Virginia, and "volunteered" three riders to accompany him: the White House Physician Presley M. Rixey, naval physician Cary T. Grayson, and TR's trusted military aide, Captain Archie Butt.

On the morning of January 13, 1909, at 2:30, Roosevelt ate a robust breakfast of rare steak and coffee. At 3:40 a.m., the four riders saddled up and headed east on Pennsylvania Avenue to Fairfax Court House, where they changed horses. It had been a hard winter, and the roads were icy ruts. Similar conditions and cranky horses took them to Warrenton just more than seven hours after leaving the White House. TR downed two cups of tea and thick soup, and then mounted up again.

On the return to Washington, a vicious blizzard struck. Under heavy snow, biting winds, and darkness, the ice-encrusted riders proceeded almost blindly—especially Roosevelt, who could see little without his spectacles, which were coated with ice. Once, the president's horse fell into a ditch, but both were unhurt. Sleet joined the snow as the riders approached Washington, over the Potomac's Aqueduct Bridge. They rode all the way to the White House, where Edith greeted four ice-creatures at the door. Her husband apologized for being late to dinner. It was 8:40 in the evening. When the ride was calculated, it was determined to have been 104 miles. All the men were in fine shape the next day, and the president's critics were silent, if not happy.

TR was not a mere physical-fitness crank. He believed that the strenuous life found its counterparts in morals, and that a flabby society revealed a culture in decline. "I wish to preach, not the doctrine of ignoble ease, but the doctrine of the strenuous life, the life of effort, of labor and strife; to preach that highest form of success which comes, not to the man who desires more easy peace, but to the man who does not shrink from danger, from hardship, or from bitter toil, and who out of these wins the splendid ultimate triumph."

## A MAN OF LETTERS

Some of the letters TR exchanged were unorthodox. For one thing, he had a problem spelling simple words, although he could generally master longer words and many scientific and biological terms. Also, he had the handwriting of a child, a sloppy child at that, compared to standard penmanship of the Victorian era. Perhaps these peculiar challenges led Roosevelt, around 1906, to join the crusade for Simplified Spelling, a fad promoted by Andrew Carnegie and others. It was basically "fonetic speling," an attempt to wash the vestiges of Germanic and Romance rules from American English. TR even ordered the Government Printing Office to adopt Simplified Spelling, but this was perhaps the shortest-lived of any Roosevelt reform.

However, as a literary man, TR was certainly the most well-read of American presidents, Jefferson not excepted. He could, and often did, read a book a day. He was what a later generation of

Burton Link in *The Pittsburgh Press*. With all his activities, and under difficult conditions, TR read at least two books a week while on safari.

teachers called a "speed reader." His retention was astounding, and his range of interests encyclopedic. Theodore Roosevelt wrote more than fifty books, and his magazine articles covered all manner of subjects. While he was president, he wrote a scholarly article on ancient Irish sagas. After leaving office he wrote lengthy art criticism of the famous Armory Show, where Cubism had its debut in America. When his son Kermit introduced him to *Children Of the Night,* an obscure book of poems, TR was so impressed that he wrote a favorable review for a major magazine, sought out the starving poet, and arranged a government job, with instructions to "think poetry first" and bureaucratic pencil-pushing second. Thus was the career of a major American poet, Edwin Arlington Robinson, begun.

Roosevelt wrote many works on American history. Without setting out to do so, because they were written or assigned in random order over many years, he eventually covered the sweep of the entire national narrative. Several of his books, like *The Naval War of 1812* and the multi-volume *Winning of the West,* continue to be regarded as standard works in their field. Listed in general order of their place in the American story (not publication dates), they include: *New York City, Gouverneur Morris, The Winning of the West, The Naval War of 1812, Thomas Hart Benton,* and *Hero Tales from American History* (with Henry Cabot Lodge). Other random titles include a biography of Oliver Cromwell, the two-volume *Life-Histories of African Game Animals* with Edmund Heller, many collections about hunting and camping, and several anthologies of articles, speeches, and essays.

A member of the American Academy of Arts and Letters, Roosevelt was also president of the American Historical Association, elected just one month after his exhaustive and contentious Bull Moose campaign for the presidency.

## THE FAMILY MAN

Childhood and its preoccupations are a separate, special, and very significant aspect of the man who was Theodore Roosevelt. For a man reared in the Victorian Age, when children were to be seen and not heard, his upbringing (and, in turn, the household of his own children) was remarkable. Theodore Senior and Mittie respected their children from their earliest ages, hiring tutors, imparting culture, and surrounding them with intellectual conversation and educational travels. But the parents also encouraged recreation and typical pursuits of childhood. Of course, the special concern paid by his father to TR's ailments and physical challenges inculcated a reverence for filial relationships.

The children of TR and Edith could be obstreperous—to the delight of cartoonists—but the chaos ultimately was managed. There were many stories: once, when Archie was sick in bed, his siblings snuck his pony Algonquin up the White House elevator to his bedroom. Another time Quentin, the youngest of the children, was cornered by a nosy reporter seeking news about the president, and the boy replied, "I see him occasionally, but I know nothing of his family life."

TR seldom missed his afternoon romps with the children. Every year at Sagamore Hill he would play Santa Claus for the village children, and he hosted monster fireworks picnics on the Fourth of July. Roosevelt frequently took his children, their cousins, and village friends on camping trips, which invariably included impromptu ghost stories around campfires, told with great theatrics by the president of the United States.

For all their precocity, however, there were strict rules and stern discipline for the children of the Roosevelt household. "The truth! FIRST!" was TR's ferocious priority when any dispute arose. And yet, even into their adolescent years, TR's children, sons and daughters alike, would kiss their father good-night.

Of course, all this was assisted by the fact that TR himself was still a child in many ways. Edith frequently said so, with a sigh. "You must remember," said Cecil Spring-Rice, the British diplomat who was best man at TR's second wedding, "the president is about six." When Roosevelt was fifty-four and planned a trip into the Brazilian Wilderness—where he charted a major, previously unknown river and almost died in the process—he dismissed warnings, saying it was his "last chance to be a boy."

When Alice Roosevelt married Congressman Nicholas Longworth, America had an advance taste of celebrity-obsession, paparazzi, and media buzz. Alice and Nick thought they were used to attention, but they became the subject of everyone's talk for some time. A T. S. Sullivant cartoon humorously depicted their trials immediately after the White House ceremony. Reproduced from the original artwork for the New York *American*.

TR's children were all gifted and interesting in their own rights, but Alice stands out as one of the great American women of her time. She was famously independent—never perfectly comfortable with her second mother—and was America's sweetheart in her early White House years. She was beautiful and rebellious; she smoked, rode in automobiles to parties (imagine!), and fell into fountains while romping with friends. The popular song "Alice-Blue Gown" was dedicated to her. TR once said, "I can run the country, or I can control Alice. I cannot possibly do both." Her parents thought that sending her on a diplomatic mission in 1905 to the Far East with Secretary of War William Howard Taft would cool her off, but on the trip she fell in love with a delegation member, Congressman

Nicholas Longworth. They married in a lavish White House ceremony, and Longworth eventually rose to be Speaker of the House. (The Longworth House Office Building is named in his honor.) Alice remained a fixture of Washington life for decades.

The wit of "Princess Alice" was sharp and frequently quoted. She mimicked President Taft's wife (whom she resented for scheming against TR), and performed devastating impersonations of her cousin Eleanor Roosevelt. She was a clever and effective campaigner against both the League of Nations and intervention in World War II. Late into her life she was constantly in demand at Washington social functions, and always a source of copy—a genetic predisposition. She never voted for her distant cousin FDR, whose politics she despised, although she was not enamored of every Republican. Told that 1940 GOP nominee Wendell Willkie was a "grass roots" candidate, she replied, "Yes. The grass of a thousand country clubs." Once her car escaped a fender-bender with a taxi, and the cabbie called Alice's driver a "black bastard." Alice rolled down her window and called the cab driver a "white son of a bitch." After she underwent two mastectomies late in life, she took to referring to herself as "Washington's topless monument."

When I was a college student in Washington, D.C., I was privileged to meet Princess Alice, and luckier still to be invited to her Dupont Circle townhouse where I saw the famous sofa pillow with the embroidered legend, "If you can't say something good about someone, come sit next to me." She died in 1980 at the age of ninety-six, and is buried in D.C.'s Rock Creek Cemetery, near the site of TR's many obstacle-walks. She remained fanatically devoted to her father all her life, even when her husband ran as a Republican from Taft's Ohio district during the 1912 Bull Moose campaign. Longworth lost by approximately 100 votes, which Alice cheerfully accepted as due to her influence.

At the other end of the spectrum of siblings was Quentin, whose group of friends, including Charley Taft, son of the Secretary of War, and boys from the local public school Quentin attended, dubbed themselves the White House Gang. In a solemn ceremony, they once voted the president of the United States an honorary member.

## A MAN OF FAITH

An important aspect of TR that curiously has been neglected by history is his fervent Christian faith. In some ways, he might be seen as the most Christian and the most religious, at least the most observant, of all the presidents.

A list evaluating presidents by this rubric would be subjective at best, and a difficult one to compute and compile. Putting TR's name at the top might surprise some people, yet that surprise might itself bear witness to the nature of his faith. It was privately held, but it permeated countless speeches, writings, and acts. His favorite Bible verse was Micah 6:8, "What doth the Lord require of thee, but to do justly, and to love mercy, and to walk humbly with thy God?"

Theodore Roosevelt was a member of the Dutch Reformed Church. He participated in missions work around New York City with his father, whether the charity was church-related or "personal," public or private—it was all God's work. TR taught weekly Sunday school classes during his four years at Harvard. Throughout his life he wrote for Christian publications. During the White House years, Edith, a strong Episcopalian, invariably attended her denomination's church across Lafayette Park, the "Church of Presidents." The president himself usually walked a little farther to worship at a humble German Reformed church, the closest he could find to the faith of his fathers.

Roosevelt called his 1912 bare-the-soul campaign speech announcing his political principles "A Confession of Faith." Later he closed perhaps the most important speech of his life, the clarion-call acceptance of the Progressive Party nomination, with the words: "We stand at Armageddon and we battle for the Lord!" That convention featured evangelical songs and closed with the hymn, "Onward Christian Soldiers."

He titled one his books *Foes of Our Own Household* (after Matthew 10:36) and another *Fear God and Take Your Own Part*. He once wrote an article for *The Ladies' Home Journal*, "Nine Reasons Why Men Should Go To Church." After TR left the White House, he was offered university presidencies and many other prominent jobs. He chose instead to become Contributing Editor of *The Outlook*, a small Christian weekly news magazine—tantamount to an extremely popular ex-president today (if we had one) choosing to edit *WORLD* magazine, instead of a higher-profile position on a mass-circulation magazine. He accepted a salary approximately one-eighth of salaries offered by magazines like *Collier's* that hoped to snag TR's services.

His first essay for the magazine, telling the public why he chose to associate himself with the journal, was quoted by *The New York Times*, citing *The Outlook's* "paying heed to the dictates of a stern morality," and its "inflexible adherence to the elementary virtues of entire truth, entire courage, entire honesty." And, he added, it had no taint of Yellow Journalism.

Roosevelt was invited to deliver the Earl Lectures at Pacific Theological Seminary in 1911, but declined due to a heavy schedule. Knowing he would be near Berkeley on a speaking tour, however, he offered to deliver the lectures if he might be permitted to speak extemporaneously, not having time to prepare written texts of the five lectures, as was the custom. It was agreed, and TR spoke for ninety minutes each evening—from the heart and without notes—on the Christian's role in modern society.

TR was not perfect, but he knew the One who is. Fond of saying that he would "speak softly and carry a big stick," it truly can be said also that Theodore Roosevelt hid the Word in his heart and acted boldly. He was a great American because he was a thorough-going good man; and he was a good man because he was a humble believer.

LETTERS FROM THE PEOPLE

# AT THE DAWN OF THE AMERICAN CENTURY

It is difficult to assess the actual effect of Roosevelt's countless reforms, the power of his personality, and the many crises he averted as president. Roosevelt is the only "great" president who achieved that status without a war, economic calamity, or severe national crisis that forced him to prove his mettle. This is probably due in large part to his ability to identify problems and battle them effectively before they became crises. For instance, Roosevelt was absolutely convinced that the nation might be headed for social war; hence his laundry-list of reforms, and public preaching about evils on the left and right. His love of the military virtues and willingness to use force were well documented; yet he frequently asserted his pride that "not one shot was fired in conflict" during the seven and a half years of his presidency (the Philippine insurrection notwithstanding). In fact, he was the first president to earn the Nobel Peace Prize. He played a significant personal role in ending or averting wars, exercising remarkable diplomatic skills, for instance, in the Russo-Japanese War and the French-German crisis over Morocco. He might have done so again if he had been president when World War I broke out.

TR was the Great Anticipator. And just as a negative cannot be proven, we will never know what America would have looked like without the presidency of Theodore Roosevelt.

Fortunately—thanks in large part to an army of cartoonists—we do know what America, and its colorful leader during that time, *did* look like.

Roosevelt's presidency ended with two events: the grand ceremony seeing the resplendent Great White Fleet off, and a small ceremony in Kentucky at the site of Abraham Lincoln's birthplace, marking the centennial anniversary of Lincoln's birth. These events closed out the Roosevelt presidency, a powerful *coda* to his efforts to establish and maintain America's status as a major power capable of defending itself.

TR once remarked that no president ever had as much fun, or could have so much fun, as he had in office. But that was only half of the story. It is likely that the American public has never, before or since, enjoyed a president as much as it enjoyed Theodore Roosevelt. Indeed, it was a bully seven and a half years.

Theodore Roosevelt, coming to the presidency at the turn of the century, embodied the optimism and confidence of the American spirit. America, a new and prosperous world leader, was confident in the man at the helm.

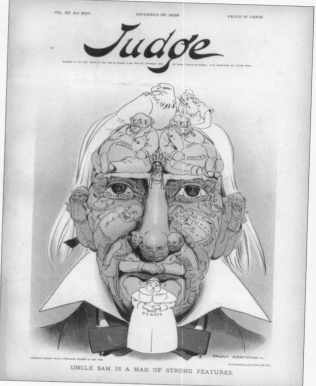

In an 1898 celebration of diversity, Grant Hamilton of *Judge* drew a cartoon of Uncle Sam's new face, comprised of ethnic groups and nationalities. Cartoonists of the day had fun at newcomers' expense, mostly because they were newcomers to the shores. Contrasts are bread-and-butter for cartoonists. Immigration reached its peak in the U.S. during Roosevelt's presidency, and he—like *Judge*—was fine with that, provided that new Americans learn the language and display undivided loyalty to America.

He arrives in "San Antone" to attend a Reunion of the Rough Riders

# PROBLEMS OF CAPITAL AND LABOR: TRUST BUSTING AND THE COAL STRIKE

IN DANGER.
PUCK.—"What are you going to do about it?"

The anti-Monopoly grievances of rural radicals like the Grange in the 1870s were adopted by many urban and establishment observers in the 1880s (this cartoon appeared in *Puck* in 1881), and led to the Sherman Anti-Trust Act of 1890. The abuses of concentrated capital and government partiality were issues long festering before TR's presidency.

"If alive to their true interests, rich and poor alike will set their faces like flint against the spirit which seeks personal advantage by overriding the laws, without regard to whether this spirit shows itself in the form of bodily violence by one set of men or in the form of vulpine cunning by another set of men. — *President Roosevelt's Speech, Sept. 7*

JACK AND THE WALL STREET GIANTS.

Cartoon by W. L. Evans of the Cleveland *Leader*. Evans had a short career as a cartoonist and a long career as designer and marketer of a successful mail-order wcartooning course that nurtured the careers of many of the succeeding generation's famous artists. The calamity depicted in the cartoon was a fair possibility. Many people were in jeopardy of freezing in the upcoming winter months, and schools and offices would have had to close in the event of a coal strike.

While there was a general consensus that trusts were a "problem," very little had been done about it before Roosevelt became president. By the turn of the century, a flurry of political cartoons and editorials reflected the public's changing attitudes. When Roosevelt decided to prosecute trusts that were in restraint of trade, the public was eager to see whether the new president could survive the resistance of the robber barons of Wall Street. Many "robber barons"—J. P. Morgan, the Vanderbilts, the Whitneys— were of Roosevelt's social set, clubs, even fox-hunting clubs and, eventually, intermarriage. They assumed, quite wrongly as events proved, that TR would overlook their transgressions.

# THE PANAMA CANAL

With its victory in the Spanish-American War, the United States could claim to be a victorious naval power, not yet a dominant one. Still, its warships patrolled a vast new territory. Its merchant marine, however, was the focus of J. S. Pughe's *Puck* cartoon, and the envy of rival commercial powers. America began the twentieth century in prosperity, and needed a canal to shorten, and protect, Atlantic-Pacific sailing.

The original caption: "Another Revelation of Strength." Uncle Sam says, "Here is a ship more powerful than my strongest ship of war. You can't resist it!"

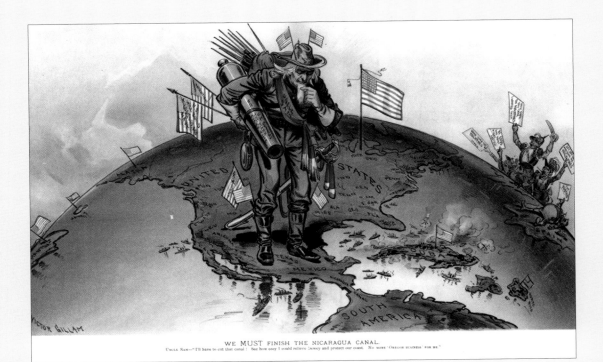

WE MUST FINISH THE NICARAGUA CANAL.

Uncle Sam—"I'll have to cut that canal! See how easy I could relieve Dewey and protect our coast. No more 'Oregon business' for me."

VICTOR GILLAM

After the Spanish-American War, the building of a canal through the Panamanian isthmus became less theoretical (illustrated by the Victor Gillam cartoon). In 1902, Congress passed the Spooner Act (introduced by Wisconsin Senator John Spooner), authorizing the president to negotiate with Colombia and buy out the old French interests in the region of Panama. This ended America's interest in an alternate Nicaraguan site, and provided the legal basis for Roosevelt's negotiations and outlays.

"ROOSEVELT'S ROUGH DIGGERS."

SUGGESTED TO THE PRESIDENT AS A WAY TO WHOOP THINGS UP AT PANAMA.

Cartoonist Billy DeBeck of *The Pittsburgh Gazette-Times* drew this prediction of History's assessment of the Panama Canal in 1914. The canal had just opened, and many people were as impressed by the speed, efficiency, and lack of corruption in the American construction project. Surely those feats were, by subsequent standards anyway, wonders in themselves. Within a few years cartoonist DeBeck forsook political cartoons and created the classic comic strip *Barney Google*.

# REELECTION

*"COMING EVENTS CAST THEIR DREAMS BEFORE."*

The large center-spread cartoon in *Judge* at Christmastide, 1903, featured this cartoon by F. Victor Gillam. The president's reveries were filled with allies and opponents, and mostly happy dreams for the future.

"SAY, BUT THAT'S MY PAIL!"

BOLTED DOWN.

*ABOVE*: To the dismay of the late President McKinley's old mentor, Mark Hanna, Roosevelt had absorbed McKinley's programs, added many of his own, and still possessed McKinley's popularity…and even his slogans. The great Charles Green Bush, in *The New York World*, 1903.

*LEFT*: This C. G. Bush cartoon shows Roosevelt quite secure in the presidential chair, despite the efforts of J. P. Morgan and Mark Hanna.

FARMER ROOSEVELT DELIVERS HIS PRIZE PRODUCE TO THE NATIONAL COUNTY FAIR.

Uncle Sam—"Good enough! That exhibit will take the prize, sure."

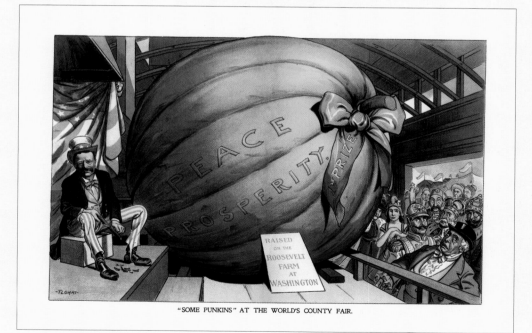

"SOME PUNKINS" AT THE WORLD'S COUNTY FAIR.

As TR ran for reelection in 1904, the worst fears of his enemies—that the "damned cowboy" would embroil America in wars, and that his Trust Busting would shake the foundations of the economy—proved groundless. The world could only marvel that the new player on the international scene was handling its affairs quite well under Theodore Roosevelt. Two election cartoons in *Judge*. The first by Zim, depicting Farmer Roosevelt arriving at a fair; the second by Emil Flohri, a portrayal of Roosevelt with his prize display, were variations on the theme.

"TERRIBLE TEDDY" WAITS FOR "THE UNKNOWN."

President Roosevelt's renomination was such a foregone conclusion that the only excitement at the Republican convention was buzz about the symbolic show of power against the Barbary Pirates ("Perdicaris Alive or Raisuli Dead"). The Democrats chose to decline the services of William Jennings Bryan once again, opting for a more conservative candidate…except that no front-runner emerged. There was talk of drafting former president Grover Cleveland, who had already run three times for the office. Quadrennial aspirants, like the senatorial fixtures David Bennett Hill of New York and Arthur Pue Gorman of Maryland, attempted to gain the nomination, but it was not to be. The party eventually turned to an obscure judge from New York State, Alton Brooks Parker. *Puck* seemed assured of the outcome, no matter who showed in the corner opposite the current champion, "Terrible Teddy."

UNCLE SAM'S ASYLUM FOR POOR, DEMENTED DEMOCRATS,
Each and every one of which has some foolish political delusion.

In 1904, the field of potential Democrat candidates to run for president against Roosevelt was rather thin—or, as seen by the great Eugene Zimmerman (Zim), rather unstable. Zim even includes two anti-imperialist Republicans, editor Carl Schurz and Senator George Frisbie Hoar, among the aspirants; the eventual nominee is not even in the asylum. It goes without saying that the cartoonist's gimlet eye gazed through the rose-colored glasses of the Republican magazine *Judge*. Zim's career actually began on *Puck*, where his style marked him as a "technical cousin" of F. Opper, in the estimation of art critic Thomas Craven. His freewheeling lines and outrageous personality delineations influenced a generation of cartoonists.

CHICAGO, JUNE 21, 1904.

"ALL IN FAVOR OF THE NOMINATION WILL SAY AYE!"

VOL. LVI. No. 1438.  PUCK BUILDING, New York, September 21, 1904.  PRICE TEN CENTS.
Copyright, 1904 by Keppler & Schwarzmann.

## Puck

"I RATHER LIKE THAT IMPORTED AFFAIR."

*LEFT*: A cartoon from *Puck* during the 1904 campaign. The magazine was traditionally Democratic, and party faithful needed its voice; in 1896 and 1900 it refused to support Bryan. So, although it generally was complimentary to President Roosevelt, during the campaign *Puck* hewed to the party line. For a reason lost to history, Grant Hamilton, the Art Editor of *Puck's* arch rival, the Republican cartoon weekly *Judge*, drew anti-Roosevelt cartoons in its pages for the duration of the campaign. Perhaps it was a contract dispute; perhaps he couldn't swallow TR's policies. Whatever the reason, he produced some handsome and effective cartoons for the Democrat cause.

"He's Good Enough For Me!"

COPYRIGHT, 1904, BY THE MAIL AND EXPRESS CO.

From the N. Y. Evening Mail          154

*RIGHT*: Homer Davenport, a Roosevelt nemesis when he drew for Hearst, switched to *The New York Mail* and became an unabashed fan of the president. "He's Good Enough For Me," one of the most famous cartoons in American political history, widely was reprinted, appeared on posters, pinbacks...and postcards like this one, mailed by the thousands. After he retired from cartooning, Davenport became an importer and breeder of Arabian white stallions; TR cut through diplomatic and trade red tape on Davenport's behalf.

The mascot of *Puck* magazine
("What fools these mortals be")
leans out from the Puck Building
on the corner of Houston and
Mulberry Streets in lower Manhattan to congratulate President
Roosevelt on his re-election. *Puck*
was the first successful American
humor magazine, founded as a
German-language weekly in 1876;
within a year it was published in
English also, and within a decade
had its own impressive headquarters building, with the nation's
largest steam lithographic presses
producing its three color cartoons
for each issue. Joseph Keppler, the
founder, died in 1894, and his son
Udo (J. Keppler Jr.) succeeded
him. In many ways he was a more
facile cartoonist than his father,
combining powerful ideas and
attractive compositions. Although
*Puck* was reliably Democratic, it
frequently praised TR. Despite its
dutiful support of Alton B. Parker
against Roosevelt, the paper
seemed quite satisfied that TR
was reelected.

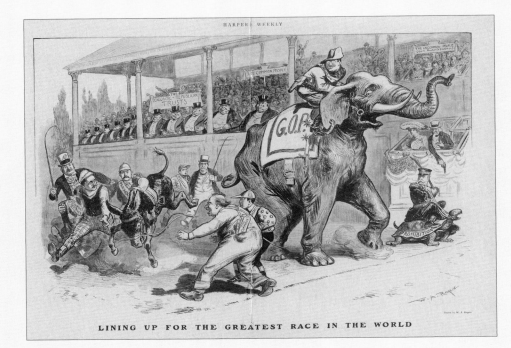

LINING UP FOR THE GREATEST RACE IN THE WORLD

*TOP*. William Allen Rogers, whose career generally coincided with TR's, drew this double-page assessment of the 1904 race—never considered much of a contest by most observers—for *Harper's Weekly*. A gaggle of Democrats are pictured as disorganized pygmies, and General Nelson A. Miles, with whom TR clashed during the Spanish-American War, is shown as a possible candidate of the Prohibition Party. (That party's nominee turned out to be a man named, ironically, Swallow.)

*LEFT*: The Democratic cartoon weekly *Life* celebrated TR's inauguration in March of 1905. The American eagle, Uncle Sam, and the Republican elephant dance happily; on the Democrat donkey kicks.

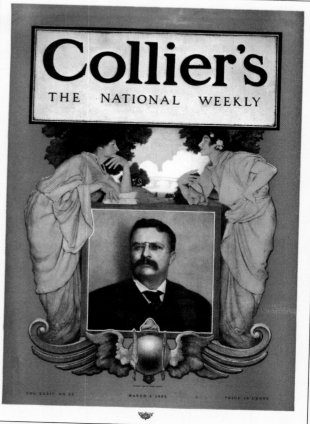

Two of the great decorative illustrators of the age were engaged by two of the great magazines of the age to commemorate the inauguration of Theodore Roosevelt in March of 1905. Edward Penfield was a designer of covers and posters in the Art Nouveau Age of the Poster. His understated portrait of TR is striking as a *Saturday Evening Post* cover design. Maxfield Parrish, legendary painter and illustrator of the same Art Nouveau period, framed the president in his trademark figures and decorations for *Collier's*.

# FOREIGN POLICY: PEACEMAKER

A SKELETON OF HIS OWN.

Many Americans were outraged by the Czar's anti-Jewish pogroms, and called on the government to intervene. *Puck* reminded Uncle Sam that he had skeletons in his own closet. The cartoonist, Joseph Keppler Jr., was also a lifelong advocate of American Indian causes.

# THE ERA OF THE MUCKRAKER

Theodore-Thomas Heine, of the German satirical magazine *Simplicissimus*, commented in 1906 on the great legislative fights between TR, the Senate, and the various meat-packing trusts over pure food regulations and monopolies' influence on food prices. Heine likened it to a glorified job of sweeping out a pigsty.

INDEPENDENCE DAY.

MORE ROUGH RIDING.

THE PRESIDENT'S MESSAGE TO CONGRESS.

*ABOVE*: An early cartoon by the great "Ding" (Jay Norwood Darling) for the *Des Moines Register* depicting Roosevelt's relations with the Senate's Old Guard in 1908.

*LEFT*: Among TR's "mundane" items to reform in the federal government when he became president was the post office, long a home to political patronage and favoritism. He had to continue the battles he inexorably fought for six years as U.S. Civil Service Commissioner.

This Harrison Cady cartoon from *Life* depicts a growing perception of reality in the Muckraking era. There were social problems, corporate evils, and union abuses in America, and Roosevelt sought to address and solve them all. He also recognized that hyperbolic radicalism was the enemy of progress.

HARRISON CADY

e Merry Go Round

ABOVE: Reproduced from the original drawing by Louis M. Glackens for *Puck*, this presents a fair portrait of TR's relationship with the financial establishment in 1907, the year of the Crash: "A Wall Street lunch before Roosevelt's name is mentioned…and after." There was a short-lived panic on Wall Street in 1907.

RIGHT: The weekly magazine *Life* was a journal of cartoons and political commentary, and its founder and editor, John Ames Mitchell, was a Harvard-educated parlor socialist. One of his books, *The Inner War*, was a novel about the "class struggle." Its illustrations were by William Balfour-Ker. His work was redrawn as line art and printed on postcards by the radical magazines *The Coming Nation* and *Appeal to Reason* of Girard, Kansas. Countless postcards like this were sent out, with an invitation to become a socialist that reads like a glee club recruitment. But the purport of the cartoon (1906), and nature of the postcard's appeal, indicate that radicalism was present and growing in mainstream American society.

Copyright by J. A. Mitchell

FROM THE DEPTHS

Most everyone who really knows, now-a-days, is a Socialist. Many have not found it out yet, but are Socialists. Are you? Study the picture It shows the Class Struggle more forcibly than the Artist dreamed.

These post cards 10 cents a dozen, 75 cents a hundred from the APPEAL TO REASON, Girard, Kansas.

# THE STRENUOUS LIFE

Cartoonist E. G. Lutz, later a pioneer in animation, in 1903 designed a parody bookplate that would be suitable for Theodore Roosevelt. It touched on some of TR's characteristics.

TR's celebrated vigor never ceased to astound the American people. Cartoon by John T. McCutcheon of *The Chicago Tribune*.

VOL. 49 · NO. 1258      NOVEMBER 25 1905      PRICE 10 CENTS

# Judge

SOMETHING TO BE THANKFUL FOR

Uncle Sam—"See here, young man; I am glad you're back, all right, but when is this thing going to stop?"

Some American citizens, and more than a few government officials, worried about TR's occasionally reckless activities and invariably taxing regimen. But the public relished their perpetually youthful president. A friend in the diplomatic corps reminded an associate that the president "is about six." And Edith frequently referred to her husband as "her seventh child."

# CONTROVERSIES

For all of TR's advocacy—including directing the Government Printing Office to adopt Simplified Spelling—the plan was rejected by the public and academia alike.

Roosevelt's short-lived crusade to reform the spelling of English was also subscribed to by Mark Twain, Andrew Carnegie, and a few others. Cartoon by E. W. Kemble in *Collier's*.

"The Roosevelt Farewell Parade": Robert Minor of the *St. Louis Post-Dispatch* makes references to TR's crusade against "Race Suicide." He frequently admonished his countrymen to have larger families; that Western societies, including America's, would lose their virility and very existence unless they resisted declining birth rates.

# THE ROOSEVELT FAMILY

THE LADIES' HOME JOURNAL

MRS. THEODORE ROOSEVELT
*From the Painting by Chartran*

AUGUST 1902                    TEN CENTS

THE CURTIS PUBLISHING COMPANY PHILADELPHIA

Edith Roosevelt was not just an equal partner in the household—having to rein in her husband as often as her other children—but by everyone's account, a valued advisor. TR consulted with Edith about everything, and rued the times he rejected her advice. They often discussed literature and the arts (he considered himself her inferior). She ran the White House as a cultural salon during her years as First Lady.

Quentin, Charley Taft (son of the Secretary of War), and friends from the neighborhood of the White House formed a club called the White House Gang. TR was solemnly elected an honorary member, and he reciprocated by joining the boys in romps and hunts and explorations of the White House's back stairwells and attic. Occasionally, the "elder member" would have to discipline the boys, like when they festooned portraits on the White House walls with spitballs. Years later, member Earle Looker wrote a book about the Gang, and cartoonist James Montgomery Flagg illustrated it.

TR as cartoonist? Not as professional as his other avocations, perhaps, but he frequently wrote picture-letters to his children: wild-game hunts from faraway places, drawings of himself playing tennis at the White House sent to children away at school, and everything in between. For years Roosevelt's biggest seller was *Letters to His Children*, which he oversaw for the editor Joseph Bucklin Bishop just prior to his death.

# A MAN OF FAITH

Cartoon by Bernard Partridge, *Punch* magazine, 1901.

"CAPTAINS COURAGEOUS."

"I feel that we should be peculiarly watchful over them, because of our own history, because we or our fathers came here under like conditions. Now that we have established ourselves, let us see to it that we stretch out the hand of help, the hand of brotherhood, toward the new-comers, and help them as speedily as possible to shape themselves and to get into such relations that it will be easy for them to walk well in the new life."—*The President's Reference to Immigrants.*

From his earliest days in public service, to the last public message TR delivered, he was stern on questions of radicalism among immigrant groups and divided loyalties, an impediment to assimilation he called "hyphenated Americanism." Yet—as with unions, corporate executives and, in fact, every other group in society—TR preached, and required, justice. Here, Joseph Keppler Jr. of *Puck* commends Roosevelt for his policies of tolerance.

# TR IN POPULAR CULTURE

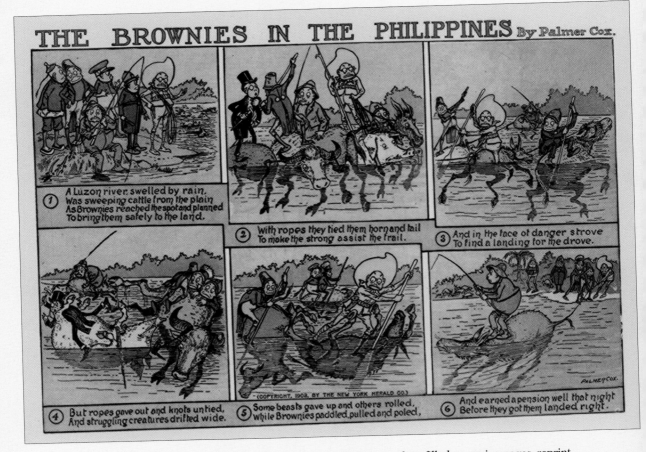

ABOVE: The Brownies were popular children's characters whose exploits filled magazine pages, reprint books, toys and games, and comic strips. Each Brownie was of a clear nationality or profession, but cavorted en masse, not as individuals speaking or with names. After the Spanish-American war, however, one little cast member was added—a dead ringer for Rough Rider Roosevelt. *RIGHT*: Three months before San Juan Hill, and with more of a navy than a Rough Rider identification, a full-page *New York World* cartoon displayed a cartoon Roosevelt in all his vaunted glory. The cartoonist was Walt McDougall, pioneer of color newspaper cartoons, and a boyhood acquaintance of TR in the fields around Oyster Bay, Long Island.

# 1901-1908: Cartoon Portfolio

The Roosevelt Bears caught on with American children (and their parents) as surely as did the plush Teddy Bear dolls themselves. There were no "official" Teddy Bear characters, but the most successful of story books (and spinoff postcards) were written by Seymour Eaton ("Paul Piper"), and illustrated by Culver, "Bart," and V. Floyd Campbell. John Randolph Bray, later a pioneer animator, produced weekly "Little Johnny and His Teddy Bears" for *Judge* magazine, for Sunday newspaper comics, and for children's books in various formats, such as the set of eight below.

Clifford Berryman of *The Washington Post* and later *The Star* was forever identified with the Teddy Bear. This is a drawing he made for a little girl who requested a sketch. Reproduced from the original drawing.

Theodore Roosevelt has been depicted on postage stamps several times. And on the 50th anniversary of the battle of San Juan Hill, a stamp commemorating the Rough Riders was issued.

# THE CARTOONISTS' BEST FRIEND

WHERE TEDDY'S ANNOUNCEMENT CAUSED JOY

A Cartoonist's Own Idea of Himself

"TEETH DRAWN WITHOUT PAIN"

# A CARTOONIST SPENDS AN AFTERNOON AT SAGAMORE HILL

The sketch Flagg made of TR on the day he wrote about here.

*In 1914, upon TR's return from Brazil, noted cartoonist James Montgomery Flagg visited Sagamore Hill to draw a portrait of the Colonel for* Harper's Weekly, *and privately to encourage him to stay active in public affairs. This is his account of the afternoon:*

His life, when he is on his own continent, is one damn caller after another!

Sagamore Hill was overrun with little governors, [political confidants], and South African explorers the other sunny afternoon, while I waited to see TR in a side room that was full of wild animals he had known.

After greeting me, his next remark was, "My full face is better than the side!"

As a matter of fact it is no such thing. Bows on, his face is strangely like a nice blond Japanese war-mask. His profile seems to belong to a different man. His super-dreadnaught head might have been done by Rodin.

I asked him if his hair was sunburnt and he said: "No, it always was the color of old rope!"

I expected [after the harrowing Brazilian experience] to see him looking played out, but, on the contrary, he was tanned, vigorous, and full of the usual pep. If monkey meat has that effect, I think, when I am feeling like the last tottering stumble of shad in the late spring, I shall go up to the Bronx Zoo and nibble a chimpanzee or two.

Those boils they talked about were probably thoroughly cowed after a short visit with him, and left him gladly at the first opportunity for quieter quarters.

He excused himself during the short sitting to say a few thousand things to some callers who were leaving. When he booms "Good-bye," his inflection makes the word sound something like "Good-boy!" The quality of his voice seems like the whanging of the "G" string on a guitar, if guitars have "G" strings—perhaps it is the "I" string.

Well, suppose he is an egotist! The ego is the necessary gasoline that drives the TR engine. [Critics] ought to remember the parts of his engine—common sense, courage, enthusiasm, broad-mindedness, integrity, scholarship, and breeding. He may not have the ten-inch upholstery of Taft or the reverse gear of Wilson, but he is Some He-Car!

…He posed for me, and when he looked at the drawing, said, "That's very good of you!" I was puzzled how to take that.

Another caricature by Flagg, ca. 1912. Reproduced from the original drawing.

With TR America had the cartoonists' presidency. Were the politically ambitious William Randolph Hearst more successful, American might have had the cartoon characters' presidency. At least this is how *Puck* cartoonist J. S. Pughe envisioned the inaugural dinner at the Hearst White House. The guests include Happy Hooligan, the Katzenjammer Kids, and Alphonse and Gaston. All these characters appeared in the newspapers owned by WRH, whose nurture of the art form make him a godfather of the funnies. A 1904 cartoon.

One of several caricatures of TR by the famous Italian tenor Enrico Caruso. The opera star and pioneer recording artist drew weekly cartoons for the newspaper *La Follia di New York*.

Homer Davenport, as a Hearst cartoonist, attacked TR vehemently. By 1904 he had left Hearst, and for *The New York Evening Mail* drew one of the most famous of all campaign cartoons: "He's Good Enough for Me" (see cartoon on page 235). A caricature of the Colonel at work, reproduced from the original drawing.

CHAPTER 9

# 1908~1912

# BIG-GAME HUNTING
# IN AFRICA . . . AND IN POLITICS

As the Roosevelt administration drew to a close, it was clear that the majority of the American public still admired, and even revered, TR. He received many expressions of support: newspapers urged another term in the White House; his staff and "Tennis Cabinet" saw no reason to have America "switch horses"; out in the hinterlands, babies were being named for him. *The New York Times*—a Democrat paper—ran the only comic strip it ever published in its long life, *The Roosevelt Bears.*

An increasingly influential congressional bloc—Republican insurgents, many of whom were in the freshman class of 1906—argued that the progress of reform would be interrupted if TR retired from the scene. Indeed, those freshmen formed the core of the GOP's increased numbers in Congress after the midterm election. Midterm gains by the party in power were (and are) rare; TR's personal popularity, and his vision for the nation (which had come to be called, collectively, "My Policies") received the credit.

The nation was not in a mere trance. Many people considered Roosevelt's guidance in the face of gathering storm clouds to be essential. Roosevelt's policies were designed

TROPHIES OF THE SEVEN YEARS' WAR.

MOVING DAY, MARCH 4th

to ameliorate society's growing disparity in wealth, to control abuses in areas of health, safety, and natural resources, and to increase national defense. A true leader, he worked to anticipate and solve national problems so that they never became crises.

But there were divisions growing in his party, as well as in the country. TR was a lame duck after his 1904 statement refusing to succeed himself in 1908. He was an ever-easier target of the entrenched Old Guard that opposed his reforms. Senators and congressmen committed slights in Congress when his messages were transmitted, and those politicians increasingly ignored his nominations. TR responded by increasing the number and length of his messages, and he increased his executive orders. More then previously, he went over the heads of Congress to the people when public pressure was necessary—the "bully pulpit" for presidential persuasion. Thus, a financial panic and short-lived recession in 1907 hurt Wall Street and Main Street, but not Pennsylvania Avenue. It was clear that the American public not only loved, but trusted, Theodore Roosevelt.

Many of his avid supporters wanted TR simply to declare his intentions, one way or the other, about the 1908 elections. His followers, the reform wing of the Republican Party, had leaders waiting in the wings, and they needed a cue if there were to be an entrance call for any of them. But TR's 1904 pledge not to

EVERY DAY IS WASHDAY NOWADAYS

By the end of Roosevelt's term, despite his "lame-duck" status, the president advocated a passel of reforms, and contended with opponents more than ever.

When the Greatest Show on Earth Reaches Rhinoceros Corners

Harrison Cady (in *Life*, 1909) imagined TR and an entourage of friends, opponents, and controversies following him to Africa.

succeed himself decided the issue…as did his natural restiveness. He needed to move on, and he thought it would be best for the nation, too. His first choice for successor was Elihu Root, cabinet member and New York legal legend, a brilliant advocate and administrator who had been one of the signatories endorsing young Theodore Roosevelt for the New York State Assembly back in 1881. TR knew, however, that Root's Wall Street connections would make him anathema to reform voters. Roosevelt nevertheless was tempted to choose him, because Root was a superb advocate: when his clients were big corporations, he served them well; if his client were the American people, he would serve them just as well. But politics doesn't work that way, and TR knew it.

Instead, TR tapped another loyal lieutenant and excellent administrator, the gargantuan William Howard Taft. The 325-pound Cincinnatian, hardly a member of TR's actual "Tennis Cabinet" but otherwise an old friend, had served in a variety of diplomatic and judicial posts under Harrison and McKinley, and was TR's Secretary of War. The genial Taft invariably endorsed Roosevelt's political agenda—"My Policies."

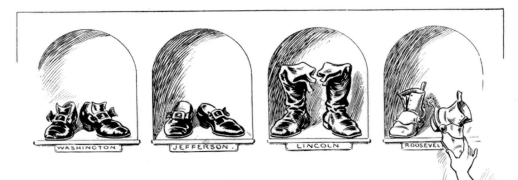

UNFILLED SHOES.

In the first issue after Taft's election in 1908, *Puck* ran this L. M. Glackens cartoon. "Unfilled Shoes" was not a slight to Taft but a show of respect (from a Democrat paper) and prediction about a remarkable president. Significantly, these are the four presidents who were still regarded as the Greats when Mt. Rushmore was completed in 1941.

The tacit support of President Roosevelt was as effective in blocking other candidates' end runs around Taft as his enormous girth would have been in a crowded hallway. Cartoonists had fun at Taft's expanse; one of them drew Taft from behind, on a speaker's platform, and labeled him "Big Built Aft." His massive size, along with such characteristics as his narcoleptic traits and famed lack of energy, made him lovable to the public. Mostly, however, Taft's nomination was assured by a nod from the president.

The Democrats almost compliantly nominated the quadrennial loser William Jennings Bryan for the presidency—a third attempt. His defeat was widely forecast. TR did not give the election proceedings his full attention, though. Except for anxiety that Taft did not press his own case strongly enough on the campaign trail, the president's focus was on other matters. Among a raft of social, not political concerns, TR pressed for spelling reform and ordered government documents to be spelt in the new way; he attacked nature writers who ascribed false characteristics to animals ("nature fakirs," he called them); he advocated large families and inveighed against "race suicide," sending letters of congratulations to parents of large broods; he reviewed books of poetry; he wrote essays on ancient Irish sagas . . . and he planned for the adventure of a lifetime in Africa.

Taft waddled his way to a smashing victory. Roosevelt, knowing that his own personality tended to eclipse other political figures in the firmament, even a large new president, reckoned that withdrawing from the United States, not just its political landscape, would help his successor establish an independent identity. Seeds of fascination planted during his boyhood trip up the Nile, as well as promptings of seasoned hunters, put an African safari in his sights. The American Museum of Natural History (of which his father was a founder) and the National Museum of the Smithsonian Institution arranged to sponsor the trip and commission the acquisition of specimens of exotic and perhaps unknown species. The legendary hunter-tracker R. J. Cunninghame led the expedition; others included naturalist Edmund Heller, explorer Frederick Selous, and, for a time during the 11-month safari, the legendary conservationist and taxidermist Carl Akeley. Theodore's own son Kermit, almost twenty, joined the expedition as hunter and photographer. In all, scores of naturalists, hunters, assistants, and native handlers comprised the party, transporting hundreds of crates holding everything from canned foods to photographic equipment and materials for analysis, skinning, and preservation of specimens.

Also included in the cargo were eighty of TR's favorite books, to be read around nighttime campfires or under the scorching sun's rests—specially bound to withstand the effects of blood, sweat, and gun oil. This "Pigskin Library" added yet another phrase to the Rooseveltian lexicon and cartoonists' drawings. Americans flocked to emulate TR's "required reading" on their home shelves. Included in his list were the Bible and the Apocrypha; several plays of Shakespeare; Mahan's *Sea Power* and Macaulay's *History*; the *Iliad* and *Odyssey*; *Chanson de Roland*; *Nibelungenlied*; Lowell's *Biglow Papers*; poems of Emerson, Longfellow, Tennyson, and George Cabot Lodge; the *Tales* of Poe; Milton's *Paradise Lost* and Dante's *Inferno*; *Autocrat of the Breakfast Table* by Oliver Wendell Holmes; *Luck of Roaring Camp* by Bret Harte; *Huckleberry Finn* and *Tom Sawyer* by Mark Twain; *The Pilgrim's Progress* by Bunyan; *The Federalist Papers*; *Vanity Fair* by Thackeray; *Our Mutual Friend* and *Pickwick Papers* by Dickens; *Alice in Wonderland* and *Through the Looking-Glass* by Carroll; Darwin, Huxley, and biblical commentaries; *Omar Khayyam*; *Don Quixote*; Montaigne's essays; and Moliere and Goethe.

SO LONG, TEDDY, TAKE KEER O' Y'RSELF!

The party made its way through "darkest Africa"—South East Africa to the headwaters of the Nile—for almost a year, and the world heard little from the former president during that time. Reporters were admonished in the strongest terms to respect TR's privacy, and no news

THE TALL TIMBER

reports emanated from those jungles and plains throughout 1909. The safari of another big-game hunter, the cartoonist and war correspondent John T. McCutcheon of *The Chicago Tribune* (the "Dean of American Editorial Cartoonists"), met up with TR's expedition to share adventures for a few days. But back home, McCutcheon's confreres were in the dark about TR's activities. They were free, of course, to speculate, and they did, joyously. Numerous cartoons depicted vicious beasts running and hiding from the approaching "Bwana Tumbo," the inexact but colorful appellation bestowed by American cartoonists. (McCutcheon reported that "Bwana Tumbo" really meant "Master with the Stomach." TR heard himself referred to as "Bwana Mkubwa," which means "Great Master.") Some cartoonists took as themes the remark of a reactionary senator who "expected every lion to do his duty."

But the Colonel (TR's post-presidential title of preference) prevailed against beasts

and disease. The party emerged in Khartoum, having identified, bagged, and processed for museums more than 11,000 specimens—from insects and tiny relatives of elephants to rare white rhinos and actual elephants. The expedition relied on game for their sustenance, during the course of collecting specimens for science and educational display, its major goal. TR wrote his accounts methodically day by day in longhand while on safari. Equal parts adventure and natural science, *African Game Trails* was serialized in *Scribner's* magazine and became a bestseller in book form.

After twelve months without her beloved husband, Edith joined Theodore in Khartoum. Following a few very private days with his wife, the Colonel slowed down not one bit. He traded khakis for formal attire, pith helmet for top hat, and commenced a prearranged tour of Europe. The world, which had become enamored of this American phenomenon—his reputation advanced as much by photos and cartoons as by news accounts—wanted to see Roosevelt for itself.

Predictably, the world got Theodore Roosevelt to the $n$th degree. In Cairo he lectured Egyptians on the pursuit of modern civilization and the British on colonial responsibilities. In Italy he and Edith stopped at the Porto Maurizio villa of her sister Emily, thence to Rome where he desired an audience with the pope. There had been, however, a local dust-up between the Methodist mission (which had referred to the Pontiff as the Whore of Babylon) and the Vatican, which warned the former president that if he called on the Methodists he would be unwelcome at St. Peter's. In a saltier variation of "a pox on both your houses," TR boycotted both with no regret; no one would dictate conditions to him. In Paris, he lectured at the Sorbonne; in England, at Oxford (the Romanes Lecture on the subject "Biological Analogies in History"). In Christiana (now Oslo), Norway, he formally received his Nobel Peace Prize and delivered a lecture, "International Peace," an early call for a league to enforce peace. (It should be noted that the draft of the League of Nations a decade later, Wilson's document that was long on rhetoric and short on sovereignty, was a perversion distinctly unacceptable to Roosevelt.) In Germany, TR reviewed the Imperial Army on horseback with Kaiser Wilhelm, who afterwards sent a set of photographs of the two, with humorous captions by the Kaiser, in English, on each photo's verso.

All in all, TR later said, he eventually felt that if he met another royal personage he would bite him. Many of them were dullards who gossiped about their fellow monarchs—their fraternal war of 1914–1918 was a few short years away—or complained to him about their spouses.

King Edward of the United Kingdom died during TR's tour of Europe's capitals and castles. President Taft designated Roosevelt the official American representative to the observances. It proved to be a bizarre display—the last flowering of Europe's ancient monarchies, a gaudy parade and funeral resplendent of pretty ritual and petty rivalries.

It is hard to believe that a short century ago, two countries, the United States and France, were the only republics among such an assembly of the world's countries. Roosevelt's frock coat and top hat stood out amongst jewels and robes, sashes and decorations, at every turn. He continued to display a plain republican's disdain of the pomp…with his trademark sense of humor.

The French representative with whom he shared a coach in the procession approached the Colonel "with tears in his eyes, tears of anger," TR later wrote. "The other guests had scarlet livery, and…ours was black. I told him I had not noticed, but I would not have cared if ours had been yellow and green. My French, while fluent, is never very clear, and it took me another half hour to get it out of his mind that I was not protesting because my livery was not green and yellow." The Colonel's accounts to friends and family of the European tour were hilarious—typical of his self-deprecatory and absurd streaks in table talk and correspondence. They were traits that endeared him to the public, and especially to cartoonists and print humorists.

Charles Dana Gibson spoke for a broad cross-section of Americans—and drew them—in his *Collier's* cartoon "Hurrah for Teddy!"

In the world's eyes, the whole show of the Royal Funeral was overshadowed by Theodore Roosevelt. Standing apart and above, he truly seemed to be the First Citizen of the World. It was with that new title on his résumé—added to his pedigree as American aristocrat, cowboy, scholar, soldier, hero, crusader, reformer, ex-president—that he returned to his native New York City.

As the only president born in New York City, TR's literal homecoming was impressive.

The parade through Manhattan was the grandest the city had seen, and has been matched by few since: Lindbergh's 1927 tribute and the 1969 New York Mets perhaps are the only rivals. Thousands of citizens thronged the streets, even remote side streets. Celebrities of all sorts were on the reception committee and mingled in the adoring crowd. There were government figures and diplomats, police and honor guard, Upper West Side

*HE'S* COMING BACK

social-register types, and Lower East Side immigrants. And there were also many rough-hewn cowboy friends and Rough Riders from every corner of the nation. Thunderous rapture echoed through the concrete corridors; confetti and banners were everywhere.

Reporters and friends, however, noted a solemnity to TR's response. "The world was at his doorstep!" But Roosevelt replied that it was a characteristic of every great wave that a depression, and often a contrary undertow, followed. He believed the more avid the adulation, the more inevitable the rejection that would come later. TR felt the legendary Roman "public slave" behind him in the carriage, holding a wreath just off his head and whispering, *Sic transit gloria mundi*—the world's acclaim is fleeting.

The Colonel faced many challenges, not the least of which were the expectations of his followers. He was fifty-one, an age younger than most presidents at the beginning of their terms. Professional employment seemed to be his least worrisome challenge; he was offered university presidencies, book contracts, even editorship of major newspapers. He accepted the invitation to serve as contributing editor of *The Outlook*, a small Christian weekly of opinion and current affairs. Its pages became his primary platform, and its offices his New York City headquarters for several years. Up until now, TR's inheritance and activities had allowed him to live comfortably, but as he wrote, "I had enough to get bread. What I had to do, if I wanted butter and jam, was to provide the butter and jam, but to count their cost as compared with other things." His work at *The Outlook*, as well as some freelance work, gave him independence of action and the reasonable confidence of a secure income, so that he would be able to pass something along to his children.

Yet there was one seemingly intractable challenge, beyond his control…perhaps. In a little more than a year, his successor in the White House had proven a hapless, and even hopeless, failure. Even presidents elected by huge majorities—and Taft's victory was even greater than Roosevelt's had been four years earlier—can be politically tone deaf, display faulty leadership skills, and have a short memory of campaign promises. They can obsess over selective causes that confuse the public, dismay supporters, and waste the currency

WHAT AN EX-PRESIDENT CAN DU WHEN HIS JOB IS THRU

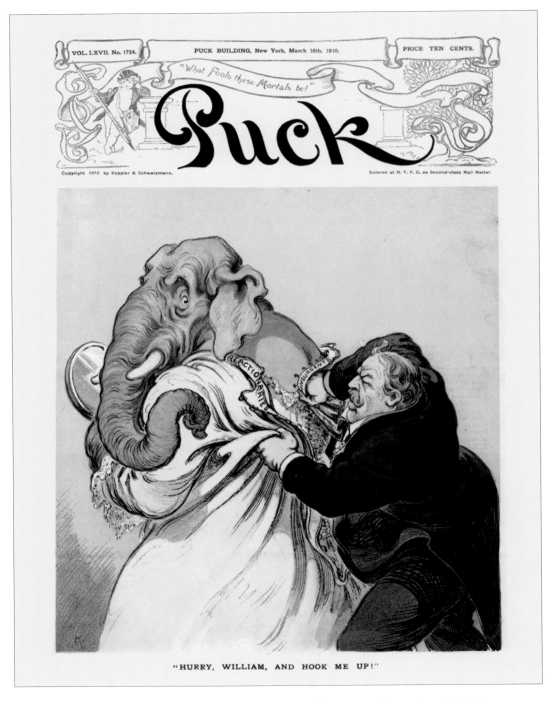

President Taft was woefully inept at keeping party factions together—where TR had been a master. Both factions besought Roosevelt's assistance after his return to America.

known as "political capital." In those terms, Taft was headed for political bankruptcy in the eyes of many people, friends and foes alike.

Such was the state of the White House upon the Colonel's return to America. Anxious and panic-stricken friends had sent letters to him in Europe, chronicling the situation. Worst of all for Roosevelt personally, Taft had drifted—some said he had hurried—away from TR's policies.

"My Policies" were now being depicted by cartoonists as abused puppies or discarded baggage. Roosevelt valued those policies because he believed they were vital to America's progress. He believed that his reforms had solved many of the nation's ills, and that the continuation of such policies would avert problems and even prevent disasters like social upheaval. America was growing more radical, in cities, on farms, and within labor unions and immigrant groups. As always, TR saw the best antidote for socialism in what he called (with Lincoln as his inspiration) "sane radicalism." Cartoonists and humorists hit the nail on the head every week: "Taft carried out Roosevelt's policies...on a slab," was one of the jabs. "President Taft is an amiable island surrounded by men who know what they want," proclaimed another. TR's supporters—allies of many years' battles as well as

When Roosevelt returned from Africa and Europe to find his successor's administration in turmoil, and TR's old allies pleading for a defense of the Square Deal policies, he determined that he would study the situation and not cause trouble for Taft. He pledged that for a month he would stay shut "like a native oyster." A difficult challenge for someone of Roosevelt's temperament. A cartoon by Billy Ireland of *The Columbus Dispatch*.

fresh activist reformers in the Rooseveltian mold—pleaded with the Colonel to defend the causes and revive his policies—that is, to re-engage in politics.

After TR's return from Europe, he responded to these contrary tugs on his loyalty and influence. He announced that on political subjects he would return to Sagamore Hill and "close up like a native oyster" for two months. He needed to assess the situation, hoping that Taft's policies were not reversals but merely different routes to the same goals. TR also sincerely desired to say nothing that could be interpreted, much less misinterpreted, against his protégé. For someone of TR's temperament, this time in seclusion was more daunting than long cattle drives, fighting Spaniards, or facing a charging elephant in the jungle. But the stakes were higher.

It was excruciating. "Will" Taft was a longtime friend whom TR loved, a man he had trusted. But Taft had dealt him innumerable personal slights. (Many were actually committed by Mrs. Taft, who never hid her disdain for Theodore and Edith.) Taft cemented alliances with TR's enemies, and there were numerous public rollbacks of reform measures and reformers. Gifford Pinchot, the nation's chief forester, exposed corruption in the Interior Department. Pinchot's revelations bordered on insubordination, and Taft sided with the Department secretary, Richard Ballinger. Pinchot was dismissed, widely seen as a sum betrayal of TR's conservation policies.

THEY ARE BOTH ON.
Which way will it go?

Even in one of the few areas where Taft maintained the Square Deal reforms—"trust-busting"—Taft's Attorney General implied that TR had looked the other way when U.S. Steel and other corporations acted to help solve the Financial Panic of 1907. The indolent Taft did not seek Roosevelt's point of view before the charge was made public; he had not thoroughly vetted all the matters appertaining; and he had not even bothered to read the legal papers, which were certain to be bombshells. The nub of the matter was that financiers during the panic had sought assurance that their assistance would not later be second-guessed or penalized. Roosevelt assented, with the knowledge and approval of advisors—including cabinet member Taft. Taft had never objected to the initial action his administration now undertook to investigate; his timing seemed designed to embarrass TR politically. Besides, Taft showed disloyalty to TR at a time when the Colonel was straining to maintain his support of the president. Perhaps worst of all was the implication, not that Roosevelt had been complicit in any illegal act, but that he had been duped by Wall Street barons.

The acts of Taft's Justice Department were bombshells. With that issue added to the others, Roosevelt found himself in a difficult position. Under Taft's inept banner, the Republicans had suffered massive defeats in the midterm elections of 1910, losing control of both houses of Congress and many governorships. The

BUCKING THE STEAM ROLLER.

only insurgent who stepped forward to challenge Taft for the 1912 presidential nomination was Wisconsin Senator Robert M. LaFollette, a quirky radical who espoused myriad causes, seldom inspiring a large following. His campaign to challenge Taft collapsed when he himself collapsed, losing control at a newspapermen's banquet and ranting abusively at his hosts for hours until the room emptied of embarrassed listeners.

The course of the primaries, by Victor Gillam in *The Denver Times.*

What had seemed like heresy to the Colonel at first now became a virtual duty: to challenge Taft for the GOP nomination. Republican officeholders, major newspapers, reformers and academics, a host of political cartoonists, and especially average citizens (as always, the constituency most special to TR) combined to create a recruiting-call that was irresistible.

Roosevelt realized that if he ran for a third term now, he risked defeat and jeopardized his place in history. It would be political suicide. His closest friends urged him to hold back. He should let Taft bumble through a second term or probable defeat, and in 1916 the White House would again be TR's for the asking, if that was his goal. But TR was not interested in this kind of personal calculation; he wanted to meet the challenge head-on, advance his principles, and lead the causes he championed. If ever TR displayed purity of purpose, devoid of raw ambition, it was in his 1912 campaign.

The limitation of one president to two presidential terms was a tradition that originated with George Washington's disinclination to succeed himself more than once. To many Americans, Washington's admonition against more than two presidential terms was sacrosanct. Ulysses S. Grant had unsuccessfully surveyed a third term, and it was a perennial, if not quadrennial, topic in politics. TR understood the trepidation, but maintained that a third non-consecutive term—especially if the public approved by election—removed any danger of entrenched influence or institutional abuse. The four terms of TR's distant cousin Franklin later prompted the adoption of the two-term amendment to the Constitution, not long after death ended FDR's marathon presidency in 1945.

Ultimately, the third-term issue, though significant, was not the major component of the opposition to TR in 1912. It was, rather, a convenient stick picked up by establishment Republicans with which to beat back the advance of reform that TR represented. It is remarkable that many conservative Republican office-holders and newspapers openly dismissed Taft's chances of re-election, yet were willing to lose with him, instead of winning with a reformer like Roosevelt. Such was the reaction against the rising tide of reform and the desperation to maintain control of the party apparatus, and to transform their basic disrespect of Taft into his humiliation.

With friends such as his "supporters," Taft still had the congressional insurgents to deal with. Almost all of them Republicans, they were largely a party within a party, and their relationship with GOP hierarchy was often strained. The group had no one identifiable chief, but many superb leaders. It subscribed to no specific charter or manifesto, but it shared common convictions and agreed to a basic, ambitious battle plan. Insurgents believed that centralized federal power held the answers to many of the problems they sought to solve, and they swore ultimate devotion to the common citizen—the unfettered individualist, able to make his or her way in the world according to God-given talents and personal responsibility. This was the type of citizen TR praised in speech after speech.

Roosevelt was still viewed as a party leader, an Establishment man, despite his reformist ways, until after the 1910 midterm elections. With a foot in both camps (the established GOP and the Insurgents) he tried to hold the Republican Party together, believing it to be the best vehicle to effect reform. The hostility of Old Guard leaders, and the effective indifference of Taft, as much as changing social and political conditions, nudged TR closer to seeing the necessity of rescuing "My Policies."

A substantial portion of America, their concerns voiced by the Insurgents, thought that President Taft was tempting revolution by looking backwards, and that Theodore Roosevelt could be—must be—empowered again to steer the nation between the two extremes of reaction and radicalism, to reform. Senators were still elected by state legislatures, not the general public, and were widely seen as "bought and paid for" by special interests. Unelected, unaccountable, and often untouchable judges were overturning hard-fought and popular laws. In response to such crises in representative governance, Roosevelt advocated the initiative, the referendum, the recall, and political primaries. These are now standard throughout the land. He favored extending voting rights to women, and was the first major politician to do so. He favored child-labor laws and workplace safety regulations, which reforms were seen as intrusive to capitalism's operation by many reactionaries of the day.

When court decisions that did not affect Constitutional matters were opposed by a majority of the public—that is, when the legislative and judicial branches disagreed—TR advocated a reform that would grant the public the ability to vote for the recall of judicial decisions. When Roosevelt proposed this reform, many of his Old Guard supporters, including longtime friends like Henry Cabot Lodge and Elihu Root, withheld their support from him, fearing that recalls of judicial decisions would lead to the recall of judges…a step on the road to mob rule, in their eyes. TR's position was that the Constitution did not create one branch to be superior to the others, and when two branches disagreed, the public (after safeguards like cooling-off periods, for certain categories of legislation) could vote to decide the issues affecting them.

In the pages of *The Outlook*, TR pressed his case. During a national speaking tour, in Osawatomie, Kansas, birthplace of John Brown, he defined his evolving creed as "The New Nationalism." Speaking before the Ohio State Legislature, he detailed his views of the initiative, the referendum, and the recall. In a speech in Carnegie Hall, he delivered his "Confession of Faith." Each step of reform was more radical, to be sure; yet he constantly gained support. Unlike many politicians, he drove his points with increasing clarity, not weasel-words (another of his phrases seized upon by cartoonists): he wanted supporters and opponents alike to know exactly where he stood.

Seven Republican governors in early 1912 wrote a public letter entreating Roosevelt to enter the race. With that, TR "threw his hat into the ring"—yet another political term he coined, to the delight of cartoonists. Although primaries were a new phenomenon, the Republicans held many of them, and Roosevelt won the vast majority of delegates so chosen. Even in Taft's home state, Ohio, the president was humiliated, roundly defeated in popular vote and losing almost every district delegate. Clearly, TR was the choice of many average Americans. It was believed that even William Jennings Bryan, the perennial Democrat candidate, might endorse Roosevelt if his own party nominated a reactionary.

Roosevelt attracted everyday voters in the primaries, but he did not capture the hearts of Republican bosses in the back rooms. Delegates selected by the primary method were overwhelmingly committed to TR; however, in the GOP Convention, roughly half the delegates were controlled by state organizations or areas of the country (such as the Deep South) where Republicans were scarcer than snowmen. Those delegates were in the pocket of the White House.

Robert Minor of the *St. Louis Post-Dispatch* viewed TR's explanation of his decision to run in 1912. Minor later founded *The Masses* magazine, then quit cartooning to become a Communist Party worker and political candidate.

An inevitable, monumental fight loomed. The Chicago Coliseum shook with tension, and the city's streets were bursting with partisans, impromptu rallies, and fistfights. The country followed every debate, every dispute, every hearing over rival delegations and credentials. The committee deciding these contests was in the hands of the White House. Reporters and cartoonists in the press gallery monitored a steady drip-drip-drip of parliamentary outrages by the bosses. Roosevelt delegates cried, "Theft" and "Thou shalt not steal!" Observers compared the actions of the credentials committee to a methodical "steamroller," crushing the people's will. Roosevelt partisans took to shouting "Toot! Toot!" to deride the convention. Convention organizers arranged to have barbed wire under the platform's bunting, fearing that speakers might be rushed. Theodore's eldest child, Alice— "Princess Alice" to the adoring public—attended the convention. She was 100 percent for her father, yet her husband Nicholas Longworth, the GOP congressman from Taft's home district, was loyal to the president. In typical Alice fashion, she managed to get right in the face of her childhood "uncles," men like Elihu Root, the convention's permanent chairman, taunting, "Toot! Toot!" Taft partisans distributed phony handbills announcing, "At three o'clock tomorrow afternoon, Theodore Roosevelt will walk on the waters of Lake Michigan."

Because of the mercurial nature of events, and the unreliable phone lines between Sagamore Hill and the Windy City, TR had decided to attend the convention, and betook an entourage by train—the first time a candidate (except for dark-horse compromise surprises) was present at his party's nominating convention. His hotel suite became a nerve center or a battle's war room, with people coming and going, emissaries trading "feelers," and reporters and cartoonists recording every rumor and bit of news. It was all a panorama of raw politics; it was glorious theater.

Eventually, the Roosevelt forces lost. The Credentials Committee narrowly seated just enough Taft delegates to give them a convention majority. The convention as a whole, as per tradition, ratified the results. But in this unprecedented situation, the disputed delegates (most of whom were Taft supporters flouting the results of their states' primaries) in effect voted on their own legitimacy. The Old Guard entertained no doubts that they were insuring the GOP's electoral doom in the fall, but it was worth it to keep control of party machinery. The Colonel's allies—delegates in Chicago, leaders who rushed to Chicago from around the country, citizens from Thomas Edison and John L. Sullivan to humble farmers and clerks—eagerly waited for TR's response, and largely urged a "bolt": an exodus from the corrupt party.

In those first heady days, and through the summer of 1912, TR knew he faced a grim alternative. On the one hand, he could not support the tainted nominee or platform of a corrupt process. But if he ran for president as an independent, he reckoned he would likely beat Taft but trail the candidate of a united Democrat party; and he, not the grandees of the Old Guard, would be blamed for the mess. To support the beneficiaries of political theft was unthinkable to Roosevelt—his righteousness was white-hot. Besides, the likelihood of defeat was, to this seasoned combatant, not reason in itself to avoid the contest. Ultimately, it was as a noble fighter for righteousness that he wished to be remembered by history, not as jeopardizing his presidency or wrecking the GOP establishment. His course was clear. He agreed to the insistent calls for a new organizing convention six weeks hence. He received assurance that there would be financial underpinning for a new party, and talked to his family and closest associates about the vituperation and sacrifices they faced.

Major newspapers (such as *The New York Mail*, *Chicago Tribune*, *Philadelphia North American*, and *Kansas City Star*) supported him. Governor Hiram Johnson of California and Senator Albert Beveridge of Indiana were with him. They were joined by a variety of civic leaders, businessmen, celebrities, reformers, and activists, in convention assembled, ironically (or appropriately) in the very site of the Republican convention. It was a foregone conclusion that the delegates met not to deliberate, but to nominate. Some observed that they assembled as if for a coronation. The party was named the Progressive

Party, but quickly became known by the cartoonists' symbol of Roosevelt's simile, the Bull Moose Party. (Newspapermen had asked him if he were up to such a fight, and he replied, "I feel as strong as a bull moose!")

The week of fervid speeches and wild enthusiasm in the Coliseum was closer to a revival meeting than a political convention. There were many prayers and hymns sung. Roosevelt's rousing, acceptance speech (the first on-site acceptance by a major presidential candidate in American history), ended with the words, "We stand at Armageddon and we battle for the Lord!" after which the entire convention hall broke into a spontaneous, lengthy parade around the perimeter, lustily singing "Onward Christian Soldiers." Even Oscar Strauss of the Macy's Department Store fortune, candidate for governor of New York and a prominent Jewish leader, joined in that demonstration.

!bɿɐwɿoꟻ Forward!

Other enthusiasts—many of the reformers and activists attracted to the movement—were liberals and radicals with whom TR was not always comfortable in this fluid, coalescing alliance. They had been allies or adversaries in the past, depending on issues and tactics of the moment; and within a few years, he would harshly condemn many of them on matters of preparedness and war, socialism and Bolshevism, and pacifism. Even during the Bull Moose campaign, he referred to these supporters as the "lunatic fringe" that every popular movement attracts. Withal, the Colonel viewed them as willing allies, not willing dupes; and he soberly sought to keep the extremists from being too extreme.

Three major parties were now in the presidential field, all paying obeisance to reform—Republicans (with an ironically progressive-*sounding* platform), Democrats, and the Bull Moose Party. Roosevelt, the veteran, seemed to present the freshest program. Taft boasted that his trust-busting was more vigorous than TR's, which was true. The Democrats rejected several conservative candidates and nominated Woodrow Wilson, the liberal New Jersey governor. Wilson, more radical than most of his supporters would have hoped, guessed, or feared, would usher in a package of statist policies and internationalist initiatives before he was finished with the presidency. Yet with this field in the race, the Socialist Party candidate Eugene V. Debs polled almost a million votes.

TR knew the immediate prize was likely a chimera. Victory seemed doomed by electoral arithmetic, and if he were elected, he would have sparse congressional support for his program. The hastily formed Progressive Party fielded few congressional or local candidates.

THE BIRTH OF THE BUTTERFLY

*OPPOSITE*: Fred G. Cooper in *Life* portrayed the Taft-Roosevelt split. *ABOVE*: J. H. Donahey in the *Cleveland Plain-Dealer*.

Nevertheless, Roosevelt was accused of blind ambition. Republican and Democrat cartoonists alike pictured TR as a Napoleon, the "Third-Term Candidate." Cartoonists who had drawn him with a "T" and an "R" in the lenses of his pince-nez spectacles now lettered a first-person singular "I" in each. Pro-Roosevelt cartoonists were for the first time outnumbered, with the attacks centered less on TR's policies and more on the third-term issue. It was a drumbeat. One newspaper, *The New York Sun*, never referred to TR as anything but "the third-term candidate," even in its news columns. The Colonel's defense, when he deigned to respond, was ineffectual: that he had meant that three *consecutive* terms were unwise for presidents; that declining a third cup of coffee should not suggest one *never* desired another cup; and so forth. His opponents, newspaper editorials, and political cartoons continued to peg away.

A Brooklyn bartender named Joseph Schrank was among those incited by the criticism, persuaded that TR's run for a third term threatened American democracy. He purchased a gun and followed the Roosevelt campaign to several cities. In Milwaukee on October 14, TR finished dinner at the Hotel Gilpatrick, prior to an appearance at a large rally. As he climbed into his open-top automobile and turned to wave to supporters, Schrank stepped forward and fired point-blank into Roosevelt's chest.

As TR later recounted, he was knocked back by the force of the bullet, and then demanded that the angry crowd bring the assailant before him. He made a mental observation that the gun was a .38 on a .44 frame—irrelevant as to the situation, but interesting to the hunter and soldier in him—coughed and found no blood, which persuaded him that the bullet was not in his lung; and then ordered the car to drive him to the Auditorium. Everyone pleaded with TR to go to the nearby hospital, but he sensed the moment's drama; this was an exquisite opportunity to demonstrate his sincere conviction that his candidacy was but one part of a crusade. He was a flag-bearer to be succeeded by another if need be; the fight was bigger than his own well-being. "I will make that speech or die," he grimly informed his worried aides.

"In the long fight for righteousness, the watchword is 'spend and be spent,'" Roosevelt had said prophetically several months earlier. "It matters little whether any one man fails or succeeds, but the cause shall not fail, for it is the cause of mankind." When he arrived at the hall, the news of the shooting had not yet reached the packed house. He was met with wild enthusiasm, but he hushed the crowd: "Friends, I shall ask you to be quiet as possible… I don't know if you fully understand that I have just been shot…. I want to take this occasion within five minutes of having been shot to say some things to our people which I hope no one will question the profound sincerity of." When he unbuttoned his jacket to take his speech from his breast pocket, the crowd—and TR himself for the first time—saw that his shirt front was bright red with blood. His typewritten speech, triple spaced and folded in thirds, had a bullet hole clear through it.

Indeed, the speech had slowed and slightly deflected the bullet, which had also passed through a metal spectacle-case. But ultimately, it was the Colonel's tremendous muscles that stopped the bullet, as doctors around the operating table at Chicago's Mercy Hospital, where TR eventually agreed to be examined after a train ride from Milwaukee, observed to their great surprise. For years TR had been known as an advocate of the "strenuous life" (which was the title of one of his books), a rabid athlete who exercised to the point of obsession. "It is largely due to the fact that he is a physical marvel that he was not dangerously wounded," one doctor said. "He is one of the most powerful men I have ever seen laid on an operating table. The bullet lodged in the massive muscles of his chest, instead of penetrating the lung."

Roosevelt delivered his speech, toward the end surrounded by aides lest the significant loss of blood manifest itself. It was a wobbly candidate who left the stage when finished, assuring his followers, "Don't worry about me. . . . It takes more than that to kill a Bull Moose!"

TR appreciated the irony of the assassination attempt. His entire life he had courted death, hunting in Maine's deep woods and Montana's snowy mountains, as cowboy, as Police Commissioner, as Rough Rider, as a president who assumed office after McKinley was fatally shot, as a big-game hunter in Africa. But now, the Colonel wrote a friend, "I feel a bit like the old maid who discovered a man under her bed one night and said, 'There you are! I've been looking for you for 40 years!'"

He recovered quickly enough to make another campaign appearance less than a month later, to an overflow crowd at Madison Square Garden. Beneath banners of Washington, Jefferson, and Lincoln, accompanied by running mate Governor Hiram Johnson of California, as well as an ocean of the common people who adored him—he made one last impassioned plea for the New Nationalism's platform of progressive conservatism, which he warned might be America's last chance to preserve the Republic as the founders planned it.

"Progressive conservatism," his version of Lincoln's "sane radicalism," was not an oxymoron but a precise program. Certainly, between the last two years of his presidency and the two years after the 1912 campaign, TR's philosophy was at its most radical. The reforms of his presidency ignited a movement of Insurgents in the GOP and in the public arena—for instance, in the pages of many newspapers and magazines—that took those reforms and accelerated them; even the Democrat Party, whose alliance with the Populists in the 1890s merged mainstream politics with radicalism, sometimes felt left behind. Disciples of TR, like Herbert Croly and Walter Lippmann (who were to found *The New Republic*), were now challenging and prodding their mentor.

Ever the traditionalist, especially as concerned the American "experiment" in republican self-rule, TR was so concerned about growing social unrest and the intransigence of the reactionary elite—"malefactors of great wealth," he called them—that he was willing to find new solutions. TR essentially sought Jeffersonian ends (that is, a nation of independent and rugged individualists), but favored Hamiltonian means (a government that boldly exercised expansive, responsible power). He inveighed, countless times, against predatory wealth and corruption in high places, while remaining critical of mob rule and socialistic policies. "The sin of greed is no lesser or greater than the sin of envy," he said. He believed the national government needed to be a referee to guarantee a level playing field—a Square Deal for all citizens. It was not a new viewpoint, but it was crystallized and energized by conditions of the day.

TR's progressive conservatism was not an oxymoron, except among those today who misunderstand history and TR's attempts to manage great social and industrial forces. There are some commentators in our day who hold that Theodore Roosevelt should be regarded, even condemned, as a father of the contemporary progressive movement, because he advocated liberal reforms (he would have said for conservative ends) in 1912, and because his one-campaign political party was called the Progressive Party.

To criticize TR for being something he was not—that is, a prophet of what modern progressivism has become—would be akin to branding progressive church suppers as subversive. He undoubtedly would condemn modern progressivism; he even condemned a contemporary progressive, Woodrow Wilson, who was to pervert many of TR's reforms, and is arguably the architect and chief culprit of the modern progressive movement. (It is interesting to note, by the way, that TR's supposed advocacy of government-run national health insurance was cited many times by liberals during the 2010 legislative wars; yet TR never advocated such a thing.)

Most of TR's predictions about the Bull Moose campaign were spot-on; he well out-polled Taft; he carried eight states to Taft's lone two; but—with the predominantly Republican nation's sympathies divided in half—Democrat Wilson was elected with a plurality of the vote. Proud of the fight he had made, TR was not sanguine about the long-term viability of the Progressive Party as a permanent vehicle.

"There are no loaves and fishes," he later wrote.

# A POPULAR PRESIDENT LEAVES OFFICE

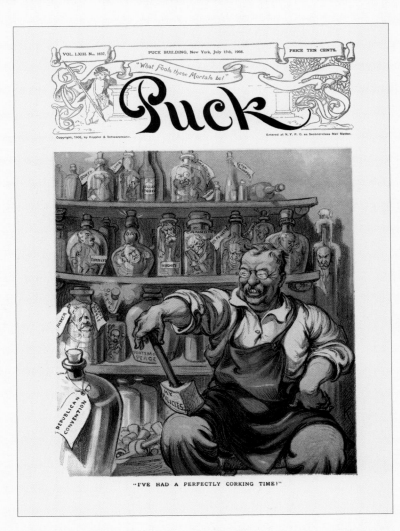

Joseph Keppler in *Puck* depicted TR in the last summer of his presidency. Ebullient, having enjoyed every moment of his days in office, he had met his challenges and opponents with zest—and bottled them up successfully.

MARTIN LUTHER ROOSEVELT.

The one person who did know Roosevelt's mind about running for reelection in 1908 was TR himself. He had pledged in 1904 not to succeed himself…and was restless for new challenges. This *Puck* cartoon portrays TR as Martin Luther, throwing an inkwell at the devil, resisting the temptation of a Third-Term crown. From a *Puck* magazine printer's proof, by Joseph Keppler.

THE DEMOCRATIC PARTY.

"DELIGHTED"

William Jennings Bryan, already twice nominated and twice defeated presidential candidate of the Democrat Party, was again nominated in 1908. Grant Hamilton in *Judge* depicted Bryan as a menace in donkey's clothing…and atop his head is the cavalry hat of TR—a reference to the challenge facing the Democrats: running against the Square Deal and TR's policy agenda record while both were wildly popular throughout the nation. The bitter irony for Bryan was that TR had appropriated important elements of Bryan's old platforms and adapted them to modern conditions.

TR hand-picked his successor, his dear friend and loyal lieutenant Secretary of War William Howard Taft. The convention nominated James Schoolcraft Sherman as vice presidential candidate. Rivals for the nomination were disappointed, but such was Roosevelt's popularity that his nod was sufficient to settle the question. The cartoon on the cover of *Life* magazine, however, confirmed that behind Taft and Sherman—and looming larger in the public perception—was the person of Theodore Roosevelt.

J. Campbell Cory in *Harper's Weekly* portrayed the dilemma, rather than the speculation, attending TR's retirement. Scattered on the floor are career options, while the Big Stick and "My Policies" are in the shadows. Indeed, Roosevelt's successor Taft would neglect those two items…to his doom and the nation's subsequent turmoil.

The caption of Cory's double-spread: "Lionization…Specula-tion…Perturbation. The Lion: 'I wish I knew what you were going to do with me.' TR (thoughtfully): 'So do I.' Chorus from window (GOP, Uncle Sam, Taft): 'So do we.'"

# A YEAR IN DARKEST AFRICA

The rest of the world was as fascinated as America was by Roosevelt–the living, breathing cowboy, Harvard scholar, naturalist, soldier, winner of the Nobel Peace Prize…and big-game hunter in what was still the "dark continent." This cartoon graced the cover of France's most notable cartoon and commentary magazine (1902–1912), *L'Assiette au Beurre*. Cartoonist d'Ostoya devoted a whole issue to a parody of the popular American institution, the dime novel, and drew a satirical biography of Roosevelt.

Natural history was TR's avocation, the subject of his first and last published works, and he never indulged in the indiscriminate carnage so common to his era. He savored the hunt and captured trophies, but never bagged an animal or bird except for food or study. Commonly regarded as one of America's two or three most prominent naturalists throughout his career, he would still be a prominent name in history even if natural history had been his sole career. Protective coloration, bird songs, and shared characteristics of species around the world—questions of antediluvian migration—were among his specialties. Yet cartoonists around the world found it easier to caricature the bloodthirsty hunter than to depict the laboratory naturalist. Especially when red ink was available to them!

The press was strongly discouraged from following TR into the jungles, but cartoonists were free to speculate. They kept Roosevelt before the public during his year-long absence, location and status unknown. James Montgomery Flagg, who a decade later painted the iconic *Uncle Sam Wants You!* poster, sketched this fantasy for the cover of *Life*.

# IN AFRICA

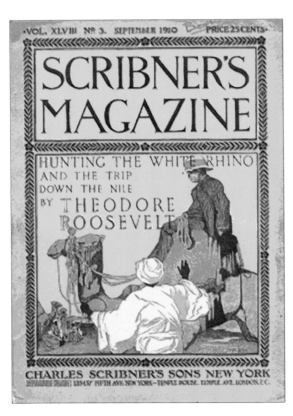

TR's scientific expedition to Africa was the stuff of legend—and of literature and poetry. Serialized in a popular monthly magazine, and later a best-selling book, his accounts of the safari were equal parts adventure, natural history, and some of the most colorful and memorable prose TR ever wrote.

KHARTOUM, March 15, 1910

*"I speak of Africa and golden joys"; the joy of wandering through lonely lands; the joy of hunting the mighty and terrible lords of the wilderness, the cunning, the wary, and the grim.*

*In these greatest of the world's great hunting-grounds there are mountain peaks whose snows are dazzling under the equatorial sun; swamps where the slime oozes and bubbles and festers in the steaming heat; lakes like seas; skies that burn above deserts where the iron desolation is shrouded from view by the wavering mockery of the mirage; vast grassy plains where palms and thorn-trees fringe the dwindling streams; mighty rivers rushing out of the heart of the continent through the sadness of endless marshes; forests of gorgeous beauty, where death broods in the dark and silent depths.*

*There are regions as healthy as the northland; and other regions, radiant with bright-hued flowers, birds and butterflies, odorous with sweet and heavy scents, but, treacherous in their beauty, and sinister to human life. On the land and in the water there are dread brutes that feed on the flesh of man; and among the lower things, that crawl, and fly, and sting, and bite, he finds swarming foes far more evil and deadly than any beast or reptile; foes that kill his crops and his cattle, foes before which he himself perishes in his hundreds of thousands.*

*The dark-skinned races that live in the land vary widely. Some are warlike, cattle-owning nomads; some till the soil and live in thatched huts shaped like beehives; some are fisherfolk; some are ape-like naked savages, who dwell in the woods and prey on creatures not much wilder or lower than themselves.*

*The land teems with beasts of the chase, infinite in number and incredible in variety. It holds the fiercest beasts of ravin, and the fleetest and most timid of those* beings that live in undying fear of talon and fang. It holds the largest and the smallest of hoofed animals. It holds the mightiest creatures that tread the earth or swim in its rivers; it also holds distant kinsfolk of these same creatures, no bigger than woodchucks, which dwell in crannies of the rocks, and in the tree tops. There are antelope smaller than hares, and antelope larger than oxen. There are creatures which are the embodiments of grace; and others whose huge ungainliness is like that of a shape in a nightmare. The plains are alive with droves of strange and beautiful animals whose like is not known elsewhere; and with others even stranger that show both in form and temper something of the fantastic and the grotesque. It is a never-ending pleasure to gaze at the great herds of buck as they move to and fro in their myriads; as they stand for their noontide rest in the quivering heat haze; as the long files come down to drink at the watering-places; as they feed and fight and rest and make love.

The hunter who wanders through these lands sees sights which ever afterward remain fixed in his mind. He sees the monstrous river-horse snorting and plunging beside the boat; the giraffe looking over the tree tops at the nearing horseman; the ostrich fleeing at a speed that none may rival; the snarling leopard and coiled python, with their lethal beauty; the zebras, barking in the moonlight, as the laden caravan passes on its night march through a thirsty land. In after years there shall come to him memories of the lion's charge; of the gray bulk of the elephant, close at hand in the sombre woodland; of the buffalo, his sullen eyes lowering from under his helmet of horn; of the rhinoceros, truculent and stupid, standing in the bright sunlight on the empty plain.

These things can be told. But there are no words that can tell the hidden spirit of the wilderness, that can reveal its mystery, its melancholy, and its charm. There is delight in the hardy life of the open, in long rides rifle in hand, in

the thrill of the fight with dangerous game. Apart from this, yet mingled with it, is the strong attraction of the silent places, of the large tropic moons, and the splendor of the new stars; where the wanderer sees the awful glory of sunrise and sunset in the wide waste spaces of the earth, unworn of man, and changed only by the slow change of the ages through time everlasting.

—TR

VOL. 57 NO. 1455     SEPTEMBER 4 1909     PRICE 10 CENTS

# Judge

ENTERED AT THE POST OFFICE AT NEW YORK AS SECOND CLASS MATTER COPYRIGHT, 1909     BY THE LESLIE - JUDGE COMPANY. TITLE REGISTERED AS A TRADE MARK

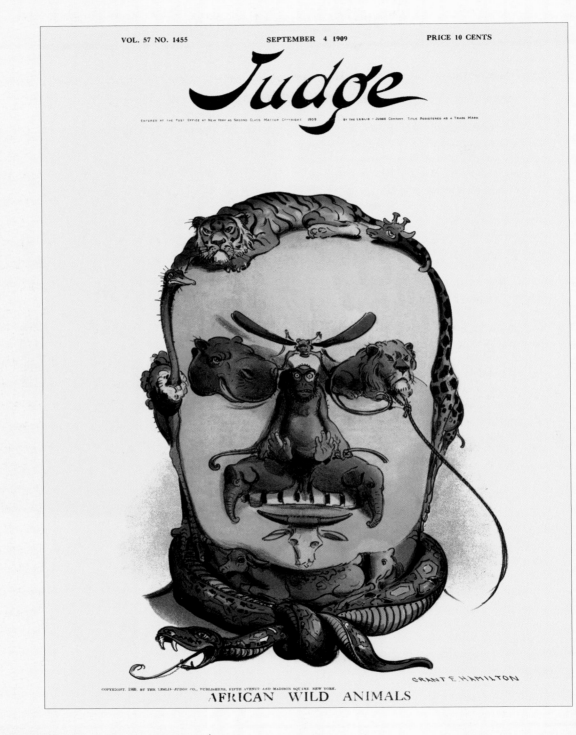

GRANT E HAMILTON

## AFRICAN WILD ANIMALS

"SAY, HONEST, IS HE REALLY GONE?"

Cartoonist L. M. Glacken's version of TR-induced jungle
fever—Friday's footprint in reverse. From *Puck*.

# THE NEW NATIONALISM

To all of TR's titles and accolades, history might add "Homecoming King." There was an unprecedented outpouring of excitement and affection when the long drought was over and the Most Interesting American was back in America. E. W. Kemble, noted as the illustrator of *Huckleberry Finn* and a delineator of rural blacks, was also a longtime political cartoonist. He most often opposed Roosevelt policies, and usually drew for Democrat papers. *Harper's Weekly* was such a publication (indeed, its editor George Harvey almost single-handedly manufactured the presidential boom of Woodrow Wilson). Yet even Kemble and *Harper's Weekly* put aside their animus and joined in the elation the whole country felt. "Teddy" was home after a 15-month absence. This cover cartoon is a lesson in cartoon iconography. Roosevelt can scarcely be seen, and no ID label is attached to him, yet the glasses and teeth, and an irrepressible vivacity, are enough for readers to recognize the central figure.

VOL. 36  NO. 915  APRIL 29 1899.  PRICE 10 CENTS

# Judge

ENTERED AT THE POST OFFICE AT NEW YORK AS SECOND CLASS MATTER. COPYRIGHT 1899 BY ARKELL PUBLISHING COMPANY. TITLE REGISTERED AS A TRADE MARK.

MUNICIPAL OWNERSHIP.

"We won't be happy until we get it."

JUDGE—"A few cities have set the good example in controlling their own franchises; let YOUR CITY follow."

If anything illustrates the turbulent nature of political discourse during Roosevelt's presidency and the Insurgent era, it is the fact that political labels and loyalties were changing rapidly. Looking ahead to 1912, even many conservative Republicans touted their anti-trust credentials. (In that regard, TR once defined a reactionary as "someone who is willing to take a progressive stand on a dead issue.") And, surprisingly, as early as 1899, the conservative Republican magazine *Judge* even took a strong stand for municipal ownership of utilities, transportation, and franchises (a.k.a. socialism). Cartoon by F. Victor Gillam.

When Roosevelt returned from the African wilds and European courts, Republicans of every stripe, old friends and opponents alike, sought his assistance to repair the damage that had been done his carefully wrought work over the fourteen months of his absence. Behind TR in the blacksmith shop is Lyman Abbott, the clergyman-editor of *The Outlook*, the Christian news and commentary magazine whose staff Roosevelt had joined. Cartoon by L. M. Glackens in *Puck*, 1910.

The worst elephant TR saw in the months after his presidency was not in Africa, but the Republican elephant, the cartoonist's symbol created by Thomas Nast in 1874. It had not taken William Howard Taft long to alienate the reformers and Insurgents—largely the Roosevelt wing—of the GOP. Ineptitude, a tone-deaf political instinct, and a willing alliance with the Old Guard combined to make Taft unpopular.

The party was splitting in two. In fact, America might have split in two but for Roosevelt's grounded perspicacity and thoughtful leadership as president; that he had succeeded to hold "Stand-Patters" and "Insurgents" together, and that he later corralled disparate forces during the high-water mark of political ferment in 1912, means that history will never know whether America would have fared differently. Since the 1870s, agrarian reformers forced many economic and social questions; and the Populist movement swallowed the Democrat Party for two decades. Similarly, reformers and Insurgents in the GOP, who both took inspiration and provided impetus for TR's reforms, often saw the Republican Old Guard, not Democrats, as the chief foe.

This cartoon (another marvelous example of cartoon iconography) shows the battered and bloodied Republican elephant, his rowboat labeled "Stand Pat," taking water. He looks longingly to TR's home, Sagamore Hill at Oyster Bay on the north shore of Long Island. It is a reminder of the remarkable, encompassing leadership of TR, that despite his sometimes radical initiatives as president, the party and public—and cartoonists—still saw him as leader of the conservative, as well as the insurgent, wings of the party.

E. W. Kemble in *Harper's Weekly*, 1910.

# THE LEADING VOICE OF RADICAL CARTOONING

America had a rich tradition of reformist cartooning, but in the Insurgent and Progressive years it took a turn for the radical. Its leader was Art Young. He drew for many magazines, but his work for *Life* and *Puck* grew radical until he left in 1912 for *The Masses*, a socialist/anarchist monthly. Later, he drew for Communist publications, but also for Hearst in the latter's right-wing years; and for *The Saturday Evening Post* and *The New Yorker*.

Young reported that this was his favorite of the cartoons he drew. "Holy Trinity" was inspired by muckraking articles by Charles Edward Russell, revealing the Episcopal Church ownership of New York tenements. Reproduced from the original artwork for *Puck*. Overleaf: A *Puck* cartoon by Young against child labor.

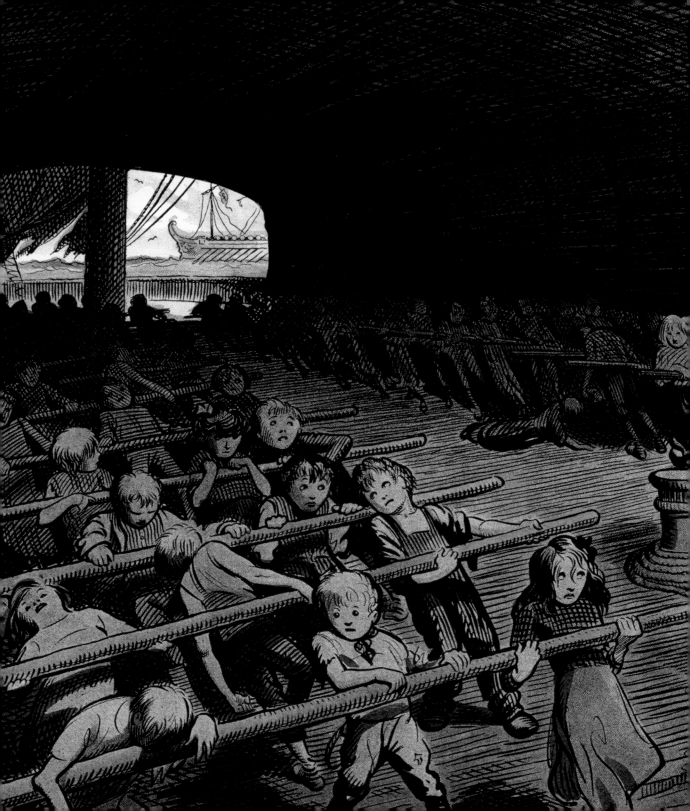

CHILD-LABOR
INVESTIGATOR
SENTIMENTALIST
CHARITY
ORGANIZATION
AND ALL MED-
DLING OLD-
WOMEN
KEEP OUT

GREED

Throughout 1910, TR largely managed to avoid criticizing President Taft…while barely managing to ignore many slights, both personal and political, dealt him by his successor. However, the Colonel spoke out on issues and wrote articles, including essays and editorials for the weekly Christian magazine of politics and current events, *The Outlook*. He continued the same advocacies and policies—"My Policies"—of his presidency, many of them taken to new levels of urgency. When reforms were undone by the Administration—for instance, in the fields of conservation and protection of natural resources—he spoke out boldly.

TR also responded to the appeals of old friends who had supported him at crucial times in the past, and of fresh public servants who had been inspired to enter politics by Roosevelt himself. There were activists in many corners of life who had risked their careers to espouse the Square Deal and TR's philosophy.

A challenge to the Colonel's effort to bridge the camps came in the fall of 1910. The Republican Party machinery in

New York State was caught in a bloody tug-of-war between the "Stand Pat" elements and the reformers. TR resisted appeals to enter the fray on behalf of the reformers, until the Old Guard laid down the gauntlet. In a gratuitous insult, the vice president of the United States, James Schoolcraft Sherman, became the nominee for the party convention's chairmanship, and he told the press that if Theodore Roosevelt (also a resident of New York) tried to chair the convention himself, he "would be beaten to a frazzle."

No longer with a party apparatus behind the Colonel—indeed, the GOP establishment daily grew more hostile to him—but by force of personality, TR attended the state convention in Saratoga and won the convention chairmanship against Taft's vice president. Roosevelt further persuaded the convention to nominate his own preferred gubernatorial candidate, Henry L. Stimson.

Cartoonist W. A. Carson of the Utica (NY) *Globe* depicted the putative frazzling victim, and well portrayed TR's trademark joy of victory. Reproduced from the original artwork.

Some cartoons write, or draw, themselves. Roosevelt's Dutch ancestry, added to the "Big Stick" that he wielded in his crusades and a trademark symbol of a popular product whose ads and labels were familiar to every American, gave rise to a natural cartoon idea. Grant E. Hamilton, the longtime Art Editor of *Judge*, drew the pastiche during TR's cross-country speaking tour presenting the New Nationalism.

# THE BULL MOOSE CAMPAIGN

THE GREAT RENUNCIATION.

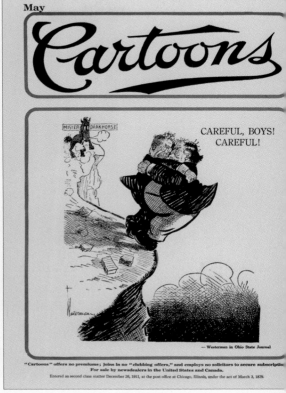

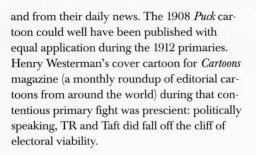

These two cartoons summarize the dilemma and the evolution of the Republican-Insurgent division during the presidency of William Howard Taft. The new president signaled his essentially conservative impulses before his inauguration, and was embraced by the Old Guard and "Stand-Patters." But many Republicans, and many ordinary citizens, never were reconciled to TR's departure—from politics and from their daily news. The 1908 *Puck* cartoon could well have been published with equal application during the 1912 primaries. Henry Westerman's cover cartoon for *Cartoons* magazine (a monthly roundup of editorial cartoons from around the world) during that contentious primary fight was prescient: politically speaking, TR and Taft did fall off the cliff of electoral viability.

"The Thieves Shall Not Win"—Roosevelt speaking from the balcony of the Congress Hotel immediately after arrival in Chicago. A brush-and-crayon drawing made on the spot by Oscar Cesare when TR broke with precedent and arrived at a presidential convention to marshal his own forces. Reproduced from the original artwork. Cesare, a facile cartoonist who drew for many New York City newspapers through the years, including *The New York Times*, was married to the daughter of author O. Henry.

Theodore Roosevelt was a gifted phrasemaker. When he announced to newspapermen during the 1912 campaign that he felt as strong as a bull moose, perhaps he knew that he was prompting the establishment of a new member of America's political bestiary. But the pens of many cartoonists—this caricature is by A. Johnson of the German weekly *Kladderadatsch*—depicted TR *as* a bull moose.

Thereby cartoonists pinpointed one of the problems of the Progressive Party in 1912: it was not so much a revolution in American politics, but a vehicle whereby supporters could advocate for their hero as an individual.

Interestingly, party leaders and the cartoonists' icons have seldom morphed. Taft, for instance, weighed more than 325 pounds, yet cartoonists—who frequently poked fun at his size—almost never yielded to the temptation to depict Taft as the Republican elephant. Likewise neither supporters nor opponents drew Democrat politicians as donkeys. But TR frequently was depicted as the Bull Moose himself.

SALVATION IS FREE, BUT IT DOESN'T APPEAL TO HIM.

THIRD-PARTY CHOIR. — "And sinners bathed beneath that flood lose all their guilty stains."

Joseph Keppler Jr., in *Puck*, pictures the split in the Republican Party in terms of religious revivals and Pentecostalism across America: TR is the evangelist, the GOP elephant is the sinner reluctant to be baptized. The caption is a direct reference to the camp-meeting gospel song, "There Is a Fountain." From 1912, during the pre-Convention battle for the soul of the GOP.

THE SAINT

SPEAKING OF HATS AND RINGS!

TEARING DOWN THE SIGN.

POLITICAL CARNIVAL

FOR MEN ONLY

I GUESS WE'VE MADE THIS SHOW FIT FOR WOMEN!

It was Theodore Roosevelt who applied the term "my hat is in the ring" to politics. Cartoonist Fontaine Fox of the *Chicago Post* gave it an even more graphic description. Fox later drew the beloved *Toonerville Trolley* comic strip, starring Mickey (Himself) McGuire and the Powerful Katrinka.

The Progressive Party was the first major American political party to endorse the right of women to vote. A cartoon by Caine in the *St. Paul Pioneer-Press*.

The hastily arranged nominating convention was held in the Chicago Coliseum approximately six weeks after the GOP "steamroller" did its work. Tickets were hard to secure; every night was standing-room only in the galleries, and overflow crowds stretched for blocks outside.

A unique fund-raising device was the issuance of "Founders' Certificates" whose receipts resembled currency. The candidates literally and figuratively spanned the continent: Roosevelt of New York and Governor Hiram Johnson of California. Each brought a full résumé and corps of followers. Hardly a rump protest, the Progressive Party startled America with the number of senators, congressmen, governors, mayors, and celebrities in its ranks.

## THE OFFICIAL DEMOCRAT CARTOONIST

It once was the practice of national parties to hire political cartoonists and distribute their work in publicity campaigns and to partisan newspapers free of charge during campaigns. Charles Macauley was the official cartoonist of the Democrat National Committee's Pictorial Publicity Department in 1912. Then on the staff of *The New York World*, Macauley drew for several newspapers and magazines throughout his career, and was to win the 1930 Pulitzer Prize. In his series of 1912 cartoons, he drew TR and Taft as "the Gold Trust Twins," parodying a popular detergent's advertising mascots; he implied that the two candidates were both tools of Wall Street.

OUT OF THE SAME DISH.

IN THE PILLORY.

"THEY ARE GOOD ENOUGH FOR ME."

The Democrats stirred the embers of Standard Oil's contribution to the GOP back in 1904. They flailed a Roosevelt aide, George W. Perkins, because he once worked for J. P. Morgan. But the public wasn't buying the idea that the Trust-Buster was in the pocket of the trusts.

Macauley continued the meme that TR was a slave to the trusts, and parodied Davenport's famous Uncle Sam cartoon of 1904, "He's Good Enough for Me."

# 1908-1912: Cartoon Portfolio

Such were the levels of extreme vituperation against TR during the Bull Moose campaign that lunatics betook themselves to do violence. In Milwaukee, a Brooklyn bartender who had been stalking Roosevelt on the campaign trail shot him in the chest at point-blank range. TR insisted on delivering his speech before seeking medical attention. Later, surgeons marveled at Roosevelt's physique—his massive chest muscles absorbed the bullet, which was never removed the rest of his days.

TR predicted to friends the outcome of the 1912 presidential campaign—he would beat Taft, and both would trail the candidate of a united Democrat party. Woodrow Wilson, late president of Princeton University and governor of New Jersey, was that Democrat candidate. Regarded as a Progressive, he was to give new meaning to the label—frequently different in substance and direction from Insurgent and Reform initiatives, and certainly a deviation in many respects from Roosevelt's own core beliefs. At that moment, after the rancorous 1912 campaign ended, the mother hen of the Democrat party could be pleased, as depicted in this cartoon by Glackens: Wilson's election was the first by a Democrat since the presidential campaign of Grover Cleveland in 1892.

HATCHED ONE AT LAST.
After Twenty Years of Unproductive Eggs.

LOOK WHO'S HERE!

The GOP ready for retirement? A lot of people thought so after the Bull Moose campaign. The Republican Party itself had been born on the graves of several dying political movements in 1854–56; and anyone could read the numbers from the presidential election. Taft carried two states, and garnered eight electoral votes. On the other hand, the Republicans still had inertia and an infrastructure of thousands of local office-holders. The Progressives, conceived in a moment of passion, had no time or resources to build from the ground up. The elephant did not remain long in the Home for Old Parties…and eventually reconciled with the wronged TR.
S. Ehrhart in *Puck*, 1912.

Elba or St. Helena ?

After the defeat of the Progressive Party, yet contemplating its impressive second-place showing, TR wondered if the public was through with him, or if his exile was temporary. "Elba or St Helena?" was drawn by Frank Wing of *The Minneapolis Journal.* Wing later was a teacher of Charles Schulz.

CHAPTER 10

# 1913~1919

# LIVING OUT
# THE GREAT ADVENTURE

The world of Theodore Roosevelt must have seemed suddenly quieter after the loss of the 1912 election. The campaign had quieted many old friendships and ruptured more than one longtime association. The political bosses who always opposed him disliked him more than ever. No longer was the public, or at least the large Republican portion of it, filled with adulation. Was Roosevelt's stature as a statesman compromised? His place in history tarnished? His "day" over?

As ever, nobody needed to worry on his behalf; this was Theodore Roosevelt. Running for the presidency of the United States of America, though important, was only one detail of his life. After the campaign, he recovered from the bullet wound in his chest and assumed the position of president of the American Historical Association; his lengthy inaugural address was on the theme "History as Literature." He resumed his friendship and correspondence with many old associates, such as his mentor Henry Cabot Lodge, with whom he began to exchange several lengthy letters each week, as if nothing ideological or political had ever interrupted their relationship (Lodge had stuck with the GOP in 1912). He also continued his editorial work for *The Outlook*, and he contracted with Macmillan publishers to write a major-length book of reminiscences, which he immediately plunged into writing. The book was published as *An Autobiography* in 1913.

During this time, TR filed a libel suit against a newspaper publisher in the Upper Peninsula of Michigan, who had written during the campaign that "Roosevelt lies, and curses in a most disgusting way, he gets drunk too, and that not infrequently, and all of his intimates know about it." For years, Democrat newspapers and political whisperers—and recently, even conservative and Republican sources—had spread stories about TR's alleged excesses. Despite the overwhelming press coverage of his every activity, and numerous attestations of Roosevelt's practically prudish personal habits, the rumors persisted. Surely many people could not help wondering at his firecracker exuberance, his constant motion, startling speaking style, and what today would be called hyperactivity.

By filing suit, TR sought to quash these rumors for two reasons: the dignity of his family; and the judgment of history. He knew if he did not conclusively refute such claims in his lifetime, they would live forever in some portions of his biographies. At enormous personal expense, TR arranged for more than two dozen character witnesses to appear in Marquette, Michigan, where the trial was held. A parade of distinguished celebrities, close associates, government officials, longtime friends, and—as a special dig at the irresponsible publisher—notable journalists, all testified to Roosevelt's propriety and sobriety. He was seldom heard to swear; he never smoked; and he hated the taste of beer and liquor, while he occasionally drank wine, though even that was watered in his glass at state dinners.

The publisher, George Newett, eventually stopped the proceedings and confessed he had no sources for his statement. His newspaper was a conservative Republican organ; he admitted to libel. The judge advised Roosevelt to press for damages—having filed suit for $10,000—but TR demanded only six cents, the minimum allowable. He only wanted to preserve his reputation.

TR had accepted a number of speaking engagements in South America. He had always wanted to visit there, and he hoped to investigate the hunting and exploring opportunities south of the equator. He sailed from New York in October of 1913 and spoke at various universities and learned societies in Uruguay, Argentina, and Brazil. The "back end" of his trip was less structured. His desire to travel and hunt had turned into an assignment from the American Museum of Natural History in New York to collect specimens and conduct studies, as he had done during his African expedition. When TR arrived in Rio de Janeiro, Brazilian Minister of Foreign Affairs Lauro Müller made a surprising proposal. If Roosevelt would consider expanding his work in the jungles, to add a new objective to his scientific work, the Brazilian government would assist. Specifically, Müller suggested that Roosevelt was well positioned, by temperament and circumstance, to spearhead an exploration deeper into the hinterlands than he had planned—deeper, in fact, than any civilized man had ever gone, to chart the course of an unknown river, the Rio da Dúvida, or River of Doubt. The expedition would seek to discover the course by which the River of Doubt flowed into the mighty Amazon. To this unique proposal TR assented. The Brazilian government assigned its own noted explorer, Colonel Cândido Rondon, to join this major expedition. Although he had been an explorer himself for decades, Rondon had only advanced into portions of the legendary river, but had never fully explored it or confirmed its role in the great interior of Brazil. The party was joined by TR's son Kermit, who had been working in Brazil as a bridge-builder and recently had recovered from a workplace accident. Kermit had been a vital member of his father's African safari four years previous.

Despite surface similarities, though, the two expeditions were hardly alike. For one thing, the geographical surfaces of Africa and Brazil were very different. Africa offered its explorers open skies, wide veldts, and abundant game. The Brazilian rain forest presented the Roosevelt party with dense, impassable jungles, daily torrential downpours that raised the humidity of already soggy underbrush and steamy air, and virtually no game for sustenance. In Africa, Roosevelt's caravan consisted of hundreds of attendants besides the naturalists; in Brazil it would be a group of twenty explorers and camp assistants. The deep forest and the river that TR was to chart overflowed with strange and hostile creatures, not the least of which was the man-eating piranha.

Near the beginning of their journey, progress was slow, depleting the food supplies, and the rain forest's animal and fish population yielded little edible meat; most of the food ran out. Lizards and monkey meat became delicacies. Traveling the river proved treacherous, to say the least. Much of the river could not be navigated because of deadly cataracts and innumerable falls; the men were obliged to carry their canoes for large stretches, hoisting them up and down cliffs on many days. Their progress, even on close river banks, could only be made by hacking a pathway through trees and dense brush. Provisions and canoes were lost. One porter drowned; another went mad and killed his companion and ran into the jungle. One day TR jumped into the rapids to save two canoes that had broken loose, and his leg was smashed between a canoe and a rock. The wound became infected, and TR developed a fever that rose to 105 degrees.

Between his infection-induced fever and the malaria that plagued nearly all the members of the expedition (they subsisted on quinine), Roosevelt was very ill—close to death. Some nights the infected Roosevelt was insensible, repeating poems like "Kubla Kahn" in his delirium. Coleridge's poem from 1797, written in an opium haze, showed what was close to the surface of the fevered Roosevelt's mind:

*In Xanadu did Kubla Khan*
*A stately pleasure-dome decree:*
*Where Alph, the sacred river, ran*
*Through caverns measureless to man*
*Down to a sunless sea.*

Once he had returned to his senses, but was still unable to walk, TR was caught putting portions of his food in other men's rations. He pleaded with Kermit to leave him in the jungle, since he was a burden to the others. Kermit refused, and TR later said that the only reason he did not use his deadly dose of morphine (an accessory on every dangerous exploration) was that he was sure the men would insist on carrying his body, anyway, to civilization.

All during the months-long, foot-by-foot trek, the scientists charted the river and took copious notes of flora and fauna. During portions of the days when travel was impossible, usually in the midst of unrelenting downpours, Roosevelt kept a record of the experience. Under small coverings, often draped in netting and wearing gauntlets as protection against vicious insects, and sometimes with a high fever, he wrote hundreds of pages of narration and observation. Once again these writings became articles in *Scribner's Monthly* and later a best-selling book, *Through the Brazilian Wilderness*. It is as riveting as anything on the long bookshelf of Roosevelt's writings. The understandable bravado of his three hunting and cowboy collections is gone, likewise the proud swagger of the memoir *The Rough Riders*. This book details the grim adventure of survival, not the exultation of big-game hunts. Typical for Roosevelt, the narration careens from descriptions of bizarre reptiles and beautiful birds to vivid stories of a deadly environment, the palpable threat of starvation, and the prospect that they would never return to civilization.

But return they did, first discovering a lone native who was gathering rubber. Soon they came upon primitive huts, then loose communities of half-clad, semi-savage peoples who knew not what to make of this band of bedraggled men. By this point the river was more passable, and the party was able to row placidly down the River of Doubt into the larger Rio Madeira. From there, they boarded a steamer to Manaos, on the Amazon. Before long, TR and Kermit sailed to New York, where they arrived on May 19, 1914. Their jungle expedition had lasted from February to April, 1914.

No longer Rio da Dúvida ("River of Doubt"), the river was renamed Rio Roosevelt; on some maps it appears as Rio Teodoro. The Roosevelt-Rondon Scientific Expedition, its official title, determined the river to be 400 miles (640 km) in length from its source in Rondônia State, emptying into the Aripuanã River and flowing from there into the Madeira River, a major tributary of the Amazon. In 1927 the National Geographic Society covered the same ground, soggy and foreboding as it was, and confirmed all of Roosevelt's findings.

William Roscoe Thayer, a friend of Roosevelt, would write that the Brazilian experience, especially its physical maladies and lingering abscesses, took ten years from TR's life. But not to have gone, responding even as it was to an almost impromptu idea, would have been for Roosevelt a contradiction of every instinct. It was TR's "last chance to be a boy."

After seven and a half months away from America, the Colonel was treated to welcome celebrations and well-wishes, though none on the scale of those following his return from Africa and Europe. Friends and family alike were shocked to see a Roosevelt much worn down by his adventures. TR had lost thirty-five pounds during the ordeal, and although he had regained some of it on the cruise homeward, he was still somewhat frail and needed a cane. Kermit also was fairly worn out by the expedition. However, the recuperation of both father and son was Rooseveltian in the extreme: in three weeks they sailed to Spain with a large family contingent for Kermit's marriage to Belle Willard, the daughter of the American ambassador to Spain.

At the end of June 1914, as Roosevelt returned to America from the wedding, he sailed from a Europe that would never be the same. Violent changes were about to rock the course of world history. A Serbian fanatic assassinated Archduke Franz Ferdinand of the Austro-Hungarian Empire in Sarajevo, Bosnia, on June 28. For a month, treaties were asserted or sublimated among European nations, monarchs and diplomats made or refreshed secret alliances, and old grievances once again were recalled. Each of the nations of Europe dug up every reason they had—or imagined they had—for waging war on their neighbors. The earlier efforts of many mediators—including Roosevelt, who had drawn up a blueprint acceptable to the aggrieved European powers in the Algeciras Conference—ultimately expired. "The Guns of August" commenced firing. President Woodrow

Wilson announced that America would be "impartial in thought as well as in action" in the impending conflict. Theodore Roosevelt advised Americans to support the president.

Wilson had focused during the first half of his term on domestic policies. The preponderance of the debate in 1912 rested on a full menu of reforms of the American political and economic systems. Taft also, except for his forays into Latin America (what became known as "Dollar Diplomacy" to act on behalf of U.S. industries or corporations), had focused primarily on internal issues during his presidency. Even a reciprocity treaty with Canada, one of Taft's pet projects, was designed to serve American farmers (many of whom were actually displeased with its provisions). So for six years, America had largely neglected foreign affairs. If the president or the Secretary of State took note of gathering war clouds in Europe, they did not respond. Besides, Wilson's skills, from his background as a professor of American Government and an author of a multi-volume history of the United States, were focused on domestic, not foreign, affairs.

The clearest illustration of Wilson's disdain of foreign policy at the beginning of his presidency was the appointment of William Jennings Bryan as Secretary of State. The Populist "Boy Orator of the Platte" had scarcely addressed international affairs since delivering anti-imperialist speeches fifteen years prior. Once in office, Bryan reverted to the spoils system—a patronage reward of the sort that had previously been among the targets of his rhetoric. In fact, Wilson owed his nomination in part to Bryan's stand at the 1912 convention, which persuaded delegates to reject any candidate beholden to both Wall Street and the patterns of political payoffs represented by Tammany Hall. Once confirmed, however, Secretary of State Bryan openly combed the diplomatic service for Republicans who could be fired, and for "worthy" Democrats who could be rewarded with positions. His machinations, once made public, were an embarrassment to the Wilson administration, particularly in Santo Domingo, where American favoritism among banking interests became a scandal. Moreover, there was a diplomatic scandal in Mexico, where the American ambassador Henry Lane Wilson was implicated in the plot to assassinate President Huerta.

# TR'S BRAZILIAN TRIP

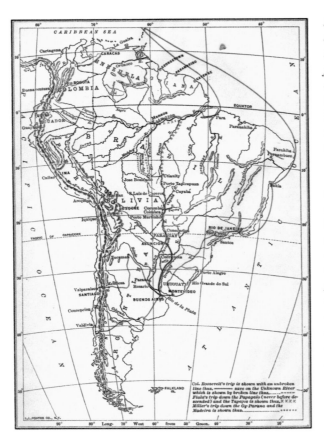

*From* Through the Brazilian Wilderness
*by Theodore Roosevelt:*

*The most beautiful music was from a shy woodland thrush, sombre-colored, which lived near the ground in the thick timber, but sang high among the branches. At a great distance we could hear the ringing, musical, bell-*

*like note, long-drawn and of piercing sweetness, which occurs at intervals in the song; at first I thought this was the song, but when it was possible to approach the singer I found that these far-sounding notes were scattered through a continuous song of great melody. I never listened to one that impressed me more. In different places in Argentina I heard and saw the Argentine mocking-bird, which is not very unlike our own, and is also a delightful and remarkable singer.*

...

*For an hour we went through thick jungle, where the machetes were constantly at work. Then the trail struck off straight across the marshes, for jaguars swim and wade as freely as marsh-deer. It was a hard walk. The sun was out. We were drenched with sweat. We were torn by the spines of the innumerable clusters of small palms with thorns like needles. We were bitten by the hosts of fire-ants, and by the mosquitoes, which we scarcely noticed where the fire-ants were found, exactly as all dread of the latter vanished when we were menaced by the big red wasps, of which a dozen stings will disable a man, and if he is weak or in bad health will seriously menace his life. In the marsh we were continually wading, now up to our knees, now up to our hips. Twice we came to long bayous so deep that we had to swim them, holding our rifles above water in our right hands. The floating masses of marsh grass, and the slimy stems of the water-plants, doubled our work as we swam, cumbered by our clothing and boots and holding our rifles aloft. One result of the swim, by the way, was that my watch, a veteran of Cuba and Africa, came to an indignant halt. Then on we went, hampered by the weight of our drenched clothes while our soggy boots squelched as we walked. There was no breeze. In the undimmed sky the sun stood almost over-head. The heat beat on us in waves. By noon I could only go forward at a slow walk, and two of the party were* worse off than I was. Kermit, with the dogs and two camaradas [camp assistants] close behind him, disappeared across the marshes at a trot. At last, when he was out of sight, and it was obviously useless to follow him, the rest of us turned back toward the boat. The two exhausted members of the party gave out, and we left them under a tree. Colonel Rondon and Lieutenant Rogaciano were not much tired; I was somewhat tired, but was perfectly able to go for several hours more if I did not try to go too fast; and we three walked on to the river, reaching it about half past four, after eleven hours' stiff walking with nothing to eat. We were soon on the boat.

...

Next day, the 3d of April, we began the descent of these sinister rapids of the chasm. Colonel Rondon had gone to the summit of the mountain in order to find a better trail for the burden-bearers, but it was hopeless, and they had to go along the face of the cliffs. Such an exploring expedition as that in which we were engaged of necessity involves hard and dangerous labor, and perils of many kinds. To follow down-stream an unknown river, broken by innumerable cataracts and rapids, rushing through mountains of which the existence has never been even guessed, bears no resemblance whatever to following even a fairly dangerous river which has been thoroughly explored and has become in some sort a highway, so that experienced pilots can be secured as guides, while the portages have been pioneered and trails chopped out, and every dangerous feature of the rapids is known beforehand. In this case no one could foretell that the river would cleave its way through steep mountain chains, cutting narrow clefts in which the cliff walls rose almost sheer on either hand. When a rushing river thus "canyons," as we used to say out West, and the mountains are very steep, it becomes almost impossible to bring the canoes down the river itself and utterly impossible to portage them along the cliff sides, while even to bring the loads over the mountain is a task of extraordinary labor and difficulty. Moreover, no one can tell how many times the task will have to be repeated, or when it will end, or whether the food will hold out; every hour of work in the rapids is fraught with the possibility of the

gravest disaster, and yet it is imperatively necessary to attempt it; and all this is done in an uninhabited wilderness, or else a wilderness tenanted only by unfriendly savages, where failure to get through means death by disease and starvation.... The conquest of wild nature demands the utmost vigor, hardihood, and daring, and takes from the conquerors a heavy toll of life and health.

THE COLONEL: NOW, LET'S SEE, WHAT'LL I DO NEXT?

After TR returned to a grateful nation after the harrowing Brazilian expedition, he recovered his vigor faster than his doctors expected...and once again became the object of speculation: What would TR do next? A cartoon by Ding Darling in *The Des Moines Register and Tribune*, 1914.

Woodrow Wilson's stated fear, that it would be "the irony of fate if my administration had to deal chiefly with foreign affairs," was increasingly echoed by nationalists and those who wanted both a strong foreign policy and an adequate military deterrent. Many bemoaned the administration's neglect of military readiness, calling for what General Leonard Wood termed the need for "preparedness." Wilson's attitude toward defense policies was reflected in his appointments, besides his appointment of Bryan. Secretary of the Navy Josephus Daniels of North Carolina conducted campaigns to ban alcohol from ships, bases, and areas around ports. He also attempted to bring all radio transmission under governmental control (famously saying in 1922 that "nobody now fears that a Japanese fleet could deal an unexpected blow on our Pacific possessions…radio makes surprises impossible"). Besides, Daniels' naval credentials were, so to speak, in drydock: Daniels was a white supremacist who had succeeded in disenfranchising registered black voters in his home state in 1898–1900; this was thoroughly compatible with Wilson's own attitude on racial segregation, which he had returned to federal facilities in the District of Columbia.

Wilson, who had no military experience and was of a pacifistic disposition, surrounded himself with others of similar tendencies. His wartime Attorney General A. Mitchell Palmer was a pacifist—whom Wilson originally wanted to nominate as Secretary of War. Declining Wilson's feeler, Palmer wrote, "As a Quaker War Secretary, I should consider myself a living illustration of a horrible incongruity." During the war itself, before becoming Attorney General, Palmer served Wilson as Alien Property Custodian, where he was accused of many acts of favoritism regarding seized German assets and their disbursements. A man who did become one of Wilson's Secretaries of War, Newton D. Baker, also was widely considered a pacifist. After his nomination, Baker (who was a classmate of Wilson in the 1890s at Johns Hopkins), declared that he was not a pacifist but, "I am an innocent…. I do not know anything about this job."

One might think that, as schoolyard bullies feel emboldened to pick on sissies, other nations would have been tempted to treat the United States with impunity. In fact several countries did. Germany, feeling squeezed by the superior British fleet around its waters, harassed and attacked American shipping, including passenger ships when plausible reports pointed to American-manufactured munitions headed for England as secret cargoes. Germany went so far as to place ads in American newspapers, warning potential travelers that ships with secret military payloads—in effect, munitions of war, using vacationing passengers as human shields—would be considered military targets. England attempted an embargo of American commercial ships headed for European ports. And the British frequently boarded American ships at sea and confiscated goods and mail, acts that have been largely forgotten by history. Britannia was still determined to rule the waves; and she ruled banking interests, transatlantic cables, and other concerns that put her in the position to be both supplicant to and mistress over the United States. Meanwhile, Mexico, which was in the midst of a long succession of revolutions and coups, spilled its turmoil over the border. Rebels raided U.S. towns, looted stores, and murdered American citizens. Pancho Villa, an opposition leader once endorsed by the United States, felt betrayed by Wilson's embrace of the latest Mexican leader. He led his bandits in cross-border incursions. The administration put General "Black Jack" Pershing in charge of troops to follow Villa into Mexico, but it was ultimately a futile effort.

In the meantime, Wilson's cherished domestic agenda was running on all pistons, thanks to Democrat majorities in Congress. The program he had dubbed "The New Freedom" differed from TR's New Nationalism, essentially holding to the Jeffersonian ideal of small towns, small farmers, and small businesses. TR accepted Bigness as a fact of modern life; rather than controlling growth, he thought the government should act as a referee. Many historians feel that, once Wilson gained power and found himself faced with reality, he incorporated Roosevelt's points of view. In truth, however, Wilson largely leap-frogged over TR's "Square Deal" perspective, and even Bryan's Populism, to a new paradigm of Progressivism, which, ultimately, did nothing to diminish the size of government or of business. In fact, although the Democrats lowered many tariffs, other "Progressive" legislation from Wilson's first term suited Big Business quite well. The Federal

Reserve Act did not break the backs of powerful financiers, but rather codified their manipulations and insulated their accountability. Wilson's first term saw a national income tax enshrined in the Constitution. The establishment of the Federal Trade Commission fulfilled some of the recommendations of the old Insurgents, but overall, Wilson's New Freedom was less a continuation of the Square Deal and New Nationalism than it was a foreshadow of the New Deal and Great Society. The Progressivism of Woodrow Wilson was of a very different kind from Theodore Roosevelt's reform agenda, with direct ties to the Progressive ideologies of our own day.

At its most basic, TR's agenda of reforms and expansion of federal power had always been aimed at reforming a system that was starting to break in two directions. In the case of the predatory rich, Roosevelt fought a corrupt system that manipulated prices and purchased politicians' votes and judges' rulings. After countless more benign attempts had failed, he saw laws and regulations as the only vehicles of reform in this area. At the other end of the spectrum, Roosevelt demanded the same standard of probity from workers. He had spoken directly to the Executive Council of American Federation of Labor during a dispute about unionized government workers in 1903:

> *I am President of all the people of the United States, without regard to creed, color, birthplace, occupation or social condition. My aim is to do equal and exact justice as among them all. In the employment and dismissal of men in the Government service I can no more recognize the fact that a man does or does not belong to a union as being for or against him than I can recognize the fact that he is a Protestant or a Catholic, a Jew or a Gentile, as being for or against him.*

A phrase that TR did not originate, but that applied to his credo, was Rugged Individualism. He proposed governmental programs as remedies and transformed Americans' view of Washington's role in the economy, to be sure. He even occasionally advocated more extreme curatives, displaying the Big Stick. But Theodore Roosevelt never would have countenanced the Welfare State. It would have been a betrayal, not a fulfillment, of his basic, lifelong principles.

In 1914 there remained remnants of the Progressive Party, loyal Bull-Moosers, across the political landscape. In the mid-term elections, many Bull Moose candidates ran for offices on the national and local levels. Still, not many political observers were sanguine about the future of the party, least of all the Colonel himself. Recognizing that Wilson's Progressivism was different than his own, and that a large-tent GOP might once again accommodate the Prodigal Sons, he was less than enthusiastic about crusading for Progressive candidates. But he kept these feelings from the public.

In certain ways, 1914–1915 was the lowest point in TR's career. He was out of power, rejected by a majority of the electorate for the first time in years. His carefully laid foundations for foreign affairs seemed to be crumbling. And the White House was misdirecting portions of his reform agenda. Worst of all, the political party that had arisen in 1912 in response to his clarion call, the Progressives, was beginning to look like a phantom army with nowhere to march. TR could be philosophical about most of these issues— except the last. He knew that public attitudes ebbed and flowed. But he could not abide the excruciating fact, as 1914 elections approached, that the Bull Moose campaign had damaged the careers and livelihoods of many of his followers. His own career would recover. He could write or teach, and was reasonably comfortable. But he felt a real obligation to other Progressive Party members, especially those who stood as candidates in 1914.

In an impressive act of humility and gratitude, he accepted speaking invitations from virtually every Progressive candidate who requested his endorsement, no matter how remote the prospect of victory. He confided to Oscar King Davis, the former Washington Correspondent of *The New York Times* who served as Secretary of the Progressive National Committee, that he owed some service to every one of these people, and he would render it. So TR put on his game face. This should not sound completely bleak, either: there were many Progressive victories, and some enthusiastic crowds. But the writing was on the wall for the party's future. Many days of the 1914 campaign saw TR—former president of the United States, recently hailed as the first citizen of the world, lately the confidant of monarchs—seated alone in the back seat of his car, as O. K. Davis drove him to the next rally in yet another small town.

About this time, during the mid-term election campaign, Roosevelt was sued for libel. In his attempts to reconcile New York State Progressives with reform elements of the Republican Party, TR characterized GOP boss William Barnes as the equivalent of Tammany Hall leaders—equally corrupt and equally willing to cut backroom deals with nominal opponents. Barnes, who had been a party worker since the 1890s, thought he had the Colonel over a barrel. Barnes was convinced he could present enough evidence of Roosevelt's own compromises and political deals through the years to nail his hide to the wall. It was not the first time an opponent of TR was warned, "Just be sure whose hide winds up on the wall."

Held in Syracuse and commencing in April of 1915, the trial and its daily press accounts kept Roosevelt's friends and foes alike riveted. Of all reporters' clippings, *The New York Times'* detailed stories are most evocative of the tense courtroom atmosphere and the sharp exchanges—and the humor and pure Rooseveltian electricity of the proceedings. With his phenomenal memory, the Colonel was able to counter most accusations and answer many questions put to him without reliance on evidence. Several times, Barnes's counsel thought they had trapped Roosevelt, and requested time to rummage through their files, only to find that TR had remembered even tiny details correctly. He repeatedly vindicated his defense of clean politics, and the defense of his employment of clean politics. Frequently the prosecution attorneys, growing more frustrated and more harried, asked the judge to have the witness refrain from making speeches...or raising his voice so often for emphasis...or gesticulating with his hands and arms...or breaking out in smiles or laughter. The judge denied the motions, saying he could not direct a witness to speak in anything other than his habitual manner.

The jury seemed to love the whole spectacle, but observers wondered whether TR's statements to reporters would hurt his case. Night after night of the trial, Roosevelt had sharply criticized Germany outside the courthouse. But the jury—several members of which were German immigrants—was not sequestered, even when a German submarine sank the *Lusitania*, a British ocean liner, killing more than a thousand people including almost 130 Americans. In the end, a verdict in TR's favor was rendered, once again clearing Roosevelt's name.

As things were changing in the world, things changed in Theodore Roosevelt's public life, too. He realized that what was being called the European War, or the Great War, was in fact a World War, and one way or another America would be brought in. (By the way, Roosevelt was one of the first to employ the term World War with regularity, beginning with his 1915 book, *America and the World War*.) He began to focus his activities almost exclusively on the necessity for America to prepare for, or against, war's eventuality. Roosevelt personally thought American intervention would come, and eventually was convinced it should come. Meanwhile, he did

Another kill: William Barnes, GOP boss of New York state, sued TR for libel. After a colorful trial, the jury exonerated Roosevelt. Robert Carter in *The New York Sun*.

not ignore domestic issues; in fact he thought a war might accelerate the implementation of some reforms, but clearly the war took center stage.

Recalling his automatic "support the president" statement when war broke out, TR later wrote in a private letter:

> *If I had been President, I should have acted on the thirtieth or thirty-first of July, as head of a signatory power of The Hague treaties, calling attention to the guaranty of Belgium's neutrality and saying that I accepted the treaties as imposing a serious obligation which I expected not only the United States but all other neutral nations to join in enforcing. Of course I would not have made such a statement unless I was willing to back it up. I believe that if I had been President the American people would have followed me. But whether I am mistaken or not as regards this, I am certain that the majority are now following Wilson. Only a limited number of people could or ought to be expected to make up their minds for themselves in a crisis like this; and they tend, and ought to tend, to support the president in such a crisis.*

Still, despite his urging the people to support the president, Roosevelt was incensed at Wilson's repeated responses to indignities by other countries: writing diplomatic notes. Wilson took pride in crafting eloquent notes that stated his position when crises came. The president of the United States countenanced insults to the flag, he refused to arm America in the face of possible danger, and he was substituting words for deeds—all with the approval of the American public.

Some of Wilson's phrases that stuck in the Colonel's craw were: "There is such a thing as a nation being too proud to fight"; "Watchful Waiting"; "Peace without Victory"; and the most repeated "warning" Woodrow Wilson could muster against the world powers, "You will be held in strict accountability." Unfortunately, this last phrase is still used by contemporary presidents, who, for decades and with the possible exception of Ronald Reagan, have been more Wilsonian than Rooseveltian. TR pointed out that even in schoolyards, nobody likes a bluffer; they are more to be despised than bullies or cowards, because the bluffer invites and enables both. In 1915, the most popular song in America was "I Didn't Raise My Boy to Be a Soldier." Where was the public that had once followed TR's lead? Edith, too, bemoaned the public's thirst for peace at the expense, even, of righteousness, saying her version of the song would be "I Didn't Raise My Boy To Be the Only Soldier."

Roosevelt switched his platform to the *Metropolitan* magazine, more of a mass-market monthly than *The Outlook*, and hammered away at issues related to the war and American defense. As 1916 approached, the minority (though a growing number) of Americans who agreed with the Colonel agitated for him to run for president. Some Republican leaders—Root and Lodge, not Taft or Barnes—worked to deliver the GOP nomination to him.

The reduced but loyal and enthusiastic contingent of Progressive Party members insisted he run once again on a third-party ticket. TR demurred, but he could not control the fanatics: they scheduled the Progressive Convention in the same city at the same time as the Republicans', hoping to force the GOP to accept TR so as to avoid committing suicide twice in four years.

It was excruciating for TR. Week by week his jeremiads were turning public opinion back his way. But he knew that if he did run as a Progressive, Wilson's re-election was guaranteed by another split opposition. In this scenario, TR could not play a role: he held Wilson in utter contempt. The Progressive Convention, feeling feisty, went ahead and nominated their hero again, in floor demonstrations that strongly resembled 1912, except that their leader was not present. He cabled the convention, thanking them for the honor, and declined the nomination in the name of uniting to support an American agenda of preparedness and integrity in foreign affairs. Among the names TR suggested in his stead, all Republicans, was Henry Cabot Lodge. His old friend, while solid on patriotic issues, was hardly a Progressive on domestic matters. The Convention was stunned. The members drifted apart. Some returned to the GOP, and some—the "lunatic fringe"—threw their weight behind radical candidates and the Socialist Party.

Most Republican leaders knew that TR would be their strongest candidate, but the wounds of 1912 were not healed. TR declared that it would simply be a mistake for America to elect him president "unless it was in a heroic mood." The public's pacific if not pacifist mindset was indeed shifting, but not yet to that extent. Another nominee was suggested by GOP power brokers: Supreme Court Justice Charles Evans Hughes. Hughes was persuaded to step down from the bench, resigning effective June 10, on which date he was nominated for president. He had been a reformer while governor of New York, but his years on the court made his current positions unknowable—a situation that Republican leaders considered a positive. His personality was famously icy, however, making him an inapt campaigner. His magnificent chin whiskers led someone to refer to him as a whisk broom with less personality. Roosevelt, meanwhile, offered his services in full to the party, and was dispatched to parts of the country where it was thought he could be effective. Week by week, that turned out to be almost everywhere. Republican voters were warming—mostly to TR and his policies, just like the good old days.

For his part, Woodrow Wilson had agreed back in 1912 to a plank in the Democrat platform that called for the nominee, if successful, to serve one term, and to work for a Constitutional amendment to limit presidents to one six-year term. That forgotten, Wilson threw himself into a campaign for a second term. He made some noises about national defense, and even marched in some preparedness parades, a little American flag held against his shoulder. Still, his

Mutual Admiration

campaign trucks carried big banners that blazoned the party's slogan and Wilson's proudest achievement: "He kept us out of war!" Peace and rumors of peace were the order of the day.

Cartoonists were very active in the campaign. The political cartoon allowed the public to grasp easily that TR was a one-man truth squad, following Wilson's appearances. TR was also a bigger draw on the campaign trail than the man he ruefully supported (he considered Hughes to have a spine only slightly stiffer than Wilson's). Democrat cartoonists underscored Hughes's lack of position by drawing him as a hammer uttering criticisms. They invented a haunting question-mark shaped figure labeled "What Would YOU have Done?" pursuing Hughes.

It was hardly a ringing defense of Wilson, but it made for good partisan cartoons. The word went out to Democrat cartoonists to depict TR as a German sympathizer; implausible as the proposition was, many such cartoons were produced. But there were some traditionally Democrat papers, like the cartoon weekly *Life*, that scored heavy hits at Wilson, frequently depicting his policy vacillations as effeminacy.

Despite the relative success of his domestic program, with a Congress behind him, and an opposition party still held together by bandages, Wilson came within a hair of being defeated for re-election. The odd duck Hughes committed a perceived slight against Governor Hiram Johnson of California, which muted the governor's enthusiasm for Hughes, and the Republican candidate lost the state by a whisker—which was just enough to give Wilson an electoral college majority. The story goes that Hughes went to bed on election night, confident of having won. The next morning, the phone rang in Hughes' residence, and one of his staff members answered, saying, "The president had a long night. He does not wish to be disturbed." The caller supposedly replied, "Well, when he wakes up, tell him he ain't president."

The Imperial German Navy continued its on-again, off-again attacks on ships it believed were delivering contraband munitions to England. Public pressure actually forced Wilson to break off relations with Germany a month before his first term ended. And a month after his second inauguration, he asked Congress "to declare that a state of war existed" between the United States and Germany. Wilson, ever the rhetorician, coined some new phrases: "the world needed to be made safe for democracy," and U.S. intervention would transform the European conflict into a "war to end all wars." Roosevelt wrote to a friend about Wilson's declaration of war, saying, "His message bears out all I have said for the past two and a half years, and condemns all he has said and done for those two and a half years."

During the hot public debates over preparedness, the Army had allowed a civilian training camp to be instituted in Plattsburgh, New York. Hewing to the tradition of a small standing army, perhaps the administration figured the Plattsburgh Training Camp would allow jingoes to blow off steam. But something happened as Colonel Roosevelt helped awaken America to the probability of war: the Plattsburgh camp and "system" grew exponentially. During 1916 and 1917, it actually became fashionable for ambitious men and young white-collar workers to train at the camp, which was kind of a National Guard operation but a little more exclusive. Bud Fisher, the cartoonist who drew *Mutt and Jeff*, was at Plattsburgh; he put his characters in uniform and signed his newspaper strips from the camp. Percy Crosby, later to draw the famous *Skippy*, was also at the camp, and mailed an army-life cartoon panel from there each day for syndication. Every week, movie houses showed newsreels with stories from Plattsburgh.

Plattsburgh's success, however, led to problems. The camp was run by General Leonard Wood, the former leader of the Rough Riders and still an associate of Theodore Roosevelt. Wood was impolitic enough to criticize Washington's lethargic armament schedule. He committed a further political sin by inviting Roosevelt to address the cheering soldiers-in-training. As a result, Wood was blackballed by the administration, despite his background as Chief of Staff of the United States Army, Military Governor of Cuba, Governor General of the Philippines, and Medal of Honor recipient. He had also created the program that eventually became the Reserve Officer Training Corps (ROTC) program. Despite widespread requests for Wood to be appointed leader of the entire U.S. contingent in France, Secretary of War Baker instead assigned Wood to train troops at Camp Funston, southwest of Manhattan, Kansas, for the duration of the war.

This insult struck many people as petty on the part of the administration. Meanwhile, TR mapped out plans to serve his country in the war effort. By the Spring of 1917, he had cre-

THE TRANSFUSION OF BLOOD

"BY GEORGE I FEEL BULLY"

When TR's services were increasingly sought during the campaign of Charles Evans Hughes (behind TR), the Republican electorate revived. But it was too little, too late. Ding Darling in *The Des Moines Register and Tribune*, 1916.

ated a list of hundreds of thousands of American men, all eager to serve in France under Colonel Roosevelt.

These men were all over draft age, so the new Selective Service system that the administration introduced to replace preparedness camps and traditional units was not threatened. Roosevelt had been able to secure from private and patriotic sources much of the funding that was needed to outfit, equip, and ship what could have been as many as four divisions. While the administration said the regular Army needed more time to reach readiness, Roosevelt's volunteers, many of whom were veterans or had trained at Plattsburgh, could have sailed sooner—at least to hold the line for the planned Allied Expeditionary Force. The Allies themselves were electrified by the news that Roosevelt, of all Americans, would lead a fresh army to assist their fight. The French leader Georges Clemenceau sent a public plea to President Wilson to allow Roosevelt's Divisions to sail for France, citing the badly needed morale boost it would provide.

Roosevelt, tired of being given the run-around by the War Department, finally requested a meeting with President Wilson himself. His request was granted. TR told the president he assumed he would not survive such a campaign at his age, but he desired to make good the war speeches of the president, and to serve his country one last time. Wilson took the matter under advisement, and later issued a short statement to the press, implying that TR was indulging in romantic fantasies. Wilson maintained that a new fighting force must meet modern conditions; Roosevelt, people were to assume, wanted to play soldier in some self-indulgent flourish.

Even against the goals of the war, America's sorry state of readiness, and the pleas of Allied military and civilian leaders, Wilson's "scientific readiness" argument might have made sense, except that military preparation progressed at a snail's pace. It was a full six

A June Wedding Announced for Chicago

The fantasy of progressive Republicans was visualized by Frank King of *The Chicago Tribune*.

months before the First Division arrived in the trenches, and it took more than twelve months after the declaration for a million U.S. servicemen to land in France. The slow pace admittedly was due in part to AEF commander "Black Jack" Pershing's insistence on rigorous training; but it was also largely the result of a woeful lack of support from the administration. Long after the declaration of war, many troops in many camps were training with wooden sticks because rifles had not been requisitioned or delivered to soldiers. Roosevelt called this scandal "Broomstick Preparedness." America had no heavy artillery, and a profound shortage of transport and warships. There were "no American airplanes fit to fly over German lines." These and many more examples abounded of what TR termed the administration's "miracle of inefficiency." Roosevelt might not have been the only American who wondered whether the pacifist-leaning president secretly hoped that the war would be over before Americans arrived, or that the threats alone of American flags would make the Central Powers capitulate.

Consigned to the home front, TR continued to write in support of the war effort. And when he thought the government was poorly managing that effort, he said so. The administration threatened to silence him and confiscate publications for which he wrote. Postmaster General Burleson was seizing magazines, threatening other periodicals, and driving several publications, like the political/cartoon monthly *The Masses*, out of business. TR dared the government to bring it on, asserting his free-speech rights. Roosevelt also appeared at bond rallies and Red Cross events and patriotic parades.

However ineffective he may have felt being excluded from the action in Europe, he was tremendously proud when his four sons were all in uniform, headed for the action. Ted and Archie had trained at Plattsburgh; Kermit, leaving his job in South America, was not able to join the AEF, so TR managed to get him assigned to British forces fighting in Mesopotamia; and young Quentin was taking flying lessons in Mineola, Long Island (at the site later named Roosevelt Field in his honor). Ethel's husband Dr. Richard Derby also served as an Army surgeon, while she served in the Ambulance Corps in France. Ted's wife Eleanor went to France to work for the Red Cross.

It was a strange time for the old Colonel. He felt like a caged lion, but did everything he could for the war effort. He wrote two more books, *Fear God and Take Your Own Part*, and *Foes of Our Own Household*. He wrote several columns every week for the *Kansas City Star*, which syndicated them at no cost to other newspapers. Meanwhile, he was surrounded at Sagamore Hill by a growing population of grandchildren, and readers may imagine how TR indulged them. Evening shadows seemed more poignant at Sagamore Hill; the Colonel was once again the idolized leader of many Americans, but right now, he cared about his boys and the war effort alone. The New York gubernatorial nomination was offered; he dismissed it, for, as he said, "My heart is with my boys."

His physical heart, however, was not doing well. Neither was almost any other portion of his body. Years of the strenuous life, compounded with a touch of yellow fever in Cuba, a serious leg wound in a carriage accident in Massachusetts, a bullet in the chest in 1912, and malaria and jungle fevers that never left him, had taken their toll. TR was unable to outrun the accumulation of ailments any longer. Not yet sixty, he looked and felt like an old man. He lost his balance from an ear infection and had to learn to walk again. He was in and out of the hospital frequently, plagued by gout and rheumatism for which doctors could provide no relief.

Despite the rigors and debilitating effects of the Brazilian rainforest exploration, TR was ready to continue his interest in worldwide nature studies. He never was able to fulfill these dreams, but he contemplated a trip to the South Sea islands; and cancelled a trip to go underwater devil-fishing in the Caribbean in order to navigate, instead, the political waters of the 1916 conventions.

Despite his ill health, political proponents told him the presidency in 1920 would be his for the asking; he vowed he would never lift a finger for it. About the same time, his doctors warned him that he might be confined to a wheelchair for the rest of his days. "All right!" he said, defiantly; "I can work that way too!" But his boys; he cared only for his boys—his sons, son-in-law, and nephews—at the moment. He laughed in bitter irony when Wilson spoke glowingly of his son-in-law who was in Paris, working for the Red

Cross. That was where his *daughter*-in-law served, TR noted sarcastically.

The Colonel read in *The New York Times* that when American troops, Ted and Archie among them, marched through Paris on the Fourth of July, crowds yelled greetings to row after row of Dough-boys, calling them "Teddies! Vive les Teddies!" a generic nickname for Americans in honor of the man they wished were there to inspire them.

Ted, Archie, and Kermit sustained serious wounds. Reports reached TR and Edith from friends in the military, and from civilian officials in France, from newspaper reports, and from wounded soldiers returning home, of how fearless—even reckless—the Roosevelt boys were, and how they were inspirations to their comrades. The Roosevelt boys received many promotions and awards. Ted was cited twice for conspicuous gallantry after being gassed in several desperate assaults, and was promoted to Lieutenant

"Roosevelt's Last Chicken," among other political policies stolen by Woodrow Wilson, in the eyes of cartoonist R. M. Brinckerhoff of *The New York Mail*, 1916.

Colonel. Kermit was awarded the British Military Cross before he was discharged in order to join the American forces in France. Archie, wounded by shrapnel, was paralyzed in one arm and sent back to the States for treatment; he was awarded the *Croix de Guerre*. Newspaper stories told of the exploits of young Lieutenant Quentin Roosevelt, engaging in dogfights with Baron von Richthofen's famed "Flying Circus." He scored a kill against one of the Red Baron's planes, and was becoming a hero in his own right.

The famous humorist Finley Peter Dunne, who had tweaked TR back during the Spanish-American War, saying that Roosevelt's book *The Rough Riders* would better have been titled *Alone in Cuba*, complimented the Colonel's sons: "The first thing you know,

History largely has forgotten that Woodrow Wilson had promised to
serve only term. Cartoonist Charles Sykes of *The Philadelphia Ledger*
depicts that platform plan from 1912 as kindling for 1916.

your four sons will put the name of Roosevelt on the map!" TR and Edith received letters
from the boys, and wrote many to them also, happy that most got through. TR imparted
some advice to Quentin, the youngest and possibly the derring-do image of his father.
Quentin was still very much the baby of the family. On his last night at Sagamore Hill—
being the last of his brothers to leave for the war—TR kissed him good-night, and Edith
went to his bedroom and tucked him in. Quentin was engaged to the heiress Flora Payne
Whitney, who was a frequent guest at Sagamore Hill; TR adjured his son to write to his
lover more often, or he should lose her—though that eventuality was hardly likely.

But a week or so after the news stories of Quentin's first aerial success, a reporter
showed up at Sagamore Hill with a heavily censored telegram *The New York Sun* had

received: "Watch Sagamore Hill for…" TR took the reporter to the veranda and shut the door. It must be Quentin—two of the others were in the hospital, and one was away from the war zone at the moment. Having no official news, Roosevelt dressed for dinner and spent as normal an evening with Edith as he could. He did not want to have her needlessly anxious.

The next morning, however, the reporter returned with the official news in his hand. Quentin had engaged two enemy planes, and was shot down behind German lines, where he was buried with full military honors. TR was quiet for a moment and then exclaimed, "But Mrs. Roosevelt! How am I going to break it to her?" Later, Quentin's parents met the reporter and delivered the state-ment he had requested. "Quentin's mother and I are very glad that he got to the front and had a chance to render some service to his country and to show the stuff that was in him before his fate befell him." The dogfight had taken place on Bastille Day.

It was hard on Colonel and Mrs. Roo-sevelt. TR told friends that Edith would carry the pain to her own grave, while she told friends that they must all share the burden Theodore would feel. A squadron of training pilots appeared in formation over Sagamore Hill, dipping

"He kept us out of war."

their wings in tribute to their fallen comrade. Condolences poured in from around the world.

TR kept his commitment to address the Republican State Convention in Saratoga two days later. With grim determination he kept to his theme: that after the war, all patriots must rededicate themselves to steering a domestic course between unrestrained capital and "the deadening formalism and inefficiency of widespread government ownership." Afterwards a friend learned that only twenty minutes before the speech, TR had received a telegram from President Wilson, confirming Quentin's death, despite lingering doubts that the reports were mistaken. TR's insistence on going through with his speech was a remarkable display of courage and self-control, the friend recalled years later.

The Roosevelts' sole consolation was their great pride in the manner of Quentin's death. Flora was at Sagamore Hill and was inconsolable. The grandchildren would innocently call out Quentin's name when they heard an airplane overhead. TR was seen in the stables, stroking Quentin's favorite horse and repeating his son's childhood nicknames. That Sunday the Roosevelts went to church and partook of Communion; it was one year, exactly, since Quentin's last Sunday in the States, and he had received the Lord's Supper at the very same rail.

It was natural that TR would have speculated on his sons' fervor to serve as a function of his own advocacies. He would have it no other way. His standards were unshakable, and so were his sons'. And yet, Theodore knew that if the war lasted long enough, none of them might return.

In a newspaper column he wrote after Quentin died—one that formed the centerpiece of his last book, *The Great Adventure*—TR wrote: "Only those are fit to live who do not fear to die; and none are fit to die who have shrunk from the joy of life and the duty of life. Both life and death are parts of the same Great Adventure."

Theodore Roosevelt was fighting through the last adventure of his many great adventures. Friends said, however, that after Quentin's death the light was gone from him. The World War ended on November 11, 1918. The U.S. mid-term elections had occurred a bare month earlier, and, unbelievably, Woodrow Wilson pleaded with voters to give him a strong Democrat Congress. He cast aside bipartisanship and ignored the fact that Congressional Republicans supported the war more solidly than members of his own party. It was to no avail: the public resoundingly repudiated the Democrats. Even Wilson's personal efforts, like recruiting the pacifist Henry Ford to run for the Senate, failed. Meanwhile, Wilson made plans to attend negotiations in Paris. Roosevelt noted that most world leaders would feel uneasy about representing their countries alone at peace talks, but Wilson kept his own counsel as he prepared for his trip. Wilson's plans for the League of Nations, although reminiscent of TR's suggestions in his Nobel Prize speech, struck many Americans—including many Democrat newspapers and magazines, and their cartoonists—as impractical and a surrender of U.S. sovereignty.

Edwin Marcus's cartoon in *The New York Times*: "This is the only trophy I need for my collection!"

At Sagamore Hill, the Colonel's physical ailments kept a sad pace with his continuing emotional distress. The whole country talked about Roosevelt as the next president, a common supposition. Even William Barnes, who had attempted to ruin TR's career with a libel suit four years previous, when asked if he thought Roosevelt would be nominated by acclamation, said, "Acclamation, hell! We'll nominate him by assault!" TR was in and out of the hospital in late 1918, returning to Sagamore Hill the day before Christmas. He continued his writing. His speeches were mostly written to be read by others, at least until his health might return.

With the war over, TR's thematic preoccupation was "Americanism," a name he gave to his movement, which was basically the old spirit behind reforms with a new focus. It was dedicated to instilling a virile righteousness at home and abroad, with the subtext of allegiance to the language, borders, and culture, that war and Bolshevism had placed in jeopardy. Since 1917 communism had been spreading, and TR recognized the threat early on, including in subversive corners of America. Immigration was running rampant, with many criminals and radicals coming into the country unscreened. And many unions were radicalized overnight, with strikes hitting major industries in the wake of the war. Americanism would be the battle cry for the future.

TR and Edith were alone at Sagamore Hill during the first week of the new year. At sunset one day he looked up and said to Edith, *apropos* of nothing, "I wonder if you will

A RUMOR HAS REACHED EUROPE

ever know how I love Sagamore Hill." When he went to sleep that night, he asked his valet, James Amos, "James, please put out the light." In the middle of the night, TR's breathing became labored. Doctors were called, but it was too late. Theodore Roosevelt was declared dead, of a blood clot, on the morning of January 6, 1919.

Archie, the only son stateside due to his injuries, cabled his siblings: "The old lion is dead."

On hearing the news, Vice President Thomas R. Marshall commented: "Death had to take him sleeping. For if Roosevelt had been awake, there would have been a fight"— probably the most accurate assessment of TR by a member of the Wilson administration.

The last speech he wrote, for delivery to the American Defense Society's mass rally in New York City on what turned out to be the day before his death, encapsulated nicely the strong views he held without wavering throughout his life. He wrote:

> *We should insist that if the immigrant who comes here does in good faith become an American and assimilates himself to us he shall be treated on an exact equality with every one else, for it is an outrage to discriminate against any such man because of creed or birth-place or origin. But this is predicated upon the man's becoming in very fact an American and nothing but an American. If he tries to keep segregated with men of his own origin and separated from the rest of America, then he isn't doing his part as an American.*

> *There can be no divided allegiance here.... We have room for but one language here, and that is the English language, for we intend to see that the crucible turns our people out as Americans, of American nationality, and not as dwellers in a polyglot boarding-house; and we have room for but one soul loyalty, and that is loyalty to the American people.*

The speech could have been written during his very days of public life, and the words were likely inculcated by his father as he grew up. What this organic unity of conviction suggests is not that Theodore Roosevelt was stuck on one small set of beliefs, nor that he was a seer, but that he grasped the full significance of the principles our country was founded on. Rather, it reminds us that biblical truths and the wisdom of the founders, combined with integrity, honor, and courage, are not just the best way for a Republic to survive, but the only way for a Republic, and a free people, to thrive.

In 1915, when William Morris drew this cover cartoon, Roosevelt made his statement that a possible presidential candidacy would be a mistake unless the nation was in a heroic mood. He was not saying that he was a hero, but that (in case anyone was in doubt) he would not be one more politician to pander to the nation's current desire for soft answers and avoidance of hard facts. Of course, opponents characterized this attitude as mere megalomania.

# UNIFICATION OF THE GOP AND THE BULL MOOSE PARTY

If It Weren't for Teddy We wouldn't Have a Bit of Fun

TR warned the political establishment that if they were interested in him as a candidate, the public would have to be in a "somewhat heroic mood." He spoke his mind. He relished the subject of "hyphenated Americans" when speaking to immigrant groups, and was savage in his attacks on Wilson. Softening his message so as not to offend "independents" was not his style. As it turned out, neither public nor political leaders were in a heroic mood in the lead-up to the 1916 campaign. In this Billy Ireland cartoon, Roosevelt is shown in contrast to his putative rivals for the nomination. From *The Columbus Dispatch*.

But He can't Make It Drink

Two cartoons from the 1916 presidential campaign that, in tandem, highlight the special facility of cartoons to make statements. Both use the cartoonist's greatest tool, the icon.

*LEFT*: The syndicated cartoon by J. Campbell Cory shows TR, former Republican, having thoroughly cowered the GOP. Roosevelt's return to the party—in a dominant role—was more evident every week during the 1916 campaign. Campaign crowds and newspaper editorials turned toward his view of Republican politics and, eventually, national policy. The whited fossil of the Progressive Party Bull Moose is a sign that TR was serious about making the GOP once again a vehicle of his policies.

*RIGHT*: In contrast, the Old Guard of the Republican establishment is pictured by Clubb of the Rochester (NY) *Herald* attempting to perform a similar "unity drive" from their side. But the Bull Moose adherents are reluctant to taste of candidate Charles Evans Hughes. Justice Hughes was lukewarm on many issues dear to Progressives and, in fact, to TR, who held his nose in order to work for the defeat of Woodrow Wilson.

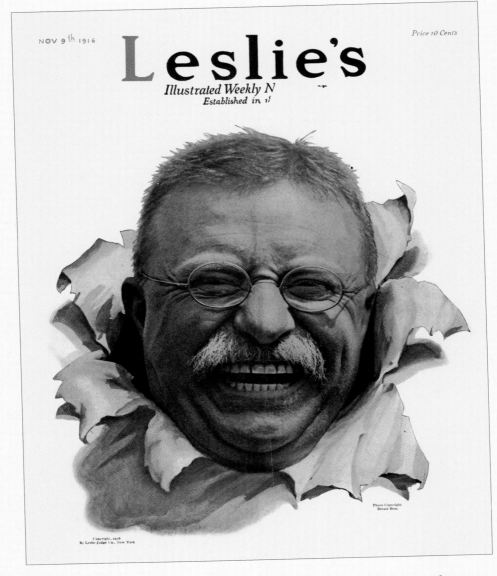

NOV 9th 1916

Price 10 Cents

# Leslie's
*Illustrated Weekly N*
Established in 1̸

Copyright, 1916
By Leslie-Judge Co., New York

Photo Copyright
Brown Bros.

Except for the whiter moustache and mileage-lines, this magazine cover, a photo/cartoon, could have appeared at any time in TR's crowded career. He continually burst on the scene…on many scenes, many stages, many platforms. The date of this *Leslie's Weekly* cover is significant: it appeared two days after the presidential election. And it went to press before the election (a close one, as it turned out) was decided. The news weekly was making the comment that, even though TR was not a candidate; despite whether Wilson or Hughes won; and no matter what issues were to come and go, Theodore Roosevelt was the preeminent figure on the national scene. And this, only a year or two removed from the lowest approvals he ever received from the American people…and four years away from the next presidential election.

# WAR IN EUROPE

A strain of the Progressive movement, mostly midwesterners, were not red-hot to intervene in the European conflict. Two who did dissent, even after war was declared, were Minnesota Representative Charles Lindbergh Sr. (whose pellucid views on the Money Trust are instructive yet today), and Wisconsin Senator Robert M. LaFollette. John T. McCutcheon, cartoonist of *The Chicago Tribune*, was influential with fellow cartoonists and a vast readership. His immortal caution, "Gold and Green Are the Fields of Peace," has been reprinted since the early twentieth century by the *Tribune*, also as prints and posters. McCutcheon himself was lukewarm on intervention in the early months of the European conflict.

### THE COLORS

Gold and green are the fields in peace

Red are the fields in war

Black are the fields when the cannons cease

And white forevermore

# THE PREPAREDNESS DEBATE: BEFORE AND AFTER AMERICA JOINS THE WAR

Wilson did Not Keep These Out of War

Cartoons like this simple but powerful drawing by Ole May recalled Theodore Roosevelt's dictum, "If I must choose between righteousness and peace, I choose righteousness." *Cleveland Leader*, 1916.

Ted Nelson, cartoonist of *The St. Paul Pioneer Press*, echoes the theme. Uncle Sam asks, "If this be peace, what d'ye call war?"

Merely an Optical Illusion, Uncle

Aunt Polly Has a Word

Tender-hearted Aunt Polly

Somebody Ought to Do Something

# UNCLE SAM: GAINING AFFLUENCE, LOSING INFLUENCE

Cartoonist Frank King of *The Chicago Tribune* hid devastating critiques behind his pleasant drawing style and good humor. In 1915, when the *Trib*'s chief political cartoonist was in Europe as a war correspondent, King drew daily cartoons that cut through to the nub of many challenges facing America: the country's material prosperity and moral laxity. In these views, perhaps better than any other cartoonist, he illustrated Theodore Roosevelt's disappointment with public opinion at the time.

King's vehicle was to re-create an Uncle Sam, to fit the reality of the nation's situation: fat, lazy, selfish, and vulnerable. This was a far cry from the "heroic mood" that TR sought in the public. King's series of cartoons was brilliant. For months they attracted widespread attention across America. The cartoonist might have gone on to greater fame as a political cartoonist, except that he created a comic strip that achieved immortality of its own, the comics' version of the Great American Novel—*Gasoline Alley*.

Political figures are seldom depicted on an equal plane with Uncle Sam; TR was an exception. This cartoon by Robert Carter can be compared to Homer Davenport's cartoon from the 1904 campaign (which became a campaign document of the GOP), with Uncle Sam resting his hand on Roosevelt's shoulder, saying, "He's good enough for me!" Here, in Robert Carter's cartoon for Frank Mumsey's *New York Sun,* the caption about TR is, "He's good enough for all."

"This, boys, is the largest weakfish ever kept alive in captivity."

"THEODORE, IF YOU DON'T STOP TAUNTING ME ABOUT UNPREPAREDNESS I'LL JUST SLAP YOU ON THE WRIST"

"IF THESE NAUGHTY MEN KEEP SINKING MY SHIPS AND BLOWING UP BUILDINGS I DECLARE I'LL JUST GO AND WRITE THEM ANOTHER LETTER. SO THERE, NOW!"

The Democrat cartoon weekly *Life* was exasperated with many of Wilson's policies, particularly his tepid response to the challenges of the Great War and affronts to American sovereignty committed by Germany and England both. The publication found itself allied with Theodore Roosevelt in spite of itself, as in the days of Insurgency and reform.

*ABOVE*: *Life*'s chief political cartoonist, William H. Walker, increasingly depicted Wilson and even Uncle Sam as effeminate—unable to muster a strong response to foreign attacks (including cross-border incursions of Mexican bandits).

In the cartoon on the opposite page, TR is shown telling the army (as he did at the Plattsburgh training Camp) and navy that the administration was a virtual "weakfish." These cartoons are from 1915 and 1916.

Other stars among *Life*'s cartoonists, most notably Harry Grant Dart, attacked the Wilson administration relentlessly, including during the largely inadequate preparation and early phases of the U.S. war effort, and into the League of Nations debate, which *Life* largely opposed.

# AMERICA IN THE WAR

Jay Norwood "Ding" Darling of *The Des Moines Register and Tribune* succinctly depicted TR's frustrated efforts to fight in World War I. Drawing the Wilson administration as a walking delegate, he shows the Army not quite prepared, and Allies drowning. The caption: "Hold up, here! You are not a member of the Life-Savers Union!" From 1917.

IT WOULD BE JUST HIS LUCK!

It was widely believed that President Wilson's prime motivation in declining TR's offer to lead troops in France was the fantasy incident pictured in this cartoon—Colonel Theodore Roosevelt personally achieving some smashing, heroic, historic breakthrough in the battlefields of the Great War.

Hundreds of thousands of men over the draft age had volunteered to go to France while the regular army trained, and leaders of the Allied military and governments pleaded for TR to lead the American invasion. Wilson would not have it. A cartoon by John Conacher in *Life*, 1917.

This cartoon, "Chorus of Allies," from the German magazine *Kladderadatsch*, illustrates the contrast between stated goals and reality in the war, and foreshadows the attitudes of America, Britain, and France in the next World War.

Pictured are the three Allies, David Lloyd George of England, Woodrow Wilson, and Raymond Poincaré of France. The caption reads: "We will never negotiate with an autocratic government—never!"

Voice of Czar Nicholas (pictured behind bars), "And if I remember rightly, they once called me 'Brother.'"

James Montgomery Flagg, the cartoonist who painted the famous "Uncle Sam Wants You" poster that is still used in U.S. military recruiting, designed a similar image, with Uncle Sam pointing a gun instead of his finger, directing his threat to the Kaiser. Recently the cartoon has been repurposed by the Tea Party as a poster caricaturizing Big Government and commemorating Tax Day. The iconic "Uncle Sam Wants You" image was also originally a cartoon cover for *Leslie's Weekly*.

### The Patriot's Response
"Had I a dozen sons, each in my love alike and none less dear than thine and my good Marcius, I had rather eleven die nobly for their country than one voluptuously surfeit out of action."—CORIOLANUS

On July 14, 1918, Lieutenant Quentin Roosevelt was shot down and killed behind enemy lines, near the village of Chamery. A captured American serviceman, Captain James E. Gee of the 110th Infantry, happened to witness the Germans' funeral, and later wrote:

*In a hollow square about the open grave were assembled approximately one thousand German soldiers, standing stiffly in regular lines. They were dressed in field gray uniforms, wore steel helmets, and carried rifles. Near the grave was a smashed plane, and beside it was a small group of officers, one of whom was speaking to the men.*

*I did not pass close enough to hear what he was saying; we were prisoners and did not have the privilege of lingering, even for such an occasion as this. At the time I did not know who was being buried, but the guards informed me later. The funeral certainly was elaborate. I was told afterward by Germans that they paid Lieut. Roosevelt such honor not only because he was a gallant aviator, who died fighting bravely against odds, but because he was the son of Colonel Roosevelt whom they esteemed as one of the greatest Americans.*

Cartoon by Boardman Robinson, *The North American Review's War Weekly*, 1918.

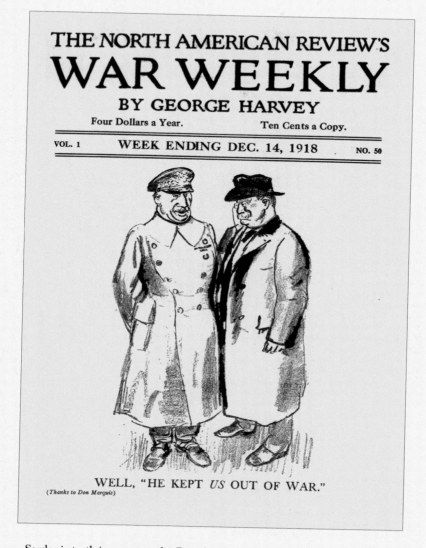

# THE NORTH AMERICAN REVIEW'S
# WAR WEEKLY
## BY GEORGE HARVEY

Four Dollars a Year.                    Ten Cents a Copy.

VOL. 1          WEEK ENDING DEC. 14, 1918          NO. 50

WELL, "HE KEPT *US* OUT OF WAR."

*(Thanks to Don Marquis)*

Sardonic truth in a cartoon by Boardman Robinson, a month after the armistice. Wilson's campaign slogan was turned around. Leonard Wood and Theodore Roosevelt, two Americans most eager to serve, and whose presence on the battlefields was implored by Allied military and political leaders—and by an army of common soldiers—were coldly denied. In their minds, and those of many Americans, spiteful politics was behind it.

# POST-ROOSEVELT AMERICA

A post-war world, a raft of new issues, and life without TR.
Cartoonists depicted the American scene as the 1920s dawned.

"O for the touch of a vanished hand
And the sound of a voice that is still!"

TR gone from national life: Cartoon by William Morris for the
George Matthew Adams Syndication Service.

**IMMIGRATION:** Immediately after World War I, America experienced inflation, a depression, a wave of HCL (High Cost of Living), unemployment due to the return of millions soldiers to the workforce, national Prohibition, and labor unrest. Strikes hit many industries, and some magazines whad to suspend publication or—like *Life*—forsake color because of striking printers.

At the nub of labor troubles was a rising tide of radicalism. Socialists and Communists were encouraged by the successful Bolshevik revolution in Russia, and infiltrated many segments of American society. At the nub of labor problems was an increase in immigration, as many of the newcomers were radicals and criminals from Eastern Europe.

A nativist response spread through the United States, captured in sentiments like "America for Americans" and Theodore Roosevelt's jeremiads against "hyphenated Americanism."

The anti-immigrant sentiment cut across the culture: Republicans and Democrats (like Billy Ireland, cartoonist of this drawing from the *Columbus Dispatch*, 1921), and former radicals, now conservatives, like newspaper publisher William Randolph Hearst.

"Officer, Call a Real Policeman!"

**LEAGUE OF NATIONS:** Edwin Marcus drew a political cartoon in 1919 about the Paris Peace Conference, that could apply to the League of Nations a few years later, or the United Nations many years in the future. This cartoon was drawn for *The New York Times,* where Marcus was staff cartoonist.

**DIPLOMACY:** *Life*'s William H. Walker made an uncanny prediction in 1918 with this drawing. It was only superficial prescience, however; the "job" done by the Treaty of Versailles actually sowed the seeds of a resurgent Germany. A negotiated peace, as Germany had been seeking, might not have created chaos, economic misery, and resentment. Since Germany's borders were never crossed, and yet she surrendered, this was a humiliating anomaly many Germans "1935 or thereabouts" could not reconcile themselves to.

1935 OR THEREABOUTS
Another visit unless the job is finished now.

On the German side, a 1915 *Kladderadatsch* cartoon predicted, "Some day the sun will rise above the stars." The cartoon was an uncanny prediction of Pearl Harbor.

Good bye!

The death of TR, allegorized by Billy Ireland of the *The Columbus Dispatch*.

**AFTERWORD**

"IT IS TRUE OF THE NATION,
AS OF THE INDIVIDUAL, THAT THE
GREATEST DOER MUST ALSO BE
A GREAT DREAMER."

~THEODORE ROOSEVELT

# AFTERWORD

Theodore Roosevelt was what we today call a "Renaissance Man." He certainly was more so than any president, including Jefferson, and is perhaps unique among all Americans in our history. Yet his uniqueness can elude us. For Lincoln, highly revered by TR for his very nature, not just his attainments, and for TR's fifth cousin Franklin D. Roosevelt, the presidency was the pinnacle of their careers. For Theodore Roosevelt, however, as great a president as he was (and he finally has been ensconced as a "great" by general consensus and numerous polls of historians), the presidency was only one aspect of his life, one detail of his biography.

Another unique aspect of TR eludes us. Many of history's "Renaissance" figures—those of multiple achievements and broad visions—tend to be defined by their field, or several fields, of specialty. But Theodore Roosevelt would have agreed with Edwin Marcus's cartoon. He was an American first, an American last, proudest to be called "American." We can think of history's other polymaths who are known by their fields of

expertise but not, primarily, their citizenship. Indeed we may find some exceptions in history, but none would be more assertive about identifying with his or her nation than Theodore Roosevelt was. To him, "American" was the noblest description he could claim.

"American" was not a cheap title to TR, nor a red-white-and-blue chip on his shoulder. Americanism was a work in progress, not to be relied upon for automatic glory. Being an American meant something special; and like anything special, it was worth fighting for. He believed it needed to be defended, periodically won, and, inevitably, reformed. Elihu Root, who variously was an ally and opponent of TR, said,

> *Review the roster of the few great men of history, our own history, the history of the world; and when you have finished the review, you will find that Theodore Roosevelt was the greatest teacher of the essentials of popular self-government the world has ever known. . . . The future of our country will depend upon having men, real men of sincerity and truth, of unshakable conviction, of power, of personality, with the spirit of Justice and the fighting spirit through all the generations; and the mightiest service that can be seen today to accomplish that for our country is to make it impossible that Theodore Roosevelt, his teaching and his personality shall be forgotten. Oh, that we might have him with us now!*

We have seen in this book how TR, drawing upon values inculcated by his father, believed that he knew what was right for America, and proceeded to act. This was not paternalism, it was conviction. Some opponents, including a few cartoonists, ascribed it to egoism. Liberals occasionally regret that TR seemed to act unilaterally in foreign affairs. Conservatives sometimes regret that the era of the strong chief executive commenced with him. But Roosevelt's motivation was the desire for a better America, a stronger America, a fairer America, where every person could rise, or fall, according to high standards of merit, struggle, and independence.

To Roosevelt the sincere patriot, these were not clichés…and they surely were not givens. He knew that despite the glorious foundations of the republic, America's future could be that of a dystopia: utopia was neither inevitable, nor, if we were to come close to it, permanent. With American citizenship as in life itself, the *process* honors the goal. Roosevelt was not a latter-day Cato, calling out that some Carthage must be destroyed; rather, he urged that a new America must be built up. *Reform*, the watchword of Roosevelt's career, was not the slogan of a public scold, but an encouragement to improve things, to always seek a better life for the next generation.

As TR himself expressed it,

A crayon sketch of the iconic Teddy Bear by the cartoonist who created him, Clifford K. Berryman. Reproduced from the original artwork.

*It is not the critic who counts: not the man who points out how the strong man stumbles or where the doer of deeds could have done better. The credit belongs to the man who is actually in the arena, whose face is marred by dust and sweat and blood, who strives valiantly, who errs and comes up short again and again, because there is no effort without error or shortcoming, but who knows the great enthusiasms, the great devotions, who spends himself for a worthy cause; who, at the best, knows, in the end, the triumph of high achievement, and who, at the worst, if he fails, at least he fails while daring greatly, so that his place shall never be with those cold and timid souls who knew neither victory nor defeat.*

"There was one cartoon made while I was President, in which I appeared incidentally, that was always a great favorite of mine. It pictured an old fellow with chin whiskers, a farmer, in his shirt-sleeves, with his boots off, sitting before the fire, reading the President's Message. On his feet were stockings of the kind I have seen hung up by the dozen in Joe Ferris's store at Medora, in the days when I used to come in to town and sleep in one of the rooms over the store. The title of the picture was "His Favorite Author." This was the old fellow whom I always used to keep in my mind. He had probably been in the Civil War in his youth; he had worked hard ever since he left the army; he had been a good husband and father; he had brought up his boys and girls to work; he did not wish to do injustice to any one else, but he wanted justice done to himself and to others like him; and I was bound to secure that justice for him if it lay in my power to do so." Cartoon by Everett E. Lowry, *The Chicago Chronicle.*

TR inspired a generation. His inspiration extended to other lands, virtually to anyone who heard about him. He inspires people yet today, in ways that other leaders have not and cannot. He taught the essentials of popular self-government, as Root said, but others have also done so. A democratic republic, as America was designed to be, is simply not a perpetual-motion machine. Even during his lifetime, TR found himself temporarily dismissed by the nation he usually inspired.

The United States needs a Theodore Roosevelt to remind it periodically of its credo, its goals, and its potential. It needs not the visionary babble of cheery politicians, but the stern encouragement and, if needed, chastisement of visionary leaders. If such high ideals will not arise every generation from the masses, thank God that, occasionally, unique individuals arise to rekindle those ideals in our souls. However, waiting for civic prophets, if not political saviors, is a risky routine. If the American public fails to remember the words of a Theodore Roosevelt and to return to the foundational truths he reaffirmed, the Republic is endangered. TR, like Washington and Lincoln before him, set the bar high for American citizens—but not too high.

A hundred years after the Most Interesting American bounded joyously across his beloved landscape, it is unclear whether Americans will show ourselves worthy of his confidence—confidence shared by our wise Founders, and imparted by God Almighty whose biblical frameworks and whose grace inspired them. It is up to us. Theodore Roosevelt did all he could do—we see it in these pages, observed in myriad ways by observers who were unique themselves. Seeing his life as his contemporaries saw it, we can understand it better and thus strive to live up to his high, American ideals.

Without realizing that it might be his own "I Have a Dream" speech, TR delivered words in early 1912 about the sacrificial fight he took up in the Progressive campaign. This speech was widely quoted six months later, when he was shot in the chest and demanded to be taken to the auditorium anyway, to deliver a speech that night. But we

The great "Ding" Darling, a friend of Roosevelt who was also a hunter and conservationist, had a short deadline when he heard the news of TR's death. He quickly sketched a drawing of a ghostly rider, borrowing from the cartoon he had done two years earlier when Buffalo Bill Cody died. He intended to draw a more substantial cartoon for later editions of *The Des Moines Register and Tribune*, but he never had to. "The Long, Long Trail" became one the most famous American editorial cartoons in history. Ding's cartoon graced walls of innumerable schoolrooms and homes. He made a limited-edition etching (above) in response to many requests.

can read those words again as his valedictory; his message to American posterity; and his advice for every citizen amongst us:

> *In order to succeed we need leaders of inspired idealism, leaders to whom are granted great visions, who dream greatly and strive to make their dreams come true; who can kindle the people with the fire from their own burning souls. The leader for the time being, whoever he may be, is but an instrument, to be used until broken and then to be cast aside; and if he is worth his salt he will care no more when he is broken than a soldier cares when he is sent where his life is forfeit in order that the victory may be won. In the long fight for righteousness, the watchword for all of us is spend and be spent. It is of little matter whether any one man fails or succeeds, but the cause shall not fail, for it is the cause of mankind.*

# ACKNOWLEDGMENTS

I have been blessed during my life with a wide assortments of interests. Many were conceived early, and some have become virtual obsessions—happily manifested in collecting; research-for-the-sake-of-research; outreaches to compatriots as I would locate them; interviews with principals when possible (sometimes scarcely possible at all). For this aspect of my personality I acknowledge with thanks, as I am glad I did uncountable times while he was alive, my father, who was himself an omnivorous cognoscente: collector, polymath, role model. I believe and recognize that I have been able to bequeath a joyful, ferocious curiosity about life to my own children Heather, Theodore, and Emily. Beyond spiritual values, I can imagine nothing of which a father can be prouder.

Two of my early interests coincided in their historical time and my avidity: cartoons and Theodore Roosevelt. With the cartoon arts, my interests ranged from collecting cartoons from the Civil War to World War I, principally; although my vision has spread earlier and later. Comic strips, too, from their prototypes, first incarnations, and golden years. When my interest advanced to illustration and other popular arts, I eventually was able to assemble virtually complete runs of the major New York newspapers from these years; of the popular news weeklies and important monthly magazines of the day; of the political and humor magazines whose work you see in these pages, *Puck, Judge, Life*, and others; and a great number of pamphlets, ads, brochures, posters, and campaign memorabilia. Professionally, I worked for a time as a political cartoonist (including for newspapers published by William Loeb, son of TR's presidential secretary).

My interest in Colonel Roosevelt began I know not when or where, but it was early. Living around New York City, and thanks once again to parents who indulged and encouraged my interests, I became an habitué of TR's birthplace museum, Sagamore Hill, the American Museum of Natural History, and other shrines. Joining my father on weekly forays to Manhattan's Book Store Row area (now vanished), I thereby began my collection of Roosevelt books and publications about the era.

…all of which, I might say, brings us to this book. Toward the end, rather now than at the beginning, of a career that combined these interests on behalf of books, articles, lectures, and exhibitions, I have published many compilations of vintage cartoons and written many histories and biographies. My interests have never waned (readers will notice that I named my only son after Theodore Roosevelt), but the time had to be just right, and the publisher Regnery History has provided the catalyst.

At the top of my list of gratefully acknowledged people are two without whom this book could have been produced as you hold it. More than fifteen years ago, when I was president of the National Foundation of Caricature and Cartoon Art in Washington, D.C., I briefly met John Olsen at a reception. He was filed thereafter in the back of my mind as an expert, and collector, in the field of political memorabilia, specifically get-out-the-vote campaigns. And I remembered that he was dedicated to TR and cartoons also. So when I located him in Iowa, and found him more interested than ever in his fields of interest, I was grateful that he signed on as Assistant Editor of this book. The only historians who do not admit to having at least one indispensible assistant, researcher, facts-checker, pulse-taker, sounding-board, devil's advocate, "reader," and matchmaker for other sources and archives…are not telling the truth, and not to be trusted as a historians. I am grateful that John has been all those things, and more—not for my sake, but for TR's, and for your sake as readers.

His counterpart on the art side is Jon Barli, my partner in Rosebud Archives. Jon has the historian's discipline, the critic's eye, and a mad man's dedication to quality. As a craftsman he is indefatigable. He almost channels the great cartoonists in this book, so devoted is he to achieving facsimiles of vintage cartoons—often, as you see, preserving occasional ragged borders and tanned stock, the better to give readers a sense of these cartoons as artifacts. His attention to detail, quality, and integrity underlies every cartoon in this book, which might otherwise look like a grimy scrapbook.

I am grateful for the "readers" along the way, Roosevelt enthusiasts, editors, or cartoon historians—or in some cases all three. Dr. Maury Foreman read every line and between every line; as always, he challenged me when I needed challenging. Jo Lauter, writing friend and prayer partner, likewise reviewed the manuscript with her husband Jim, honoring me (and the man whose October 27 birthday she shares) with diligence. Richard Samuel West, historian of cartoons and politics, reviewed the manuscript and offered valuable suggestions. Sharon Kilzer, Project Director of the Theodore Roosevelt Center at Dickinson (ND) State University, reviewed Chapter Four (about TR's Bad Lands period) and offered vital suggestions about facts and interpretations. I am constrained to note that she emphasizes that TR could apply the term "cowboy" to himself, but often drew the distinction that he was a rancher, and his men were cowboys whose duties he often shared. Gary Gervitz, who maintains the splendid website *The Almanac of Theodore Roosevelt*, read the first chapters and likewise offered helpful suggestions.

In the course of writing a book like this, and compiling the illustrations, there have been others through the years whom I must acknowledge. At Regnery History—for whose parent imprint I have had lifelong admiration and from whose writers I have received instruction in my ways through the years—my editor Mary Beth Baker and Art Director Amanda Larsen have been creative, supportive, and patient. Harry Crocker, who first evinced interest in this project, is obviously a wise man, and has lent support to *BULLY!* in many ways. This book would have been shorter, smaller, and paler in the hands of other publishers; Harry has had the vision. And Alex Novak, not least of all, has overseen this book in his first wave of Regnery History as a new imprint, and has been responsive and supportive. This has been a team effort.

My literary representative, Greg Johnson of WordServe Literary Agency, has believed, and encouraged, and in fact badgered with magnificent persistence. A fan of American history, Greg now has a new brother, TR, in his band of heroes. I am grateful to him beyond measure. Other people have supported with facts, advice, and prayers, equally welcomed by this writer, some of them through the years: Heather and Pat Shaw; Theodore Christian Marschall; Emily and Norman McCorkell; Betty and Barbara Marschall; Bill Loeb; Diane Obbema; Norm and Penny Carlevato; Marlene Bagnull; Becky Spencer; Hope Flinchbaugh; Tom Heintjes; Ed Norton of Oyster Bay; Jeff Dunn; Bill Sharpless; Mark Rhodes; Veronica Ronyets; Bob Paulson; William Newman; Ed van Kloberg; Alan Neigher; Lynne McTaggart. My mentors at the American University, where I received my degree in American History, were Dr. Albro Martin and Dr. Charles McLaughlin. Their commitment to excellence and their fierce integrity matched the unselfish personal interest they displayed toward an aspiring protégé. My gratitude is reflected—I trust—on every one of these pages.

For the many suggestions I have received and corrections I have made, I again offer thanks; but any mistakes of fact, and all opinions, are my own.

When I was young, there was a nitwit notion abroad in the land that "Teddy" Roosevelt was a buffoon who played cowboy and soldier, imposed his ego on other people in any given environment, and was, generally, a Bull Moose in a china shop. In part he had been eclipsed by cousin Franklin in an America that might have elected FDR to seventeen more terms if health and calendar had not intervened; and by popular-culture caricatures like "Crazy Cousin Teddy" who buried bodies in the basement he believed to be the Panama Canal (in the Frank Capra/ Cary Grant movie *Arsenic and Old Lace*). A Pulitzer-Prize biography of the 1930s carped and was back-handed in its treatment of TR. The final nail in the coffin lid that would not stay shut was the sudden anti-Americanism that engulfed America, including campuses like my own, in the 1960s. TR fought in a war, and successfully; he used guns and shot animals; he believed in expansion and manifest destiny; he was a patriot who advanced "Americanism" and waved the flag; he elbowed America around the Caribbean. Hence, he became a virtual devil in much of academia, especially contrasted to Woodrow Wilson, who was painted as a dreamy internationalist and idealist who, if he had not been thwarted by Neanderthals at home and abroad, would have delivered heaven on earth.

Admiration for Theodore Roosevelt actually took some effort, sometimes bravery, in those days. By and by, however, people remembered that TR was one of the four presidents on Mount Rushmore. Liberals began to realize that expanded powers of the presidency, occasionally a good thing, largely commenced with TR. Conservatives remembered that Roosevelt was a thoroughgoing patriot—and that his muscular foreign policy actually advanced American interests. Liberals and conservatives both, in times of environmental concerns, learned that TR's nurture of the wild spaces, of flora and fauna, was an unimaginable blessing to the nation. The debates surrounding the Vietnam War and the Panama Canal Treaty started to remind people of foreign policies not built on bluff and weakness; people grew nostalgic for a president like Theodore Roosevelt. The respect of the historical community, begun around the time of Roosevelt's centennial, increased as biographers like Carleton Putnam, David McCullough, and Edmund Morris—no disparagement is meant to others I cannot start listing—produced first-rate works about a first-rate figure. Ronald Reagan called TR his favorite president. So did Bill

Clinton. So did George W. Bush. Eventually, those "historians' polls" conducted by Siena College and others, where Theodore Roosevelt once placed barely in the top third…now see him in the Top Five; recently, Number Two, ahead of Lincoln and Washington. (Historians gave him top honors in areas of imagination, integrity, intelligence, luck, background, and being willing to take risks, in the latest Siena poll.) TR is the subject of more biographical treatments than any American other than Lincoln.

Welcome home, Colonel Roosevelt. In fact it might be America that has returned–to a place where TR's standards and inspirations are considered worthy of study. Whether they are matters of curiosity or conviction remains to be seen. I have been the recipient of grand, if passive, assistance in order to do this book: cartoonists I have admired; family members (Princess Alice) and friends (Bill Loeb) who could tell me about the man TR; historians whose standards I emulate and biographers who have written splendid accounts of TR. Recent biographers have been a bumper crop of admirable historians, but I must list the inspirations of my formative years: Butterfield, Lorant, Hagedorn, Wagenknecht, and Putnam.

I have listed friends and assistants and inspirations. Yet there is one acknowledgment whose presence in this part of a biography would seem to be redundant, and, at least, self-evident; yet biographers seldom speak the obvious. To Theodore Roosevelt himself I acknowledge an impact on my life that transcends another assignment to write another book. TR has affected my life and attitudes. He is a guide whose directions still seem clear to me. In my larger political philosophy and my more personal, family-circle civic discussions, he is a model. WWTRD? is a question that I pray more and more Americans will be asking as we pull away from the American Century. Yes, I can thank him in this unorthodox manner, but it is not only his impact on me that I acknowledge here. May this book provide for new readers what earlier works did for me—a window that opens to a greater knowledge of the Most Interesting American.

# BIBLIOGRAPHY

## BOOKS ABOUT THEODORE ROOSEVELT

Aadland, Dan. *In Trace of TR: A Montana Hunter's Journey.* Lincoln: University of Nebraska Press. 2001.

Abbott, Lawrence F. *Impressions of Theodore Roosevelt.* Garden City, NY: Doubleday, Page & Company, 1919.

Adams, Henry. *The Education of Henry Adams.* Boston: Massachusetts Historical Society, 1918.

Amos, James E. *Theodore Roosevelt, a Hero to His Valet.* New York: The John Day Company, 1927.

Anderson, Robert Gordon. *Leader of Men.* G P Putnam's Sons, 1920.

Andrews, Mary Raymond Shipman. *His Soul Goes Marching On.* New York: Charles Scribner's Sons, 1922.

(anonymous) *Cartoons of the War of 1898 with Spain, From Leading Foreign and American Papers.* Chicago: Belford, Middlebrook & Co., 1898

(anonymous) *The Chicago Record's War Stories, by Staff Correspondents.* Chicago: Chicago Record, 1898.

Beale, Howard K. *Theodore Roosevelt and the Rise of America to World Power.* Baltimore, MD.: Johns Hopkins Press, 1956.

Beer, Thomas. *The Mauve Decade.* New York: Alfred A Knopf, 1926.

Beisner, Robert L. *Twelve Against Empire.* New York: McGraw-Hill, 1968.

Berman, Jay Stuart. *Police Administration and Progressive Reform: Theodore Roosevelt as Police Commissioner of New York*. Westport, CT.: Greenwood, 1987.

Bishop, Joseph Bucklin. *Charles Joseph Bonaparte, His Life and Public Services*. New York: Charles Scribner's Sons, 1922.

Blanchard, Newton C., Chairman, Committee of Governors, et al. *Proceedings of a Conference of Governors*. (Conservation Conference). Washington, D.C.: Government Printing Office, 1909.

Blum, John Morton. *The Republican Roosevelt*. Cambridge: Harvard University Press, 1954.

Bowers, Claude. *Beveridge and the Progressive Era*. Boston: Houghton Mifflin, 1932.

Brands, H. W. *T. R. The Last Romantic*. New York: Basic Books, 1997.

Brinkley, Douglas. *The Wilderness Warrior: Theodore Roosevelt and the Crusade for America*. New York: HarperCollins, 2009.

"Bronco Bill" (supposed "Corporal, Company Q, Rough Riders" of Los Angeles) *Teddy (In Five Canters)*. Title-page cartoon by Culver; Privately printed. Los Angeles, 1903.

Brough, James. *Princess Alice*. Boston: Little, Brown, 1975.

Bryan, William Jennings. *A Tale of Two Conventions*. New York: Funk and Wagnalls Company, 1912.

Bullitt, William C. and Sigmund Freud. *Thomas Woodrow Wilson, a Psychological Study*. Boston: Houghton, Mifflin, 1967.

Burns, James MacGregor and Susan Dunn. *The Three Roosevelts: Patrician Leaders Who Transformed America*. New York: Atlantic Monthly Press, 2001.

Burroughs, John. *Camping and Tramping with Roosevelt*. Houghton, Mifflin, 1907.

Burton, David H. *Taft, Roosevelt, and the Limits of Friendship*. New Jersey: Fairleigh Dickinson University Press, 2005.

———. *Theodore Roosevelt: Confident Imperialist*. Philadelphia: University of Pennsylvania Press, 1969.

Busch, Noel F. *T.R.: The Story of Theodore Roosevelt and His Influence on Our Times*. New York: Reynal & Company, 1963.

Butt, Archibald W. *Taft and Roosevelt: The Intimate Letters of Archie Butt, Military Aide*. 2 vols. Garden City, NY: Doubleday, Doran and Company, 1930.

——. *The Letters of Archie Butt, Personal Military Aide to President Roosevelt.* Edited by Lawrence F. Abbott. Garden City, NY: Doubleday, Page and Company, 1924.

Butterfield, Roger. *The American Past.* New York: Simon and Schuster, 1947.

Caroli, Betty Boyd. *The Roosevelt Women.* New York: Basic Books, 1998.

Case, Carleton B. *Good Stories About Roosevelt. The Humorous Side of a Great American.* Chicago: Shrewesbury Publishing Company, 1920.

Cashin, Herschel V. *Under Fire With the 10th U.S. Cavalry.* Chicago: American Publishing House, 1902.

Chace, James. *1912: Wilson, Roosevelt, Taft & Debs – the Election that Changed the Country.* New York: Simon and Schuster, 2004.

Chalmers, David M. *Neither Socialism Nor Monopoly: Theodore Roosevelt and the Decision to Regulate the Railroads.* Philadelphia: J. B. Lippincott, 1976.

Chambers, John Whiteclay. *The Tyranny of Change: America in the Progressive Era, (1890-1920).* 2d ed. New Brunswick, NJ: Rutgers University Press, 2000.

Charnwood, Godfrey (Lord). *Theodore Roosevelt.* Boston: Atlantic Monthly Press, 1923.

Chessman, G. Wallace. *Governor Theodore Roosevelt: The Albany Apprenticeship, 1898-1900.* Cambridge: Harvard University Press, 1965.

——. *Theodore Roosevelt and the Politics of Power.* Boston: Little, Brown, 1969.

Choate, Joseph Hodges. *The Life of Joseph Hodges Choate as Gathered Chiefly from His Letters.* New York: Scribner's, 1927.

Clymer, Kenton J. *John Hay: The Gentleman as Diplomat.* Ann Arbor: University of Michigan Press, 1975.

Cobb, William T. *The Strenuous Life: The Oyster Bay Roosevelts in Business and Finance.* New York: William E Rudge's Sons, 1946.

(Collier's Weekly staff) *The Illustrated History of the War with Spain.* New York: Peter F Collier, 1898.

Collin, Richard H. *Theodore Roosevelt, Culture, Diplomacy, and Expansion: A New View of American Imperialism.* Baton Rouge: Louisiana State University Press, 1985.

——. *Theodore Roosevelt's Caribbean: The Panama Canal, the Monroe Doctrine, and the Latin American Context.* Baton Rouge: Louisiana State University Press, 1990.

Collins, Michael L. *That Damned Cowboy : Theodore Roosevelt and the American West, 1883-1898.* 1989.

Congden, C. H. *Progressive Battle Hymns*. New York: National Progressive Convention Committee, 1912.

Cooper, John Milton, Jr. *The Warrior and the Priest: Woodrow Wilson and Theodore Roosevelt*. Cambridge: Belknap Press of Harvard University Press, 1983.

Cordery, Stacy. *Alice: Alice Roosevelt Longworth, from White House Princess to Washington Power Broker*. New York: Viking, 2007.

Cortissoz, Royal. *The Life of Whitelaw Reid*. New York: Scribner's, 1921.

Crane, Stephen. *Wounds in the Rain*. New York: Frederick A Stokes, 1900.

Creelman, James. *On the Great Highway: The Wanderings and Adventures of a Special Correspondent*. Boston: Lothrop, 1901.

Croly, Herbert D. *Marcus Alonzo Hanna: His Life and Work*. New York: Macmillan, 1912.

——. *The Promise of American Life*. New York: Macmillan, 1909.

Cutright, Paul Russell. *Theodore Roosevelt the Naturalist*. New York: Harper and Brothers, 1956.

——. *Theodore Roosevelt: The Making of a Conservationist*. Urbana: University of Illinois Press, 1985.

Dalton, Kathleen M. *Theodore Roosevelt: A Strenuous Life*. New York: Alfred A. Knopf, 2002.

Darling, Jay Norwood (Ding). *Condensed Ink*. Des Moines: The Register, 1914.

——. *Peace and War Cartoons*. Des Moines: The Register, 1916.

——. *The Education of Alonzo Applegate*. Des Moines: The Register, 1910.

Davis, Oscar King. *Released for Publication: Some Inside Political History of Theodore Roosevelt and His Times, 1898-1918*. Boston: Houghton Mifflin Company, 1925.

Davis, Richard Harding. *Cuba in War Time*. Illustrated by Frederic Remington. New York: Robert Howard Russell, 1899.

Dawes, Charles Gates. *A Journal of the McKinley Years*. Chicago: Lakeside Press, 1950.

DeKay, Ormonde, Jr. *Meet Theodore Roosevelt*. Illustrated by Jack Davis. New York: Step-Up Books, 1967.

Dennett, Tyler. *John Hay: From Poetry to Politics*. New York: Dodd, Mead, 1933.

——. *Roosevelt and the Russo-Japanese War*. Garden City, NY: Doubleday, Page and Company, 1925.

Du Val, Miles P., Jr. *And the Mountains Will Move: The Story of the Building of the Panama Canal.* Stanford, CA.: Stanford University Press, 1947.

Dupuy, Trevor N., Curt Johnson, and David L. Bongard. *The Harper Encyclopedia of Military Biography.* New York: HarperCollins, 1992.

Dyer, Thomas G. *Theodore Roosevelt and the Idea of Race.* 1980.

Eaton, Seymour ("Paul Piper"). *More About Teedy B and Teddy G, the Roosevelt Bears.* Philadelphia: Edward Stern & Company, 1907.

——. *The Travels and Adventures of the Roosevelt Bears.* Philadelphia: Edward Stern & Company, 1906.

Einstein, Lewis. *Roosevelt: His Mind in Action.* Boston: Houghton Mifflin Company, 1930.

Esthus, Raymond A. *Theodore Roosevelt and the International Rivalries.* Claremont CA: Regina Books, 1970.

Evans, George, cartoonist (anon.) *The Rough Rider.* New York: Classics Illustrated Comics, Number 141A, Gilberton Company, 1957.

Felsenthal, Carol. *Alice Roosevelt Longworth.* New York: G P Putnam's Sons, 1988.

Flack, Ambrose. *Room for Mr. Roosevelt.* New York: Thomas Y Crowell, 1951.

Freidel, Frank. *The Splendid Little War.* Boston: Little, Brown, 1958.

Gable, John Allen. *The Many-Sided Roosevelt: American Renaissance Man.* Middleburg, the Netherlands: Roosevelt Study Center, 1986.

——. *The Bull Moose Years: Theodore Roosevelt and the Progressive Party.* Port Washington, NY: Kennikat Press, 1978.

Gardner, Joseph L. *Departing Glory: Theodore Roosevelt as Ex-President.* New York: Charles Scribner's Sons, 1973.

Garraty, John A. *Henry Cabot Lodge.* New York: Knopf, 1953.

Gatewood, Willard B., Jr. *Theodore Roosevelt and the Art of Controversy: Episodes of the White House Years.* Baton Rouge, LA: Louisiana State University Press, 1970.

Gerson, Noel B. *TR.* Garden City: Doubleday and Company, 1970.

Gibson, William M. *Theodore Roosevelt Among the Humorists : W. D. Howells, Mark Twain, and Mr. Dooley.* Knoxville: University of Tennessee Press, 1980.

Gilman, Bradley. *Roosevelt, the Happy Warrior.* Boston: Little, Brown, 1921.

Goldman, Eric F. *Rendezvous with Destiny: A History of Modern American Reform.* New York: Knopf, 1952.

Grant, George. *The Courage and Character of Theodore Roosevelt.* Nashville, TN: Cumberland House, 2005.

Grondahl, Paul. *I Rose Like a Rocket: The Political Education of Theodore Roosevelt.* New York: Free Press, 2004.

Gros, Raymond. *TR in Cartoon.*, Cleveland, Saalfield, 1910.

Hagedorn, Hermann. *A Theodore Roosevelt Round-Up.* Roosevelt Memorial Association, 1958.

———. *Roosevelt in the Bad Lands.* Boston: Houghton Mifflin Company, 1921.

———. *The Boys' Life of Theodore Roosevelt.* Harper and Brothers, 1918.

———. *The Bugle That Woke America.* New York: The John day Company, 1940.

———. *The Free Citizen.* New York: Macmillan, 1956.

———. *The Roosevelt Family of Sagamore Hill.* New York: Macmillan Company, 1954.

———. *The Theodore Roosevelt Treasury. A Self-Portrait from His Writings.* New York: G P Putnam's Sons, 1957.

———. *Theodore Roosevelt. A Biographical Sketch.* New York: Roosevelt Memorial Exhibition Committee. Columbia University. Privately printed, 1919.

Hale, Annie Riley. *Rooseveltian Fact and Fable.* New York: Broadway Publishing Company, 1908.

Hale, William Bayard. *A Week in the White House with Theodore Roosevelt: A Study of the President at the Nation's Business.* New York: G. P. Putnam's Sons, 1908.

Harbaugh, William Henry. *Power and Responsibility: The Life and Times of Theodore Roosevelt.* New York: Farrar, Straus and Cudahy, 1961.

(Harper's Weekly staff) *Harper's Pictorial History of the War with Spain.* New York: Harper and Brothers, 1899.

Hay, Samuel P. *Conservation and the Gospel of Efficiency: The Progressive Conservation Movement, 1890-1920.* Cambridge: Harvard University Press, 1959.

Henry, Will. *San Juan Hill.* New York: Random House, 1962.

Hofstadter, Richard. *The Age of Reform: From Bryan to FDR.* New York: Knopf, 1955.

Horn, Maurice, Editor, and Richard Marschall, Associate Editor. *The World Encyclopedia of Cartoons.* New York: Chelsea House Publishers, 1980.

House, Edward Mandell (as "Anonymous"). *Philip Dru, Administrator.* New York: B W Huebsch, 1912.

Howe, M. A. DeWolfe. *George von Lengerke Meyer: His Life and Public Services.* New York: Dodd, Mead, 1920.

Howland, Harold. *Theodore Roosevelt and His Times: A Chronicle of the Progressive Movement.* New Haven: Yale University Press, 1921.

Iglehardt, Ferdinand. *Theodore Roosevelt: The Man as I Knew Him.* New York: The Christian Herald. 1919.

Irwin, Wallace. *The Teddysee.* B W Huebsch, 1910.

Jeffers, H. Paul. *Colonel Roosevelt: Theodore Roosevelt Goes to War, 1897-1898.* Hoboken: John Wiley & Sons, 1996.

Jeffers, H. Paul. *Commissioner Roosevelt: The Story of Theodore Roosevelt and the New York City Police, 1895-1897.* Hoboken: John Wiley & Sons, 1994.

———. *In the Rough Rider's Shadow.* New York: Presidio, 2002.

Jessup, Philip. *Elihu Root.* New York: Dodd, Mead, 1938.

Johnston, William Davison. *The Words of Theodore Roosevelt.* Mount Vernon: Peter Pauper Press, 1970.

———. *TR: Champion of the Strenuous Life.* New York: Farrar, Straus & Cudahy, 1958.

Josephson, Matthew. *The Politicos.* New York: Harcourt, Brace and Company, 1938.

———. *The President Makers.* New York: Harcourt, Brace and Company, 1940.

Keller, Morton, editor. *Theodore Roosevelt: A Profile.* New York: Hill and Wang, 1967.

Kennan, George Frost. *American Diplomacy, 1900-1950.* Chicago: University of Chicago Press, 1951.

Koenig, Louis W. *Bryan: A Political Biography of William Jennings Bryan.* New York: Putnam's, 1971.

Kohlsaat, H. H. *From McKinley to Harding.* New York: Charles Scribner's Sons, 1923.

Kolko, Gabriel. *Railroads and Regulation, 1877-1916.* Princeton, N.J.: Princeton University Press, 1965.

Kraft, Betsy Harvey. *Theodore Roosevelt, Champion of the American Spirit.* New York: Clarion Books, 2003.

Kushner, Howard I. and Anne Hummel Sherrill. *John Milton Hay: The Union of Poetry and Politics.* Boston: Twayne Publishers, 1977.

Landis, Frederick. *The Angel of Lonesome Hill. The Story of a President.* New York: Charles Scribner's Sons, 1910.

Lang, Lincoln A. *Ranching with Roosevelt, By a Companion Rancher*. Philadelphia: Lippincott, 1926.

Leary, John J., Jr. *Talks with R. T. from the Diaries of John J. Leary, Jr.* Boston: Houghton Mifflin Company, 1920.

Leech, Margaret. *In the Days of McKinley*. New York: Harper and Bros. 1959.

Leopold, Richard W. *Elihu Root and the Conservative Tradition*. Boston: Little, Brown, 1954.

(Leslie's Weekly staff) *Leslie's Official History of the Spanish-American War*. New York: Leslie's Weekly, 1898.

Letwin, William. *Law and Economic Policy in America: The Evolution of the Sherman Antitrust Act*. New York: Random House, 1965.

Lewis, William Draper. *The Life of Theodore Roosevelt*. Philadelphia: John C. Winston Company, 1919.

Lippmann, Walter. *Men of Destiny*. Illustrated by Rollin Kirby. New York: The Macmillan Company, 1927.

Lodge, Henry Cabot. *Theodore Roosevelt: A Memorial Address*. Washington: Government Printing Office, 1919.

——, editor. *Selections from the Correspondence of Theodore Roosevelt and Henry Cabot Lodge, 1884-1918*. New York: Charles Scribner's Sons, 1925.

Longworth, Alice Roosevelt. *Crowded Hours*. New York: Charles Scribner's Sons, 1933.

Looker, Earl. *Colonel Roosevelt: Private Citizen*. New York: Fleming H. Revell, 1932.

——. *The White House Gang*. New York: Fleming H. Revell, 1929.

Lorant, Stefan. *The Life and Times of Theodore Roosevelt*. Garden City, NY: Doubleday, 1959.

Lucas, E. V. *Edwin Austin Abbey, Royal Academician: The Record of His Life and Work*. New York: Charles Scribner's Sons, 1921.

(Macauley, Charles R). *Campaign Cartoons Issued by Democratic National Committee, 1912*. Privately compiled, bound, and presented with inscription to Thomas H. Owen of Democratic National Committee by cartoonist Macauley of *New York World*. Proofs of cartoons by Macauley; also Nelson Harding, W. A. Rogers, James Donahey, et al. Author's Collection.

MacIntryre, Niel. *"Great Heart": The Life Story of Theodore Roosevelt*. New York: William Edwin Rudge, 1919.

Manners, William. *TR and Will: A Friendship That Split the Republican Party*. New York: Harcourt Brace & World, 1969.

Marks, Frederick W., III. *Velvet on Iron: The Diplomacy of Theodore Roosevelt*. Lincoln: University of Nebraska Press, 1979.

Marshall, Edward. *The Story of the Rough Riders*. Illustrated by R. F. Outcault. New York: G W Dillingham Company, 1899.

Martin, Albro. *Enterprise Denied: Origins of the Decline of American Railroads, 1897-1917*. New York: Columbia University Press, 1971.

McCullough, David G. *Mornings on Horseback. The Story of an Extraordinary Family. a Vanished Way of Life, and the Unique Child Who Became Theodore Roosevelt*. New York: Simon and Schuster, 1981.

——. *The Path between the Seas: The Creation of the Panama Canal, 1870-1914*. New York: Simon and Schuster, 1977.

McCutcheon, John T. *Drawn from Memory*. Indianapolis, IN: Bobs-Merrill, 1950.

——. *In Africa*. Indianapolis, IN: Bobbs-Merrill, 1910.

——. *TR in Cartoon*. Chicago: McClurg, 1910.

McDougall, Walt. *This Is the Life!* New York: Knopf, 1927.

McIntosh, Burr. *The Little I Saw of Cuba*. New York: F Tennyson Neely, 1899.

Millard, Candice. *The River of Doubt: Theodore Roosevelt's Darkest Journey*. New York: Doubleday, 2005.

Miller, Helen Topping. *Christmas at Sagamore Hill*. New York: Longmans, Green, 1960.

Miller, John. *The Big Scrum: How Teddy Roosevelt Saved Football*. New York: Harper, 2011.

Miller, Nathan. *Theodore Roosevelt: A Life*. New York: William Morrow, 1992.

Millis, Walter. *The Martial Spirit*. Cambridge: The Literary Guild, 1931.

Moore, J. Hampton. *Roosevelt and the Old Guard*. Philadelphia: Macrae Smith, 1925.

Morris, Edmund. *Colonel Roosevelt*. New York: Random House, 2010.

——. *The Rise of Theodore Roosevelt*. New York: Coward, McCann & Geoghegan, 1979.

——. *Theodore Rex*. New York: Random House, 2001.

Morris, Sylvia Jukes. *Edith Kermit Roosevelt*. New York: Coward, McCann and Geoghegan, 1980.

Mowry, George E. *The Era of Theodore Roosevelt and the Birth of Modern America, 1900-1912*. New York: Harper and Brothers, 1958.

——. *Theodore Roosevelt and the Progressive Movement*. Madison: University of Wisconsin Press, 1946.

——. *The Era of Theodore Roosevelt, 1900-1912.* 1958.

Mullins, Linda. *The Teddy Bear Men.* Cumberland MD: Hobby House Press, 1987.

National Progressive Convention Committee. *National Progressive Convention Program.* 1912.

Neilson, Winthrop. *The Story of Theodore Roosevelt.* Illustrated by Edward A Wilson. New York: Grosset & Dunlap, 1953.

Neustadt, Richard E. *Presidential Power.* New York: Macmillan, 1980.

Nevins, Allan, and Frank Weitenkampf. *A Century of Political Cartoons.* New York: Charles Scribner's Sons, 1944.

Nevins, Allan. *Henry White: Thirty Years of American Diplomacy.* New York: Harper & Brothers, 1930.

O'Toole, Patricia. *When Trumpets Call: Theodore Roosevelt After the White House.* New York: Simon and Schuster, 2006.

Oliver, Lawrence J., ed. *The Letters of Theodore Roosevelt and Brander Matthews.* Knoxville, TN: University of Tennessee Press, 1995.

Opper, Frederick Burr. *John, Jonathan, and Mr Opper.* London, Grant Richards, 1903.

——. *Willie and His Papa.* New York: Grosset and Dunlap, 1901.

Peck, Harry Thurston. *Twenty Years of the Republic, 1885-1905.* New York: Dodd, Mead & Company, 1920.

Penick, James L. *Progressive Politics and Conservation: The Ballinger-Pinchot Affair.* Chicago: University of Chicago Press, 1968.

Pinchot, Gifford. *Breaking New Ground.* New York: Harcourt Brace and Company, 1947.

——. *The Conservation Diaries of Gifford Pinchot.* Durham, NC: The Forest History Society, 2001.

Post, Charles Johnson. *The Little War of Private Post.* Boston: Little, Brown, 1960.

Pringle, Henry F. *The Life and Times of William Howard Taft.* New York: Farrar and Rinehart, 1939.

——. *Theodore Roosevelt: A Biography.* New York: Harcourt, Brace and Company, 1931.

Putnam, Carleton. *Theodore Roosevelt: The Formative Years, 1858-1886.* New York: Charles Scribner's Sons, 1958.

Putnam, George Haven. *Memories of a Publisher.* New York: G P Putnam's Sons, 1915.

Reisner, Christian F. *Roosevelt's Religion.* New York: The Abingdon Press, 1922.

Remey, Oliver E., Henry F. Cochems, and Wheeler P. Bloodgood. *The Attempted Assassination of Ex-President Theodore Roosevelt.* Milwaukee: O E Remey, 1912 (reprinted 1978 by Roger H. Hunt, Madison, WI).

Renehan, Edward J. *The Lion's Pride: Theodore Roosevelt and His Family in Peace and War.* New York: Oxford University Press, 1998.

Rhodes, James Ford. *The McKinley and Roosevelt Administrations.* New York: The Macmillan Company, 1922.

Riis, Jacob A. *How the Other Half Lives: Studies Among the Tenements of New York.* New York: Charles Scribner's Sons, 1890.

———. *Theodore Roosevelt the Citizen.* New York: The Outlook Company, 1904.

Rixey, Lilian. *Bamie: Theodore Roosevelt's Remarkable Sister.* New York: David McKay, 1963.

Robinson, Corinne Roosevelt. *My Brother Theodore Roosevelt.* New York: Charles Scribner's Sons, 1921.

Rogers, W. A. *A World Worth While.* New York: Harper and Brothers, 1922.

Roosevelt, Eleanor B. (TR's daughter-in-law). *Day Before Yesterday.* Garden City: Doubleday and Company, 1959.

Roosevelt, Kermit, editor. *Quentin Roosevelt, a Sketch with Letters.* New York: Charles Scribner's Sons, 1921.

———. *The Long Trail.* New York: The Review of Reviews, 1921.

Roosevelt, Mrs. Theodore, and Mrs. Kermit Roosevelt, Richard Derby, and Kermit Roosevelt. *Cleared for Strange Ports.* New York: Charles Scribner's Sons, 1927.

Roosevelt, Nicholas. *Theodore Roosevelt: The Man As I Knew Him.* New York: Dodd, Mead and Company, 1967.

Roosevelt, Theodore (TR's son) and Kermit Roosevelt. *East of the Sun and West of the Moon. With Illustrations from Photographs Taken by K.R.* New York: Charles Scribner's Sons, 1926.

———. *All in the Family.* New York, London: G. P. Putnam's Sons, 1929.

Rosewater, Victor. *Backstage in 1912. The Inside Story of the Split Republican Convention.* Philadelphia: Dorrance & Company, 1932.

Ruddy, Daniel. *Theodore Roosevelt's History of the United States.* Smithsonian Books/ HarperCollins, 2010.

Samuels, Peggy, and Harold Samuels. *Teddy Roosevelt at San Juan.* College Station: Texas A&M University Press, 1997.

Schlesinger, Arthur M., Jr., ed. *History of U.S. Political Parties.* New York: Chelsea House, 2002.

Scott, James Brown. *Robert Bacon: Life and Letters*. Garden City, New York: Doubleday, Page, 1923.

Sewall, William Wingate. *Bill Sewall's Story of TR*. New York: Harper and Brothers, 1919.

Shaw, Albert. *A Cartoon History of Roosevelt's Career*. New York: Review of Reviews Co., 1910.

Shookster, Linda. "The Role of Theodore Roosevelt's Family in the Founding of the New York Orthopedic Hospital." *Theodore Roosevelt Association Journal*. Vol. 28, Number 3, 2007.

Sinclair, Upton. *The Jungle*. New York: Doubleday, Page, 1906.

Smith, Albert E. *Two Reels and a Crank*. Garden City: Doubleday and Company, 1952.

Steffens, Lincoln. *The Autobiography of Lincoln Steffens*. New York: Harcourt, Brace and Company, 1931.

Stoddard, Henry L. *As I Knew Them*. New York: Harper and Brothers, 1927.

Straus, Oscar Solomon. *Under Four Administrations: From Cleveland to Taft*. Boston: Houghton Mifflin, 1922.

Street, Julian. *The Most Interesting American*. New York: Century Company, 1916.

Sullivan, Mark. *Our Times*. New York: Charles Scribner's Sons, 1926-1935 (six volumes).

Tate, James P. *The Army and Its Air Corps: Army Policy Toward Aviation 1919-1941*. Maxwell Air Force Base, Alabama: Air University Press, 1998.

Taussig, Frank W. *A Tariff History of the United States*. New York: G P Putnam's Sons, 1914.

Teague, Michael. *Mrs L. Conversations with Alice Roosevelt Longworth*. Garden City: Doubleday & Company, 1981.

Teichmann, Howard. *Alice*. Englewood Cliffs: Prentice-Hall, 1979.

Thayer, William Roscoe. *The Life and Letters of John Hay*. Boston: Houghton Mifflin Company, 1915.

———. *Theodore Roosevelt: An Intimate biography*. Boston: Houghton, Mifflin, 1919.

Towne, Charles Hanson, ed. *Roosevelt as the Poets Saw Him*. With an Introduction by Corinne Roosevelt Robinson. New York: Charles Scribner's Sons, 1923.

Trani, Eugene P. *The Treaty of Portsmouth: An Adventure in American Diplomacy*. Lexington: University of Kentucky Press, 1969.

Valaik, J. David. *Theodore Roosevelt, an American Hero in Caricature*. Privately printed, 1993.

Verney, Kevern. *The Art of the Possible: Booker T. Washington and Black Leadership in the United States, 1881-1925*. New York: Routledge, 2001.

Viereck, George Sylvester. *Roosevelt, a Study in Ambivalence.* New York: Jackson Press, 1919.

Vietze, Andrew. *Becoming Teddy Roosevelt: How a Maine Guide Inspired America's 26th President.* Maine: Down East Books, 2010.

Vorpahl, Ben Merchant. *My Dear Wister.* Paolo Alto: American West Publishing, 1972.

Wagenknecht, Edward. *The Seven Worlds of Theodore Roosevelt.* New York: Longmans, Green and Company, 1958.

Walker, Dale L. *The Boys of '98.* New York: Forge, 1998.

Washburn, Charles G. *Theodore Roosevelt: The Logic of His Career.* Boston: Houghton Miffin Co., 1916.

Washington, Booker T. *Up from Slavery.* New York: Doubleday, Page and Co., 1901.

Watts, Sarah. *Rough Rider in the White House: Theodore Roosevelt and the Politics of Desire.* Chicago: University of Chicago Press, 2006.

West, Richard Samuel. *Satire on Stone.* University of Illinois Press, 1988.

White, G. Edward. *The Eastern Establishment and the Western Experience: the West of Frederic Remington, Theodore Roosevelt, and Owen Wister.* Austin: University of Texas Press, 1989.

White, William Allen. *Autobiography.* New York: Macmillan, 1946.

———. *Masks in a Pageant.* New York: Macmillan, 1928.

Wiegand, Wayne A. *Patrician in the Progressive Era: A Biography of George von Lengerke Meyer.* New York: Garland Publishing, 1988.

Willis, Jack. *Roosevelt in the Rough.* New York: Ives Washburn, 1931.

Wilson, Dorothy Clarke. *Alice and Edith.* Garden City, NY: Doubleday, 1989.

Wilson, R. L. *Theodore Roosevelt, Outdoorsman.* New York: Winchester Press, 1971.

———. *Theodore Roosevelt: Hunter-Conservationist.* Missoula: Boone and Crockett Club, 2010.

Wister, Owen. *Roosevelt: The Story of a Friendship, 1880-1919.* New York: Macmillan Company, 1930.

Wood, Frederick S., ed. *Roosevelt As We Knew Him: The Personal Recollections of One Hundred and Fifty of His Friends and Associates.* Philadelphia: John C. Winston Company, 1927.

Young, Art. *On My Way.* New York: Horace Liveright, 1928.

———. *His Life and Times.* New York: Sheridan House, 1939.

## BOOKS BY THEODORE ROOSEVELT

*The Works of Theodore Roosevelt*. National Edition, 20 volumes. Edited by Hermann Hagedorn. New York: Charles Scribner's Sons, 1926:

I. *Hunting Trips of a Ranchman. Ranch Life and the Hunting Trail.* II. *The Wilderness Hunter. Outdoor Pastimes of an American Hunter* part 1. III. *Outdoor Pastimes of an American Hunter* part 2. *A Book-Lover's Holidays in the Open.* IV. *African Game Trails.* V. *Through the Brazilian Wilderness. Papers on Natural History.* VI. *The Naval War of 1812.* VII. *Thomas Hart Benton. Gouverneur Morris.* VIII. *The Winning of the West* part 1. IX. *The Winning of the West* part 2. X. *Hero Tales from American History. Oliver Cromwell. New York.* XI. *The Rough Riders. Men of Action.* XII. *Literary Essays.* XIII. *American Ideals. The Strenuous Life. Realizable Ideals.* XIV. *Campaigns and Controversies.* XV. *State Papers as Governor and President.* XVI. *American Problems.* XVII. *Social Justice and Popular Rule.* XVIII. *America and the World War. Fear God and Take Your Own Part.* XIX. *Foes of Our Own Household. The Great Adventure. Letters to His Children.* XX. *Autobiography.*

*The Letters of Theodore Roosevelt.* Edited by Elting E. Morison, John M. Blum, Alfred D. Chandler Jr., Sylvia Rice, et al. Cambridge: Harvard University Press, 1951-1954.

Volume 1–*The Years of Preparation, 1868- 1898*; Volume 2–*The Years of Preparation, 1899-1900*; Volume 3–*The Square Deal–1901-1903*; Volume 4–*The Square Deal–1903-1905*; Volume 5–*The Big Stick–1905-1907*; Volume 6–*The Big Stick–1907-1909*; Volume 7–*The Days of Armageddon, 1909-1914*; Volume 8–*The Days of Armageddon, 1914-1919.*

## SELECTED BOOKS BY TR. MANY INCLUDING MATERIAL NOT IN THE MEMORIAL EDITION OR LETTERS

*An Autobiography.* New York: Macmillan, 1913.

*Biological Analogies in History.* New York: Oxford University Press, 1910.

*Cowboys and Kings.* Cambridge: Harvard University Press, 1954.

*History as Literature, and Other Essays.* New York: Charles Scribner's Sons, 1913.

*Letters from Theodore Roosevelt to Anna Roosevelt Cowles, 1870-1918.* New York: Charles Scribner's Sons, 1924.

*Letters to Kermit from Theodore Roosevelt, 1902-1908.* Edited by Irwin, Will. New York: Charles Scribner's Sons, 1946.

*New Nationalism.* New York: Outlook Company, 1910.

*Notes on Some of the Birds of Oyster Bay; and Summer Birds of the Adirondacks.* New York: Privately printed facsimiles of TR's first published writings, 1925.

*Outlook Editorials.* New York: The Outlook Company, 1909.

*Pocket diary, 1898: Theodore Roosevelt's private account of the War with Spain. A facsimile edition of the manuscript accompanied by extracts from his published recollections and illustrated with photographs.* 1998.

*Presidential Addresses and State Papers and European Addresses.* Homeward Bound Edition. New York: The Review of Reviews Company, 1910. 8 volumes.

*Progressive Principles: Selections from Addresses Made During the Presidential Campaign of 1912, Including The Progressive National Platform.* Edited by Elmer H. Youngman. New York: Progressive National Service. 1913.

*Realizable Ideals: The Earl Lectures.* San Francisco: Whittaker & Ray-Wiggin Co., 1911.

*Roosevelt in the Kansas City Star: War-Time Editorials by Theodore Roosevelt.* Edited by Ralph Stout. Boston: Houghton Mifflin Company, 1921.

*Selections from the Correspondence of Theodore Roosevelt and Henry Cabot Lodge, 1884-1918.* New York: Charles Scribner's Sons, 1925.

*The Free Citizen: A Summons to Service of the Democratic Ideal.* Edited by Harmann Hagedorn. New York: MacMillan Company, 1956.

*The Roosevelt Policy.* Griffith, William, editor. New York: The Current Literature Publishing Company, 1919.

*The Successful Life. Compiled From the Speeches of Theodore Roosevelt During his European Tour.* London: Hodder & Stoughton, 1910.

*Theodore Roosevelt and His Time, Shown in His Letters.* Edited by Joseph Bucklin Bishop. New York: Charles Scribner's Sons, 1920.

*Theodore Roosevelt on Race, Riots, Reds, Crime.* Compiled by Archibald B. Roosevelt. West Sayreville, NY: Probe Research, 1968.

*Theodore Roosevelt Cyclopedia.* Edited by Albert Bushnell Hart and Herbert Ronald Ferleger. Oyster Bay: Theodore Roosevelt Association, 1941.

*Theodore Roosevelt's America: Selections from the Writings of the Oyster Bay Naturalist.* Edited by Flarida A. Wiley. With Introductory Essays by John Burroughs, et al., and a Foreword by Ethel Roosevelt Derby. New York: Devin-Adair, 1955.

*Theodore Roosevelt's Diaries of Boyhood and Youth.* New York: Charles Scribner's Sons, 1928.

*Theodore Roosevelt's Letters to His Children.* Edited by Joseph Bucklin Bishop. New York: Charles Scribner's Sons, 1919. Letters from 1898-1911.

## PERIODICALS CONSULTED

Magazines: *Puck* (1876-1918); *Judge* (1881-1921); *Life* (1883-1922); *Cartoons Magazine* (1911-1920); *Truth* (1894-1898); *The Outlook* (1909-1913); *Harper's Weekly* (1871-1919); *Leslie's Weekly* (1876-1918); *Collier's* (1902-1912); *The Metropolitan* (1914-1918); *The New Republic*, 1914-1917; *North American Review War Weekly* (1918); *Jugend*, Munich (1896-1919); *Simplicissimus*, Munich (1896-1919); *Kladderadatsch*, Berlin (1901-1919); *L'Assiette au Beurre* (Paris), 1902-1912; *Ulk*, Berlin (1901-1910); *Lustige Blätter*, Berlin (1901-1918); *Wieland*, Munich (1915-1917); various American cartoon magazines of the 1880s including *Chic, Wasp, Texas Siftings*; and of the 1890s, including *Vim, The Bee, Twinkles, Types.*

Journals of cartoon history, political Americana, history: *Nemo, the classic comics library; The Puck Papers; Target; Hogan's Alley, Journal of the Cartoon Arts; The Keynoter, The Standard; The Historian (Phi Alpha Theta journal); American Heritage* (1954- ).

Newspapers: New York *American* (1896-1919); *New York Evening Journal* (1898-1906); *New York World* (1893-1912); *New York Herald* (1893-1919); Chicago *Inter-Ocean Color Supplement* (1892-1895); *Pearson's War Pictures* weekly (1898). Various issues of *Philadelphia Inquirer, Cincinnati Enquirer, Boston Globe*, Philadelphia *North American, Stars and Stripes*, Paris (1918-1919).

Theodore Roosevelt Association. *Theodore Roosevelt Association Journal* (1975- ).

## RESOURCES

Theodore Roosevelt Association
P.O. Box 719, Oyster Bay, NY 11771
www.theodoreroosevelt.org

Theodore Roosevelt Center
Dickinson State University
291 Campus Drive
Dickinson, ND 58601
http://www.theodorerooseveltcenter.org

Almanac of Theodore Roosevelt
http://www.theodore-roosevelt.com

TR media channel on YouTube
http://www.youtube.com/user/trmediafanatic

# CITATIONS

In the interests of brevity and clarity, source citations for cartoonists and cartoons that are identified in captions, and periodical titles and dates that clearly appear in the illustration, are not here referenced. Cartoons will be identified by publication-source and year, as well as month and day if possible. Some cartoons have been reprinted from anthologies, magazine compilations, and reprint books of their time, and therefore a precise date cannot always be affixed. Likewise, many of the illustrations are from vintage scrapbooks or collections of clippings; in those cases, the author has ascertained the closest date by context of subject matter and the cartoonist's style. Images absent from the citations were judged to be self-explanatory as to source. For cartoons from compilations where no page numbers are assigned, "n.p." is used. Book titles are abbreviated; readers may refer to the Bibliography for complete data.

All the cartoons in *BULLY!* are from the collection of Rick Marschall, with the exception of the cartoons that filled important gaps in the narrative, or upgraded images of poor quality in the author's collection: Page 293, John Olsen: and pages 33, 43, 133, 144, 174, 255 (right), and 312, courtesy Richard Samuel West / Periodyssey. Thanks to Rich West, noted cartoon historian, and Kayt Thompson for all courtesies.

## FOREWORD

### CARTOONS:

**Page 2**: line drawing by Franklin Booth, unknown publication, n.d., 5. Poster by Hubbell Reed McBride, 1924.

### TEXT:

"Aggressive fighting for…": *The Works of Theodore Roosevelt*, National Edition (hereinafter *Works*) XV, 33. **Page 4**: "…romped crazily with his children": Wagenknecht, *The Seven Worlds of Theodore Roosevelt* (hereinafter *Wagenknecht*), 172–73 and *passim*. Of course this commitment was observed when TR was home and events provided, though this seldom was missed: Wagenknecht reports of a White House meeting with President McKinley that TR passed up because of a promise to romp with his boys (page 172). **Page 6**: "Imagine [him] at the desk…": William Bayard Hale, *A Week in the White House* (hereinafter *Hale*), 14.

## CHAPTER 1

### CARTOONS:

**Page 16**: Family crest: William T. Cobb, *The Strenuous Life* (hereinafter *Cobb*), 97. **Page 21**: North Dutch Church member roll: *Cobb*, 19.

### TEXT:

**Page 14**: "Claes bought a 50-acre…": Farming and glass importation were to be Roosevelt family occupations; also manufacture of hardware, flour, and chocolate. But banking and real estate investment provided most of what became a modest fortune. *Cobb, passim*; also http://www.navvf.org/lambert-manhattan.html. **Page 15**: "How much this time?" Corinne Roosevelt Robinson, *My Brother, Theodore Roosevelt* (hereinafter *Robinson*), 15; "The best man I ever knew…": Theodore Roosevelt, *Theodore Roosevelt, An Autobiography* (hereinafter *TR Auto*), 7.

**Page 16**: "Bamie suffered from…": Linda Shookster, 2007, "The Role of Theodore Roosevelt's Family in the Founding of the New York Orthopedic Hospital" (hereinafter *Shookster*), 4. **Page 17**: "It was this summer…": *TR Auto*, 17; "On the stagecoach ride…": *TR Auto*, 27–28. **Page 18**: "You have the mind…": *Robinson*, 50; "The upstairs back piazza…": http://www.nps.gov/nr/travel/presidents/t_roosevelt_birthplace.html ; "Ask me anything…": There are numerous examples of TR remembering faces from years before, and facts from obscure sources. It appears he had what would be clinically defined as a photographic memory. Edmund Morris (in *Col. Roosevelt*, hereinafter Col. Roosevelt) provides no fewer than thirty examples in footnote 51 of Chapter 5. **Page 20**: "Now look here…": Putnam, *Theodore Roosevelt: The Formative Years* (hereinafter *Putnam*), 140, 219; "Do you see that girl…": Kathleen Dalton, 2002, *Theodore Roosevelt: A Strenuous Life* (hereinafter *Dalton*), 71. **Page 21**: "… left camp to…": Vietze, *Becoming Theodore Roosevelt* (hereinafter *Vietze*), 17, 18, 48; also see http://www.maine.gov/doc/parks/history/biblepoint/history.htm .

## CHAPTER 2

### CARTOONS:

**Page 31**: Original art by Arthur Burdett Frost, June 15, 1875. This is the drawing style Frost used in the wildly popular *Out of the Hurly-Burly*, a book written by Max Adeler, the cartoonist's first major success. For half a century Frost was to dominate several tracks: serious magazine illustration in the *Graphic*, *Harper's Weekly*, and *Collier's*; cartoons for the *Graphic*, *Harper's Weekly*, *Scribner's*, and *Life*; sporting prints and rural scenes for portfolios and advertising; and book illustration—a hundred books, by Lewis Carroll, Frank Stockton, Joel Chandler Harris (*Uncle Remus*), H. C. Bunner, Mark Twain, Will Carleton, et al., and his own popular *Stuff and Nonsense* and *The*

*Bull Calf.* Author's collection. **Page 34**: August 30, 1896. Keppler often based cartoons on European legends, and (German) music, especially operas–here the Romantic *Erl King* of Goethe (and Schubert's memorable piano piece). **Page 36**: January 29, 1879.

### TEXT:

**Page 28**: "Thee's health began…": Theodore Roosevelt, *The Letters of Theodore Roosevelt* (hereinafter *Letters*), I, 30; "…the best friend I ever had": Other sincere effusions are found in a letter to his father quoted in Wagenknecht (165), "I do not think there is a fellow in College, that has a family that mean as much as you all do me, and I am *sure* that there is no one who has a Father who is also his best and most intimate friend, as you are mine"; "the best man I ever knew…": *TR Auto*, 7. **Page 29**: "I shall always live my life as he would want…": TR also wrote after his father's death, "I can conscientiously say that I have done nothing of which I do not think father would approve if he were alive" (Wagenknecht, 165); "He met John…": *Robinson*, 6. "I feel that…": *Dalton*, 68.

### CHAPTER 3
### CARTOONS:

**Page 43**: This cartoon likely is the first to mention Theodore Roosevelt, and possibly the first to depict him. The ambiguity derives from cartoonist Worth's reference to Roosevelt's legislative bill without labeling the Assemblyman… or caricaturing him well. It is the author's opinion that the mustachioed face outside the prison courtyard is supposed to be Roosevelt. **Pages 46 and 47**: Thomas Nast in *Harper's Weekly,* April 19, 1884 and May 10, 1884, respectively, are often thought to be the first national cartoons depicting Theodore Roosevelt. The "whipping-post" cartoon in *Judge* notwithstanding, the cartoons in *Puck* of February 20 and March 26 [see

page 56] predate Nast's cartoons. **Page 52**: reprinted in a *New York World* story about influential American political cartoons, March 21, 1897. **Page 54**: April 13, 1881. **Page 55**: Joseph Keppler in *Puck*, 1881. **Page 56**: Cartoons by Friederich Grätz. The first of the two *Puck* covers was published within a week of the death of TR's mother and wife. **Page 57**: *Puck*, April 16, 1884. **Pages 58 and 59**: Bernard Gillam in *Puck*; full title, *Phryne Before the Chicago Tribunal: Ardent Advocate* [Whitelaw Reid, Editor of the *New York Tribune*]: "*Now, gentlemen, don't make any mistake in your decision! Here's Purity and Magnetism for You—can't be beat!*" **Page 60**: November 5, 1884.

### TEXT:

**Page 40**: "briefly clerking in…": *Dalton*, 78. **Page 41**: "…emulating his father's charitable visits around the city": Putnam chronicles more fully than any other biographer the bond between father and son, and the deep Christian commitment of each. Thee's charity rounds, Teedie's accompaniment, and TR's ultimate inability to emulate one-on-one missions work: *Putnam, supra*. "Nothing but my faith in the Lord Jesus Christ could have carried me through this, my terrible time of trouble and sorrow," TR wrote months after his father's death. *Putnam*, 151. **Page 44**: "…derisively pictured as applauding…": David McCollough, *Mornings on Horseback* (hereinafter *McCollough*), 256; "If you try anything like that, I'll kick you…": *Putnam*, 252; "When another assemblyman made fun…": *Putnam*, 274. **Page 47**: "He was invited…": *Dalton*, 82. **Page 48**: "I rose like a rocket…": Edmund Morris, *The Rise of Theodore Roosevelt* (hereinafter *Rise TR*), 184. **Page 49**: "Alice is dying…": There are (slightly) conflicting accounts of how many telegrams were sent to TR in Albany, and which of TR's siblings met him at the door. Confusion in such inconsequentials is understandable. This doorway "greeting" is the family version that has prevailed. "The light has gone out of my life": TR's Private Diary, image at http://lcweb2.loc.gov/ammem/trhtml/trdiary3.html. **Page 50**: "She was beautiful… ": Lorant, *The Life and Times of Theodore Roosevelt* (hereinafter Lorant), 196; "I shall come back to my work at once": Wagenknecht, 166.

## CHAPTER 4

### CARTOONS:

**Page 65**: cover of *Judge's Library*, December 1896. **Page 73**: November 10, 1886. **Pages 74 and 75**: May 25, 1887.

### TEXT:

**Page 63**: "…visiting chapels in the Newsboys' Lodging House": TR gradually abandoned his father's practice of visiting homes and missions in the city. It is clear (*Putnam, supra*; *Wagenknecht*, 111 and Chapter Five, 181–95) that their faiths, equally strong, were exercised in different manners. **Page 67**: "In another incident…": http://www.theodore-roosevelt.com/trsorbonnespeech.html; "Black care…": (*Works* 1926, I, 329). **Page 68**: "An astonished local… ": "Theodore Roosevelt; His Prompt Pursuit and Capture of Three Thieves in Dakota," *New York Times*, April 25, 1886. **Page 71**: "The cattle-men keep…": Theodore Roosevelt, *Hunting Trips of a Ranchman* (Hereinafter *Ranchman*), 19.

## CHAPTER 5

### CARTOONS:

**Page 82**: *Puck*, November 16, 1892. **Page 85**: Keppler in *Puck*, January 21, 1891. **Page 95**, Dalrymple in *Puck*, 1889. **Pages 96–97**, Dalrymple in *Puck*, 1889. **Page 99** (left): Thomas Nast in the *Daily Inter-Ocean*, October 2, 1892. One of the first cartoons printed in color in an American newspaper. It gives the lie to the false history concerning yellow inks being obstreperous, leading to the Yellow Kid four years later. **Page 100**: Illustrations from Jacob Riis,

*How the Other Half Lives*. **Page 102**: Charles Jay Taylor in *Puck*, July 24, 1895. Taylor drew political cartoons for *Harper's Weekly*, briefly, and for *Puck* for fifteen years beginning in 1886; but his considerable contributions were in the field of short-story illustration (of Bunner's work, principally) and creating a rival to the glamorous Gibson Girl, the "Taylor-Made Girl." **Page 103**: August 8, 1896. **Page 104** (top): August 18, 1895. **Page 105**: J. S. Pughe in *Puck*, 1897. **Pages 106–107**: *Puck*, September 18, 1896. **Page 108** (top): C. G. Bush, *New York Herald*, April 19, 1896; (bottom): August 8, 1896.

### TEXT:

**Page 80**: "How close a number…": http://m.whitehouse.gov/about/presidents/benjaminharrison. **Page 83**: "[TR] would come…": Hagedorn, *The Boys' Life of Theodore Roosevelt* (hereinafter *Boys' Life*), 155. **Page 86**: "What? And me going home to my bunnies?": *Rise TR*, 493. **Page 87**: "Of course I told…": Nathan Miller, *Theodore Roosevelt* (hereinafter *Miller*), 232. **Page 88**: "…raise less corn and more hell!": Roger Butterfield, *The American Past* (hereinafter *Butterfield*), 259. **Page 89**: "Cross of Gold" speech: quoted in *Butterfield*, 271. **Page 92**: "It is not difficult…": Theodore Roosevelt, *American Ideals* (hereinafter *Am Ideals*), 19.

## CHAPTER 6

### CARTOONS:

**Page 112**: W. A. Rogers in *New York Herald*, May 7, 1898. **Page 113**: *The Chicago Record's War Stories* (hereinafter *Record*), 149. **Page 118**: *New York Journal*, May 4, 1898. **Page 120**: *Record*, 177. **Page 125**: F. Victor Gillam in *Judge*, 1898. **Page 128**: Charles Dana Gibson in *Scribner's Magazine*, 1898. **Page 130**: June 29, 1898. **Page 131**: July 27, 1898. **Pages 134–35**: Grant Hamilton in *Judge*, September 17, 1898. **Page 137**: *New York Journal*, July 31, 1898. **Page 138**: August

6, 1898. **Pages 142–43**: Grant Hamilton in *Judge*, June 4, 1898.

## TEXT:

**Page 114**: "If I must choose…": Theodore Roosevelt, "Theodore Roosevelt on the Danger of Making Unwise Peace Treaties," *New York Times*, October 4, 1914. **Page 117**: "…backbone of a chocolate éclair": Peck, *Twenty Years of the Republic*, 642; see also Rhodes, *The McKinley and Roosevelt Administrations*, 57. **Page 118**: "He thinks he…": *Lorant*, 290. **Page 120**: "You provide the pictures, I'll provide the war": James Creelman, *On the Great Highway*, 178. The exchange, a legend of American journalism, has never been substantiated by documentation, and frequently has been challenged. Its endurance is due in part to its colorful audacity in a conflict, and a field replete with such tales; but also it accurately reflects Remington's disappointment over fly-infested misery, and little revolutionary romance, in pre-war Cuba, and Hearst's bellicose self-assurance. **Pages 121–22**: "Come on, boys! We've got the Yankees on the run!": Trevor N. Dupuy, et al., *The Harper Encyclopedia of Military Biography*, 794. **Page 124**: "The entire command moved forward": Herschel V. Cashin, *Under Fire With the 10th U.S. Cavalry*, 207–8; "Roosevelt was right…": *Lorant*, 290. **Page 128**: "I am proud…": Edward Marshall, 1899, *The Story of the Rough Riders* (hereinafter Marshall), 252. **Page 129**: "It has been a splendid little war": John Hay to Theodore Roosevelt, July 27, 1898.

## CHAPTER 7
### CARTOONS:

**Page 150**: December 22, 1898. **Page 153**: Albert Levering in *Life*, August 30, 1900. **Page 156**: June 19, 1900. **Page 159**: J. Campbell Cory in the *New York World*, 1901. **Page 162**: Grant Hamilton in Judge, October 29, 1898. **Page 163**: *New York World*, March 26, 1899. **Pages 164–65**: *Judge*, October 22, 1898.

**Page 168**: From clippings of the *Willie and His Papa* series by F. Opper in the *New York Journal*, not collected in the Grosset and Dunlap reprint book of the day. **Page 169**: J. S. Pughe in *Puck*, June 29, 1898. **Page 170**: Winsor McCay in the *Cincinnati Enquirer*. McCay also freelanced anti-imperialist cartoons to *Life* magazine at the time, his initial national exposure. Author's Collection.

## TEXT:

**Pages 150–51**: "…religiously fulfilled this pledge": William Draper Lewis, *The Life of Theodore Roosevelt* (hereinafter Lewis), 153. **Page 154**: "When the subject…": *TR Auto*, 290.

## CHAPTER 8
### CARTOONS:

**Page 174**: Joseph Keppler in *Puck*, January 28, 1903—President Roosevelt extending support to Black America, at the feet of Lincoln. One of President Roosevelt's first acts in office was to invite Booker T. Washington to dine at the White House. Southern states were outraged, but TR wanted to signal his lack of prejudice, his openness to Americans of all backgrounds, and—mostly—his desire to consult with a broad spectrum of citizens. He continued to discuss federal appointments with Washington throughout his presidency. **Page 177**: James Montgomery Flagg in *Life,* February 23, 1905. **Page 182**: John T. McCutcheon, *TR in Cartoon* (hereinafter *McCutcheon Cartoons*). n.p. **Page 183**: W. H. Walker in *Life,* May 4, 1905. **Page 189**: The original cartoon that started a tradition. This Clifford Berryman cartoon was a vignette in a larger group of commentary-cartoons. When it became famous, Berryman re-drew it several times, altering the bear's size and anxiety… but not its charm. Berryman was a fixture in the nation's capital and among cartoonists and politicians for a generation. **Page 195**: clipping from *Judge*, ca. 1914. **Page 198**: George Rehse, *St. Paul Pioneer Press,* ca. 1907. **Page 201**, starting upper left: covers from April, May, June, and February 1905. Kemble, known primarily as a comic illustrator and delineator of blacks, mostly was a cartoonist of chameleon-like sympathies, depending on his publisher (Art Young once caricatured him as a prostitute in a bordello). But his muckraking cartoons for *Collier's* were as forceful as any cartoons he, or any other American cartoonist, ever drew. **Page 208**: Keppler in *Puck*, July 7, 1906. The title is "Vacation." **Page 213**: T. S. Sullivant in New York *American*. Reproduced from the original drawing in Author's Collection. **Page 217**: *McCutcheon Cartoons*, n.p. **Page 219**: Keppler in *Puck*, January 1, 1902, a few weeks after he assumed the presidency. **Page 220**: *McCutcheon Cartoons*, n.p. **Page 221**: February 9, 1881. **Pages 222–23**: Keppler in *Puck*, September 30, 1903. **Page 224**: Keppler in *Puck*, January 13, 1904. **Page 225**: J. S. Pughe in *Puck*, August 17, 1898. **Page 226**: F. Victor Gillam in *Judge*, June 19, 1898. **Pages 226–27**: Keppler in *Puck*, November 14, 1906. **Page 228**: reprinted in *Cartoons Magazine*, December 1913, 631. **Page 229**: F. Victor Gillam, *Judge*, December 26, 1903. **Page 230** (top): November 11, 1903; (bottom): December 20, 1903. **Page 231** (top): by Zim, October 3, 1903; (bottom): by Emil Flohri, September 23, 1905. Years after serving as a mainstay for *Judge*, where he did political and social cartoons and theatrical portraits for *Judge's* sister magazine *Film Fun*, Flohri became one of Walt Disney's first employees in Hollywood. Flohri painted the lush watercolor backgrounds for some of Disney's impressive first *Silly Symphonies* shorts. **Page 232**: *Puck* cover, June 1, 1904. **Pages 232–33**: Eugene Zimmerman (Zim) in *Judge*, 1904. **Page 234**: Keppler in *Puck*, June 15, 1904. **Pages 236–37**: Keppler in *Puck*, November 9, 1904. **Page 238** (top): W. A. Rogers in *Harper's Weekly*, July 2, 1904; (bottom): November 9, 1904. **Page 240**: July 29, 1903. **Page 241**: November 16, 1904. In the light of TR's subsequent Nobel Peace Prize, it is interesting to note cartoonist

Hamilton's skepticism of TR's pacific capacities; the title of this back-page *Puck* cartoon is "Too Good To Be True." **Page 242**: July 2, 1906. **Pages 244–45**: July 29, 1903. **Pages 246–47**: Harrison Cady in *Life*, August 1, 1908. **Page 249**: Caricature by Charles Johnson Post, n.p., reproduced from the original drawing in Author's Collection. Post was a volunteer in the Spanish-American War whose posthumous memoirs present a jaded view of a soldier who was not a Rough Rider. **Page 250**: August 20, 1903. **Page 251**: *McCutcheon Cartoons*, n.d. **Page 252**: Zim in *Judge*, November 25, 1905. **Page 253**: Bartholomew in *Minneapolis Journal*. **Page 256**: Illustrations from Earl Looker, *The White House Gang*, 1929. **Page 257**: TR picture-letter, *Liberty Magazine*, article "All in the Family," by TR II, May 4, 1929, 27; see also Hagedorn, *Roosevelt Family of Sagamore Hill*, 256. **Pages 258–59**: Joseph Keppler Jr. in *Puck*, July 1, 1903. **Page 260**: *New York Herald*, August 9, 1903. **Page 262**: *Roosevelt Bears*, syndicated to various newspapers, 1906. **Page 265**: (upper left): Brewerton in *Atlanta Journal*; reprinted in *Cartoons Magazine*, April 1912, 73; (right): W. Kemp Starrett, *Albany Knickerbocker-Press,* reprinted in *Cartoons Magazine,* March 1914, 333. **Pages 268–69**: June 29, 1904.

**TEXT:**

**Page 180**: "A special blessing over the life I am to lead here": *Robinson*, 206–7; "It would be a far worse…": Henry Cabot Lodge, editor, *Selections from the Correspondence of Theodore Roosevelt and Henry Cabot Lodge* (hereinafter *Roosevelt-Lodge Letters*), I, 506. **Page 181**: "Without honesty, popular government is a repulsive farce," Theodore Roosevelt, "Applied Good Citizenship," *The Outlook* 99:611, November 11, 1911. **Page 182**: "…jargon of street kids of the day": The enthusiastic compliment "bully" was not coarse but common, and filtered upward to polite society for a period. John Hay wrote, in a letter to the great American illustrator and painter Edwin Austin

Abbey, "I have gone twice to Boston to look at your *Galahad* series, with new pleasure and admiration each time. You have done the job, old man. You have made your unquestionable place in the art of this generation. And the Shakespeare drawings! I saw a few of them at a picture shop here. They are bully, as my children say, in a language which I used to think hideous, but which seems to be current now in the best society." Quoted in Lucas, *Edwin Austin Abbey*, II, 293 (February 11, 1896). **Page 183**: "... certainly justified in morals": Joseph Bucklin Bishop, *Theodore Roosevelt and His Time* (hereinafter *Bishop*, I, 278); "What I need...": *Wagenknecht*, 235–36. **Page 184**: "TR, who later confided...": Walter Wellman. "The Inside History of the Great Coal Strike," *Collier's Weekly*, Vol. 30, No. 3, 6–7. **Page 185**: "It dawned on me...": *TR Auto*, 468. **Page 186**: "If we have done...": *Bishop*, Vol. 1, 184–85. **Page 187**: "Not unless we...": *Bishop*, I, 184–85. **Page 188**: "...when you know all the facts": *Lorant*, 416; "I have not...": Lorant, 416. **Page 189**: "I am no longer...": Miller, 436. "Under no circumstances ...": *TR Auto*, 387; "How I wish father...": *Bishop*, 363; "Speak softly...": Theodore Roosevelt, *The Strenuous Life* (hereinafter *Strenuous*), 288; "Nine-tenths of wisdom...": Speech at Lincoln, NE, June 14, 1917, http://www.theodoreroosevelt.com/images/research/txtspeeches/707.pdf. **Page 194**: "If I must choose... ": "Theodore Roosevelt on the Danger of Making Unwise Peace Treaties," *New York Times*, October 4, 1914. **Page 196**: "... building of the canal through Panama": TR to S. Small, December 29, 1903; "I took the Isthmus": Daniel Ruddy, *Theodore Roosevelt's History of the United States* (hereinafter Ruddy), 266; also see James Ford Rhodes papers, Massachusetts Historical Society, Boston, dinner book, December 1, 1911. **Page 198**: "In utilizing and conserving the natural resources...": Address to the National Editorial Association, Jamestown, Virginia, http://www.theodoreroosevelt.org/life/conservation.htm. **Pages 203–4** . "You may

recall...": National Edition, XVI, 424. **Page 205**: "The opposition to reform...": Theodore Roosevelt, *American Ideals* (Hereinafter: *Am. Ideals*), 149. **Page 206**: "...every side was like an electric battery," quoted in *Theodore Roosevelt Cyclopedia* (hereinafter *Cyclopedia*), xiii; "You have to hate ...": Harbaugh, *Power and Responsibility* (hereinafter: *Harbaugh*), 490. **Page 207**: "In case we... ": *TR Auto*, 45. **Pages 209–10**: "I wish to preach...": "Strenuous Life" speech, Chicago, Illinois, April 10, 1899, National Edition, XIII. **Page 212**: "I see him occasionally ... ": Earl Looker, *White House Gang* (hereinafter *Looker*), 62; "The Truth! First!" One of Quentin's childhood friends recalls the father/president meting out punishment with the admonition, "The truth! The truth! Next time, remember, be quicker with the truth!" (*Looker*, 19); "...the president is about six": Betsy Harvey Kraft, *Theodore Roosevelt, Champion of the American Spirit* (hereinafter *Kraft*), ix; "last chance to be a boy...": *Wagenknecht*, 11. **Page 213**: "I can run ...": Owen Wister, *Roosevelt: The Story of a Friendship,* (hereinafter *Wister*), 87. **Page 214**: "The grass of a thousand country clubs": Stacy Cordery, *Alice Roosevelt Longworth* (hereinafter *Cordery*), 371; "...white son of a bitch": Cordery, 463; "Washington's topless monument": Cordery, 468, quotes, "Washington's topless octogenarian." Both startling statements made the circuit at the time. **Page 216**: Roosevelt chose *The New York Times* as the vehicle to announce, and explain, his choice to work at *The Outlook* (March 5, 1910). **Page 218**: "...not one shot was fired in conflict": In his book *America and the World War*, TR stated his justifiable boast about his presidency this way: "Not a single shot was fired at any soldier of a hostile nation," National Edition, XVIII, 134.

## CHAPTER 9
### CARTOONS:
**Page 274** (top): "Ding" Darling, *The Education of Alonzo Applegate* (hereinafter *Ding*), n.p.; (bottom):

# CITATIONS

William H. Walker in *Life*, February 25, 1909. **Page 275**: *Ding*, n.p. **Pages 276–77**: Harrison Cady in *Life*, May 6, 1909. **Page 278**: November 4, 1908. Glackens was the brother of famed Ashcan School artist (member of "The Eight") William Glackens. **Page 280**: *Ding*, n.p. **Page 281**: Mark Fenderson in *Life*, April 15, 1909. Fenderson was a pioneer of the Sunday color newspaper comic supplements. **Page 282**:An example of the hundreds of celebratory merchandised items (this celluloid button highly prized by collectors today) spawned by Roosevelt-mania that surrounded TR's return from Africa and Europe. **Page 285**: *McCutcheon Cartoons*, n.d. **Page 287**: June 4, 1908. **Page 289**: Reprinted in *Cartoons Magazine*, May 1913, 279. **Page 290 and 291**: clippings from *Judge* ca. 1912. **Page 292**: *Cartoons Magazine*, March 1912 , 7. **Page 293**: Keppler in *Puck*, May 15, 1907. **Page 295**: *Cartoons Magazine*, March 1912, 4. **Page 298**: Fred G. Cooper in *Life*, May 23, 1912. **Page 299**: J. H. Donahey, *Cleveland Plain Dealer*, reprinted in *Cartoons Magazine*, September 1912. **Page 309**: April 15, 1909. **Pages 312 and 313**: L. M. Glackens in *Puck*, March 16, 1910. **Pages 316–17**: L. M. Glackens in *Puck*, August 3, 1910. **Page 318**: Kemble in *Harper's Weekly*, 1910. **Page 319**: Art Young, *Puck*, ca. 1909. **Pages 320–21**: Art Young in *Puck*, August 4, 1909. **Page 322**: W. A. Carson in Utica *Saturday Globe*, 1910, reproduced from the original drawing, Author's Collection. **Page 324**: L. M. Glackens in *Puck*, June 3, 1908. **Page 325** (right): Reprinted in *Cartoons Magazine*, October 1912, 52. **Pages 326–27**: August 7, 1912. **Page 327** (left): Fontaine Fox, *Chicago Post*, reprinted in *Cartoons Magazine*, May 1912, 33; (right): Caine, *St. Paul Pioneer-Press*, reprinted in *Cartoons Magazine*, September 1912, 57. **Page 329**: Charles R. Macauley, *Campaign Cartoons Issued by Democratic National Committee, 1912*. **Page 330**: L. M. Glackens in *Puck*, 1912. **Page 331**: S. Ehrhart in *Puck*, July 24, 1912. **Page 332**: "My Best Cartoon," Frank Wing, *Cartoons Magazine*, August 1914, 329.

**TEXT:**

**Page 282**: "…expected every lion to do his duty": TR, amused or not, quoted senators who wished him ill, cordially or not. A front-page story in the *Adams County Union-Republican* (Iowa) cites a Washington dispatch from the *Atlanta Constitution*: *President Roosevelt is quoted as asserting that Wall Street hates him. "When I go to Africa," said the president in talking to a party of Georgians who called on him, "Wall Street expects every lion to do his duty. Wall Street hates me with fervid sincerity, not because of any general denunciation of railroads and corporations, but because I have done things"* (December 16, 1908). **Page 284**: "…with tears in his eyes": Theodore Roosevelt, *Cowboys and Kings* (hereinafter *Cowboys*), 113. **Page 286**: "I had enough…": *TR Auto*, 55; "…amiable island…" said Senator Jonathan Dolliver, Iowa,

http://lib-cdm5.iowa.uiowa.edu/uipress/bdi/DetailsPage.aspx?id=99. ("Amiable man" was supplanted in public jests by the image of a huge, aimless, floating mass.) **Pages 289–90**: "…close up like a native oyster": Edmund Morris, *Colonel Roosevelt* (hereinafter *Colonel*), 87. **Page 295**: "… threw his hat into the ring": *Colonel*, 170. **Page 296**: "Taft partisans distributed… ": Frederick S. Wood, *Roosevelt As We Knew Him* (hereinafter *Wood*), 273. **Page 297**: "I feel as strong as a bull moose!" Mark Sullivan, *Our Times*, IV, 506. **Page 298**: "We stand at Armageddon…": *Colonel*, 198. **Page 301**: "It is largely…": *Bishop*, 338; "There you are!" Letter to Henry Cabot and Nannie Lodge, *Letters*, VII, 632, October 28, 1912. **Page 303**: "There are no loaves …": Henry F. Pringle, *Theodore Roosevelt: A Biography* (hereinafter *Pringle*), 400. **Page 322**: The Sherman forces and TR traded "frazzle" barbs at each other, *The Outlook*, October 8, 1910, 307.

### CHAPTER 10
#### CARTOONS:

**Page 343**: "Ding" Darling, *Condensed Ink*, n.d. **Page 349**: Robert Carter in *New York Evening Sun*, reprinted in *Cartoons Magazine*, December 1913, n.p. **Page 352**: French, *Chicago Record-Herald*, reprinted in *Cartoons Magazine*, November 1913, 484. **Page 353**: Clubb, Rochester Herald, reprinted in *Cartoons Magazine*, November 1913, 483. **Page 355**: "Ding" Darling, *Peace and War Cartoons*, n.p. **Page 356**: Reprinted in *Cartoons Magazine*, February 1916, 182. **Page 359**: Robert M. Brinkerhoff, *New York Evening Mail*, reprinted in *Cartoons Magazine*, August 1916, 196. **Page 361**: Ding Darling, *Des Moines Register and Tribune,* reprinted in *Cartoons Magazine*, December 1916, 850. **Page 363**: Ed Marcus in *The New York Times,* ca. 1917. **Page 364**: A. B. Walker in *Life*, June 7, 1917. Walker was the brother of *Life*'s chief political cartoonist W. H. Walker. **Page 368**: Billy Ireland, *Columbus Dispatch*, reprinted in *Cartoons Magazine*, August 1916, 190. **Page 369** (left): J. Campbell Cory, *Brooklyn Citizen*, reprinted in *Cartoons Magazine*, June 1916, 846; (right): Clubb in *Rochester Herald*, reprinted in *Cartoons Magazine*, September 1916, 379. **Page 372** (right): reprinted in *Cartoons Magazine*, December 1916, 805; (left): reprinted in *Cartoons Magazine*, December 1916, 811. **Page 373** (top left): reprinted in *Cartoons Magazine*, October 1915, 640; other cartoons reprinted in *Cartoons Magazine*, December 1915, 949; Charles Sykes cartoon reprinted in *Cartoons Magazine*, April 1916, 505. **Page 374**: "He's Good Enough For All," Robert Carter in *New York Evening Sun*, reprinted in *Cartoons Magazine*, August 1916, 320. It is interesting to note that such cartoons appeared about TR although the presidential campaign was in full swing, and he was not one of the candidates; Wilson as Weakfish, February 10, 1916. **Page 375** (left): Uncle Sam as sissy, March 2, 1916; (right): January 6, 1916. **Page 376**: *Cartoons Magazine*, July 1917, 89. **Page 377**: John Conacher in *Life*, June 7, 1917. **Page 378**: Reprinted in *Cartoons Magazine*, October 1917, 441. **Page 380**: July 27, 1918. **Page 383**: Reprinted in *Cartoons Magazine*, September 1919, 437. **Page 384**: Marcus in *New York Times* Mid-Week Pictorial, April 13, 1919. **Page 385** (bottom): reprinted in *Cartoons Magazine*, December 1915, cover; (top): July 4, 1918.

#### TEXT:

**Page 336**: "Roosevelt lies…": *Colonel*, 243. **Page 341**: "…impartial in thought… ": *Colonel*, 380. **Page 342**: "The most beautiful…": Theodore Roosevelt, *Through the Brazilian Wilderness* (hereinafter *Brazilian*), 32; "For an hour… ": *Brazilian*, 114; **Page 343**: "Next day the… ": *Brazilian*, 300. **Page 344**: "nobody now fears … ": http://ncsu.edu/sma/instructional-material/dropwknc-88-1-fm/history-of-wknc-88-1-fm; "As a Quaker War Secretary… ": Stanley Coben, *A. Mitchell Palmer: Politician* (hereinafter *Coben*), 71; "I am an innocent…": James P. Tate, *The Army and Its Air Corps* (hereinafter *Tate*), 3. **Page 346**: "I am President… ": Statement to AF of L, September 29, 1903, Memorial Edition, XXIII, 289. **Page 348**: "Just be sure whose hide winds up on the wall": William Roscoe Thayer, *Theodore Roosevelt, An Intimate Biography*, 401. **Page 350**: "If I had been President… ": *Bishop*, Vol. II, 372. **Page 351**: "I didn't raise… ": Hermann Hagedorn, *The Roosevelt Family of Sagamore Hill* (hereinafter *Family*). **Page 354**: "… to declare tha …" Wilson speech to Congress, April 2, 1917; "the world needed…": *Colonel*, 484. **Page 357**: "Broomstick Preparedness," National Edition XIX, 267. **Page 359**: "All right! I can work that way too!": Nathan Miller, *Theodore Roosevelt*, 564. **Page 360**: "The first thing you know… ": A paraphrase. The humorist said: "Colonel, one of these days those boys of yours are going to put the name of Roosevelt on the map" (*Colonel*, 527). **Page 361**: "Watch Sagamore Hill for… ": Miller, 561; "But Mrs. Roosevelt!": Miller, 562; "Quentin's mother and I… ": *Miller*, 562. **Page 362**:

"the deadening formalism … ": Before Republican State Convention, Saratoga Springs, NY, July 18, 1918, National Edition XIX; "Only those are fit to live … ": *Colonel*, 537. **Page 363**: "Acclamation, hell!": *Miller*, 559. **Page 365**: "I wonder if … ": *Kraft*, 163; "James, please put … ": James E. Amos, *Theodore Roosevelt, a Hero to His Valet* (hereinafter *Amos*), 156; "The old lion is dead": Sylvia Jukes Morris, *Edith Kermit Roosevelt* (hereinafter *EKR*), 434; "Death had to … ": quoted in William Roscoe Thayer, *Theodore Roosevelt: An Intimate biography*, 450; Last speech TR wrote to be read to the American Defense Society mass rally in New York City: "We should insist that if the immigrant who comes here does in good faith become an American and assimilates himself … ": Letter by then former president Roosevelt on January 3, 1919, to the president of the American Defense Society. It was read publicly at a meeting on January 5, 1919. Roosevelt died the next day, January 6, 1919, http://msgboard.snopes.com/politics/graphics/troosevelt.pdf.

## AFTERWORD
### CARTOONS:

**Page 390**: Edwin Marcus in *Life,* 1919. **Page 393**: Lowry drew this cartoon, TR's favorite, ca. 1906, when he was also producing *Binnacle Jim* and other comic strips for the World Printing Company. **Page 395**: From a limited-edition, signed etching by "Ding" (therefore, reverse image of original cartoon), ca. 1919.

### TEXT:

**Title Page**: "It is true of the nation, as of the individual, that the greatest doer must also be a great dreamer": Speech in Berkeley, CA, 1911. **Page 391**: "review the roster … ": Elihu Root, "Theodore Roosevelt," *North American Review*, Vol. 210,757. **Page 392**: "It is not the critic … ": 1910 Speech at the Sorbonne, Paris: "The Man in the Arena," http://www.theodoreroosevelt.com/trsorbonnespeech.html. **Page 393**: "There was one cartoon … ": *TR Auto*, 390. **Page 396**: "In order to succeed …": Carnegie Hall speech, "The Right of the People to Rule," published in *The Outlook* 100, 626.

**Compiled By Rick Marschall and John Olsen**

# INDEX

*Page references in italics refer to illustrative material.*

# ABOUT THE AUTHOR

Rick Marschall has written or edited sixty-five books, and hundreds of magazine articles, mostly in the field of American popular culture. A former political cartoonist, he has been an editor at three newspapers and at Marvel Comics, and a script writer for Disney Comics. His vintage-cartoon reprint projects have won awards in the United States, France, Germany, and Italy. Marschall has spoken overseas on behalf of the U.S. Information Service of the State Department, and in 1995 he was consultant to the U.S. Postal Service for the 20-stamp commemorative series, *American Comic Classics.*

Marschall is a member of Phi Alpha Theta, the national history honorary society (for "Conspicuous Attainments and Scholarship in the Field of History"). He holds a BA in American History from the American University in Washington, D.C., and his Master's Thesis (American Studies) was on the early American graphic satire magazines. His specialty is the period between the Civil War and World War I, with emphasis on Abraham Lincoln and Theodore Roosevelt. His collection of vintage newspapers and magazines, political and paper Americana, cartoon and advertising items, books and original artwork, is among the largest of such private collections in America. *Bostonia* magazine has called Marschall "perhaps America's foremost authority on popular culture."

Marschall established Rosebud Archives, specializing in reclaiming vintage American graphic art in various media, with Jon Barli (www.rosebudarchives.com, where additional citations and material about *BULLY!* can be found). Lately Marschall has been active in the Christian field, producing a weekly blog, Monday Morning Music Ministry, and writing a biography of Johann Sebastian Bach for Thomas Nelson Publishers (2011). He currently edits the sesquicentennial e-downloads of *Harper's Weekly*, the Civil War era newspaper (http://www.harpersweekly-thecivilwaryears.com) and is Contributing Editor to *Hogan's Alley, The Journal of the Cartoon Arts.*

www.RickMarschallArts.com

**NOTE:** More cartoons, extended information on the life and times of Theodore Roosevelt, notes on cartoon history, and "bonus material" (for instance the complete text and art to *The Teddysee* by Wallace Irwin, 1910) can be accessed at www.RickMarschallArts.com/BULLY.

Any of the cartoons in this book can be obtained as prints, posters, framed art, stationery, and apparel images, and in many other gift and display formats through:

www.RosebudArchives.com